Limits to Soviet Power

Edited by

Rajan Menon
Lehigh University

Daniel N. Nelson
University of Kentucky

Lexington Books
D.C. Heath and Company/Lexington, Massachusetts/Toronto

Library of Congress Cataloging-in-Publication Data

Limits to Soviet power.

Includes index.
1. Soviet Union—Politics and government—1982–
2. Soviet Union—Foreign relations—1975–   .
3. Power (Social sciences). I. Menon, Rajan, 1953–
II. Nelson, Daniel N., 1948–   .
DK288.L54   1989   320.947   86–45368
ISBN 0–669–13226–8 (alk. paper)
ISBN 0–669–20221–5 (pbk. : alk. paper)

Published simultaneously in Canada
Printed in the United States of America
Casebound International Standard Book Number: 0–669–13226–8
Paperbound International Standard Book Number: 0–669–20221–5
Library of Congress Catalog Card Number 86–45368

The paper used in this publication meets the minimum requirements of
American National Standard for Information Sciences—Permanence of
Paper for Printed Library Materials, ANSI Z39.1984.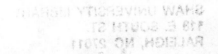

89 90 91 92 8 7 6 5 4 3 2 1

Contents

Preface

Power is a fascinating concept. There are few notions more readily accepted or more frequently used in academe and government. There are obvious reasons for the acceptance and use of the concept of "power." It is the most general word in English to connote an ability to influence and control others. At the same time, it implies a very specific and tangible capacity or force, especially at the nation-state level.

The Soviet Union has unquestionably become more "powerful" in absolute and relative terms since World War II. This enlargement of power is suggested less by the accumulation of delivery systems and nuclear warheads than by the USSR's global presence. Greater Soviet involvement in the world is an empirically verifiable phenomenon. Soviet power (i.e., influence and control), however, is more difficult to identify and verify. Since World War II, the Soviet Union has gained many allies and client states around the globe and, since the early 1970s, has heightened its presence in many African, Asian, and Latin American locales. Yet, as the U.S. experience in Vietnam suggested, the ability to project military forces around the world does not translate into control over events. Neither did the Soviets find that billions of rubles and two decades of diplomatic effort ensured influence in Egypt.

Soviet military intervention in Afghanistan is not debatable, but whether or not that invasion evinces Soviet "power" is certainly questionable. That the Soviet Union insisted on the renewal of the Warsaw Pact in 1985 is fact, but the Pact is not necessarily symbolic of Soviet strength. The Soviet Union does, indeed, have a massive economy with large energy reserves, but these aggregates must be assessed in light of the economy's inefficiencies.

The purpose of this book is not to assert that there *are* limits to Soviet power but, through an examination of selected aspects of Soviet foreign and domestic policy, to understand what limits there are and to assess their significance and severity. We began this project with the safe assumption that the vast size of the Soviets' nuclear arsenal and considerable energy reserves, their vigorous and communicative new leadership in the person of Mikhail Gorbachev, their record of forceful interventions in Eastern Europe, Afghanistan, and Africa, and other indicators of ability to exert influence and control in world affairs were recognizable to most Americans. We asked contributors, therefore, to consider if, and how, Soviet power was constrained.

Because of the breadth of material we cover in this book, our contributors are drawn from diverse academic disciplines. Such a project required a truly interdisciplinary approach. Most of the scholars involved in *Limits to Soviet Power* have, at one time or another, been consultants to business or government, and our contributors now in government have also been faculty members. We sought to assemble, in other words, a "team" that encompassed a wide analytical and experiential background.

We have organized *Limits to Soviet Power* simply—a section with four chapters on "Internal Constraints" on Soviet power and a section with another three chapters on "External Constraints." This dichotomy errs, of course, by its simplicity. Many elements discussed (for example, in Dina and Martin Spechler's chapter, "The Economic Burden of the Soviet Empire") could easily be classified as "external constraints." The categories of "domestic" and "external" are therefore not analytically precise; instead, dividing the book in such a manner is meant to distinguish in a general manner between elements that limit the creation and maintenance of power vis-à-vis the projection of power.

Rajan Menon's "Introduction" places into a theoretical context the issue of Soviet power. The components of a specifically Soviet form of power are identified and related to the broader concerns of power as a concept in international relations. Menon poses questions about the parameters of Soviet influence and control now that the Soviet Union has become a truly global actor.

Martin and Dina Spechler, Stephen White, Martha Olcott, and Judith Thornton have written about economic, leadership, ethnic, and technological factors that impinge on the creation and maintenance of the Soviet Union's ability to influence and control events around the world. As mentioned previously, none of these categories are mutually exclusive, and chapters such as Thornton's and the Spechlers' intersect at many points. Yet, the four authors in part I offer distinct perspectives on Soviet power. The "political economy" of Soviet foreign policy vis-à-vis Eastern Europe is examined in the Spechler chapter. Stephen White's chapter is a thorough look at the capacities of Gorbachev's leadership in light of his first three years in office; if the Soviet Union is to act as a global power, it must be led as one, and White's analysis gives us cause to reassess our expectations. Ethnic and nationality issues are the domain of Martha Olcott's chapter. Whatever the Communist party's goals for global involvement and influence, the Soviets' own multinational society could be a great impediment or a huge asset. The Soviet Union is, in many ways, not at all Russian. Olcott's analysis identifies the constraints that may be placed on Gorbachev's leadership and Soviet power. To close part I,

Judith Thornton offers a much-needed consideration of the Soviet Union's problems in obtaining, absorbing, and controlling technological advances, and how those problems affect the creation, maintenance, and projection of power.

In part II, Soviet "global" involvements are the subject of three chapters by Christopher Jones, Michael Klare, and Mel Goodman. Christopher Jones discusses the Warsaw Treaty Organization (WTO or Warsaw Pact) from the standpoint of Soviet efforts to exert control via mechanisms of the Pact, and he considers problems encountered by them in those efforts. Michael Klare's analysis concerns Soviet ability to project power—a task that necessitates estimates of naval and air components available to bring Soviet forces elsewhere, as well as evaluations of Soviet intentions to utilize such capabilities. Mel Goodman examines specific Third World countries in which the Soviet Union has, or has had, considerable presence. Goodman's contribution turns on the debate about whether the Soviet Union enhances or wastes its power by supporting poor client states in the Third World.

"Paradoxes of Soviet Power," a concluding chapter written by Daniel N. Nelson, identifies parameters of Soviet influence and control around the world, offering a hierarchy of limitations on Soviet "globalism." Nelson poses hypotheses that might explain variations in Soviet power over time and by region or locale. Contributions in this book and other data are used as preliminary "tests" for those hypotheses.

The editors wish to acknowledge gratefully the interest and patience of Jamie Welch-Donahue of Lexington Books in this project, and the cooperation of all contributors. Our thanks to Lehigh University for providing the financial support for preparing the index. The final version of the manuscript was typed at the University of Kentucky by Kim Hayden, to whom we are most grateful. For comments and useful discussions on the subject of the book, we thank Melvyn Leffler (University of Virginia), John Oneal (University of Alabama), and Bruce Moon (Lehigh University).

Introduction:
On Assessing Soviet Power

Rajan Menon

his book is about constraints, both internal and external, on Soviet power. The literature on power analysis demonstrates the danger of proceeding as if the concept is obvious and needs no elaboration. So central is the concept of power to this book that I begin by discussing the theoretical issues germane to it and, on that basis, offering a working definition. This is followed by a discussion of the elements of Soviet power, which focuses on the causes and consequences of the Soviet Union's heavy reliance on the military aspects of power and its relative weakness in other forms of power.

Defining Power

In their classic text, *Power and Society,* Harold Lasswell and Abraham Kaplan defined power as the ability to shape the behavior of others by making it necessary for them to take account of you in their decision making.[1] This is a "causal conception" of power, quite similar to Bertrand Russell's pithy definition that power is but "the production of intended effects."[2] In drawing a distinction between *power* and *influence*—a term often used as a synonym—Lasswell and Kaplan maintain that "Power is a special case of the exercise of influence: it is the process of affecting the policies of others with the help of (actual or threatened) severe deprivations for nonconformity with the policies intended."[3] Thus, as opposed to influence, which is exerted through gentler forms of suasion, power is wielded by the actual or potential ability to inflict some form of hardship on others.

The use of the word *power,* especially in world politics, evokes military images: it seems inextricably linked to weapons, destruction, and death. Perhaps because they realized this, Lasswell and Kaplan stressed that power is not simply another word for violence and that the use of power does not boil down to affecting the "physical safety and well being" of others.[4] If power is the capacity to shape the behavior of others by being able to cause hardship and to affect outcomes in areas deemed important by them, it can, to be sure, be achieved through military means. But it can also be attained by economic, political, and ideological instruments.

A shortcoming of the Lasswell-Kaplan approach is that it is applicable only to the *coercive* manifestation of power. This occurs when A induces B to do something that B was not predisposed to do and that entails costs (economic, political, or military). Although such situations do arise in world politics, because of (1) states' sensitivity to infringements of their independence and (2) the various means available to resist such blatant uses of power, they are not commonplace. The typical form of power in the politics among nations is *complementary:* A provides B the means (whether tangible, as in money or weapons, or intangible, as in expressions of solidarity) to do something that benefits both parties.[5] To give an example apposite to the topic of this book, such power was exercised during the 1975–76 Angolan civil war when the Soviet Union ferried to the MPLA (Popular Movement for the Liberation of Angola) the armaments and Cuban soldiers that helped it to defeat its rivals.

A working definition broad enough to subsume these two forms of power, as well as the connotations given to the term by the other contributors to this book, is as follows: a state has power when it possesses the means relevant to shaping the decisions and conduct of others such that certain benefits accrue to it. It can shape the decisions and actions of others in three ways: (1) by providing or denying certain resources that affect their behavior, (2) by threatening to do so in a credible manner, thus affecting their policies or those of other states involved in the situation, and (3) by being able to provide or deny—without actually doing so or even threatening to—certain resources valued by others, thus forcing them to take its preferences into account on matters known to be of importance to it. This third and indirect version of power is pervasive in international politics and is essentially what Carl Friedrich long ago termed "the rule of anticipated reactions."[6]

Facets of Soviet Power

Because the topic of Soviet military capabilities occupies so central a place in U.S. political debates and deliberations, and due to the expansion of Soviet nuclear and conventional forces in the decades since World War II, Americans' discussions about Soviet power invariably focus on the military dimension. That Soviet military prowess has grown considerably since 1945 is undeniable. So, too, is the proposition that the production and application of the military instruments of statecraft constitute the Soviet Union's strong suit or area of comparative advantage. There is, however, a corollary to these observations that is recognized but often glossed over: in the nonmilitary means of statecraft, the Soviet Union not only lacks comparable effectiveness, but it is also surpassed by its principal competitors: the United States, Western Europe, and Japan. That is, the Soviet Union's status as a superpower is starkly and indisputably apparent only if power be equated, rather crudely and narrowly, with the means to "kill people and destroy things."[7] Bearing in mind the Lasswell-Kaplan insistence that the means of exercising power are varied and not limited to the capacity to inflict violence, it is apparent that the power resources of the Soviet Union lack versatility. A look at the non-military elements of Soviet power illustrates this proposition.

Soviet spokesmen have always emphasized the appeal of the Soviet economic and political system as a major source of their country's influence. Yet this must now be regarded as a diminishing asset. In the West, the Soviet economic model has become a byword for inefficiency and ill-used potential. In the developing world, where, in the early post-World War II years, it excited attention as a route to rapid industrialization and a more equitable distribution of societal wealth, its allure has faded. The Third World states most influenced by it—Afghanistan, Angola, Ethiopia, Mozambique, and South Yemen, referred to in Soviet parlance as the "states of socialist orientation"—are among the poorest, most unstable, and least developed. The economically most dynamic developing countries—South Korea, Singapore, and Taiwan—have adopted state capitalistic economic strategies, have few significant economic ties with the Soviet Union, and are involved in extensive business transactions with Japan and the West. Some influential Soviet specialists recognize that the appeal of the Soviet model has been strongest in countries least significant to the outcome of the Soviet–U.S. geopolitical competition.[8] Mikhail Gorbachev's scant reference to the states of socialist orientation in his February 1986 political report to the 27th Party Congress suggests that such assessments may be percolating upward from Soviet academe to the leadership.[9]

This does not mean that the Soviet Union will abandon radical states in the Third World. Since the advent of Gorbachev, it has continued to deliver large quantities of arms to Angola's MPLA government to support its war against Jonas Savimbi's National Union for the Total Liberation of Angola (UNITA) guerrillas, who are backed by South Africa and the United States.[10] In Afghanistan, mired in a quicksand-like war, the Soviet Union participated in negotiations sponsored by the United Nations. These talks led ultimately to the April 1988 Geneva Accords, which provide for the withdrawal of Soviet forces from Afghanistan over a period of nine months.[11] Yet the Soviet Union intends to continue providing the People's Democratic Party (PDPA) of Afghanistan with arms, economic aid, and advisors while it seeks to draw the guerrilla resistance into negotiations aimed at power sharing. Whether this strategy works or not—and success seems unlikely—it shows that the Soviet leaders, while they have decided to end their war in Afghanistan, are still prepared to commit resources to try and shape the political outcome in that country. Also, despite writings by Soviet scholars and speeches by Soviet leaders reflecting concern about the expense of dependent states in the Third World, in 1986 the Soviet Union increased economic aid significantly to Vietnam and Cuba, chief recipients of Soviet assistance.[12] The expectation that economic problems at home will prompt the Soviet leaders to make a quick and general renunciation of existing commitments is much too simplistic. It ignores, for example, the importance of military installations to which the Soviet Union has gained access in dependencies such as Angola, Cuba, and Vietnam.[13]

Yet Soviet scholarly analyses and the content or tenor of speeches by Andropov (to the Central Committee in June 1983) and Gorbachev (before the 27th Party Congress in February 1986) reflect pessimism about the Third World states of socialist orientations' economic prospects, political stability, and significance for the outcome of East–West competition. The result could well be a reassessment of the Angola-Ethiopia-South Yemen approach to policy in the developing areas and a reaffirmation of the India-Nigeria-Brazil strategy, which emphasizes the greater geopolitical importance of large, capitalist, emergent powers in the Third World. This is the context in which Foreign Minister Shevardnadze's visits in 1986–87 to Argentina, Brazil, Thailand, Indonesia, and Mexico should be seen. A policy guided less by the allure of socialist orientation and more by *Realpolitik* may also explain why, as of June 1988, India is the only Third World country Gorbachev has visited. There have been four meetings between Rajiv Gandhi and Gorbachev since March 1985 and over this period, 2.5 billion rubles in Soviet loans have been provided to India.[14] Efforts to improve relations with Israel and Saudi Arabia, plus the establishment of diplomatic relations with Oman and the United Arab Emirates in 1985, again suggest the influence of balance-of-power, as opposed to chiefly ideological, considerations.

But the imbalance among the components of Soviet power and the consequent status of the military aspect as the strong suit make it difficult for the Soviet Union to court the emerging powers in the Third World. With the exception of India, none will look to the Soviet Union as a principal arms supplier; thus the key instrument of Soviet policy, arms sales, will be ineffecive. And the Soviet weakness in the economic facets of power will aggravate the problem, for these countries will turn, as they do even now, chiefly to Japan, Western Europe, and the United States for industrial imports, investment, and the transfer of technology.[15] This comparative disadvantage, to reverse Ricardo, will be compounded by the absence of the Soviet Union from multilateral economic forums (GATT, the World Bank, and the International Monetary Fund), its irrelevance in the negotiations on resolving the problem of Third World debt, and the inability of the Soviet economy to emerge as a model considered worthy of emulation by the most dynamic developing nations. Thus the consequences of the imbalanced nature of Soviet power and the links between the malaise of the Soviet Union's economy and the effectiveness of its foreign policy are again illustrated. A Soviet policy in the Third World that seeks to focus on the emergent powers requires successful internal reforms that strengthen the effectiveness of Soviet economic instruments of statecraft.

Much more apparent that the impediments to Soviet effectiveness in the Third World is the frustration of Moscow's desire to be the leader, or at least the *primus inter pares,* of a transnational socialist movement. Nationalism among socialist countries, far from having been eroded by the theoretical injunctions of Marxism-Leninism to think and act in terms of class allegiances, remains robust, divisive, and inimical to the establishment of a coalition of ideologically like-minded states headed by the Soviet Union.

The schisms between the Soviet Union, Tito's Yugoslavia, Mao's China, and Hoxha's Albania—a series of quarrels that ushered in what political scientists term "polycentrism" within the socialist world—were successful rebellions by states that rejected the Soviet Union's control despite being within the shadow of its power. In addition to such open and total defiance, the Soviets have, despite being providers of arms and aid, had to accommodate the stubborn nationalism and political cantankerousness of Nicolae Ceauşescu's Romania and Castro's Cuba. (The former, for example, failed to follow the rest of the Soviet bloc in severing diplomatic ties with Israel after the 1967 Middle East War, maintained cordial ties with China despite the Sino–Soviet animosity of the 1960s and 1970s, and refuses to allow Warsaw Pact troops to be stationed or maneuver on its soil.[16]) A theoretical point germane to power analysis that must be made here is the need to distinguish between *presence* on the one hand and *power* or *influence* on the other. The former, as is often assumed, does not automatically yield the latter.

The preceding argument cannot, of course, be taken so far as to maintain that the Soviet Union is devoid of all ideologically rooted power. After all, despite periodic upheavals in Eastern Europe, Moscow has maintained its hegemony. To do so, it has used the advantages of superior military might, proximity, and the close ties that have been built since 1945 between the Soviet and Eastern European economies. The institutional embodiments of such controls are the Warsaw Pact and the Council for Mutual Economic Assistance (CMEA). But ideological mechanisms have also undoubtedly played a role in maintaining bloc cohesion. A political status quo in Eastern Europe favorable to the Soviet Union is based on a complex power structure of military officers, administrators, police and security personnel, and ideologists, trained—either in the Soviet Union or in their home countries—with reference to Soviet ideological norms and procedures. Along with the Soviet Union, this dependent bureaucracy has a vested interest in opposing upheavals that threaten its power and privileges.[17] Ideological means, then, have played a role in allowing the Soviet Union to achieve and safeguard one of its principal geopolitical goals: having a subordinate and politically similar glacis along its western frontier, which it views as a traditional invasion route used by its enemies.

Yet in assessing the role of ideology in establishing and securing Soviet predominance in Eastern Europe, a distinction must be made between that region's political elites and the mass citizenry. The former have acquired a stake in the status quo and perhaps internalized some of the ideological norms of their Soviet counterparts. But, as the upheavals since 1945 in East Germany, Hungary, Czechoslovakia, and Poland demonstrate, the same cannot be said of the Eastern European masses. At this level, especially in Poland, antipathy toward the Soviet Union remains a basic feature of local nationalisms. Despite over forty years of ideological indoctrination, it is still a potent force and an enduring challenge to Soviet dominance. It is this nationalism, together with the Sino–Soviet split, that spawned the now familiar observation that the Soviet Union is the only country surrounded by hostile communist neighbors. It is this nationalism that has led Western analysts to wonder how reliable Soviet commanders would find the conscript troops of Eastern Europe to be, particularly in a prolonged war.[18] It is this nationalism that has led the Soviet leaders, as Christopher Jones argues in his chapter, to devise various means through which the Warsaw Pact can ensure Soviet control over Eastern Europe by protecting the indigenous pro-Soviet *nomenklatura* (bureaucratic elite) from upheavals initiated either by reformist or revolutionary forms of opposition.

Power has, of course, economic aspects as well. Indeed, one cannot erect an analytical wall between economic and military power. Activities in which the Soviet Union has great strengths—the manufacture of armaments, the export of weapons worldwide, the provision of military advisors to client states—show that the two are closely intertwined. This is why analyses documenting this or that deficiency in the Soviet economy need, for discussions relating to Soviet power, to be put in proper perspective. True, the Soviet economy is only 54 percent the size of the U.S. economy.[19] And, although, as a long-term average, its growth rate compares favorably to that of Western economies, it has been beset by a slowdown that has persisted since the 1950s.

Remarkably, however, the Soviet Union's economic maladies have not prevented it from emerging as a military-political power on a par with its archrival, the United States. It has closed the nuclear gap with the United States and maintains vast nuclear and conventional forces on its eastern and western frontiers adequate to meet its security goals vis-à-vis China and NATO. Despite the travails of the Soviet economy, Moscow has also been able to bear the costs of aid to Eastern Europe, Cuba, Afghanistan, and Vietnam.[20] Indeed, as Dina and Martin Spechler show later in this book, the burden of such commitments may have been declining since the early 1980s and Moscow's efforts to control it will involve limiting future undertakings, not eliminating quickly a series of present ones.

Several important changes have occurred during the 1980s in Soviet aid policy in the Third World: a steep decline in the rate of growth of economic assistance; efforts to phase out subsidized oil exports to Cuba, Vietnam, and Mongolia; and calls for greater efficiency and self-reliance on the part of recipients. Yet with the cost of military and economic assistance to developing countries estimated at roughly 1 percent of Soviet GNP, the *economic* burden ought not to be exaggerated.[21] Perhaps more significant is a reassessment of the *political* gains made from past commitments to regimes now regarded as having limited significance in the global balance of power.

There is, nevertheless, an imbalance between the economic and military components of Soviet power. In the traditional areas of world politics—those having directly to do with military power and security—the Soviet Union's vast military might has unquestionably made it a superpower. But, as the writings on international political economy and economic statecraft show, power in international politics derives from being an important participant in a host of economic issues as well: global monetary matters, foreign aid and investment, commercial lending, trade negotiations, and the functioning of international organizations such as the World Bank and the International Monetary Fund.[22]

On the one hand, a state heavily involved in such issues must contend with the reduced autonomy that results from becoming enmeshed in an interdependent global economy.[23] On the other hand, the ability to figure in and shape outcomes in these fields is an important source of power precisely because economic interdependence makes them so salient to states. One need only ponder the reasons for Japan's increasing importance in world politics to realize this. The Soviet Union's marginal status in matters relating to global finance, trade, and investment has limited its ability to use the economic aspects of power to further its foreign-policy goals.[24]

A specific example involves the limits imposed on Soviet policy in the Middle East by Soviet weakness in the economic elements of power. The region is close to the Soviet Union and is one in which, as Soviet representatives repeatedly assert, the Soviet Union has vital interests. The Soviet Union is heavily engaged there: it has signed security treaties with several states in the area, it has access to ports and airfields in some regional states, its arms and military advisors are sent in large numbers to various Arab states, and it is engaged in several diplomatic efforts aimed at expanding its influence. However, its policy rests heavily on military-political instruments. Were it in a position to offer the states of the region large volumes of banking and investment capital plus technological assistance on a par with that provided by the West and Japan, its policy would be buttressed by more diverse instruments. Indeed, the existence of millions of Soviet Central Asian Muslims with religious and cultural links to the region would provide the Soviet Union a special advantage in utilizing the economic tools of diplomacy.[25]

Reforming for Power

To use Paul Dibb's apt characterization, the Soviet Union is an "incomplete superpower," potent in the military instruments, but weak in the others.[26] But does this matter? It could be argued that the Soviet leaders realize that military power is their strong suit and believe that the economic, ideological, and cultural forms of power are too fuzzy and, if not irrelevant, are certainly less consequential than raw military might.

I believe this view is mistaken. It rests on the preoccupation in the U.S. political debate with the military aspects of East–West competition. Following from this is the assumption that the size of the Soviet arsenal must mean that the Kremlin leaders denigrate the importance of the nonmilitary bases of power. Yet Soviet ideology and military doctrine, while certainly not belittling the role of force in world politics, by no means equate success in foreign policy with military predominance. Indeed, as some recent studies show, despite its militaristic overtones, the Soviet term *correlation of forces* does not simply mean "the balance of military power."[27] Instead, it refers as well to the economic, technological, ideological, and political conditions within which East–West competition is waged. Soviet scholars are explicit in making the point, for example, that Soviet global influence depends on its ability to demonstrate economic and technological advances. In the words of one:

> A critical role in the influence of real socialism . . . is played by the course and outcome of the economic rivalry between socialism and capitalism. Real socialism has had considerable success in this rivalry. . . . However, complex problems stand in the way of the new system's influence. . . . These . . . are primarily bound up with the certain slowing of economic growth . . . and with the increasing difficulties of shifting to an intensive type of development, mastering . . . effective management, etc.[28]

A similar point is made by the *Izvestia* commentator, Alexander Bovin. He notes that the failure to implement radical reforms to rejuvenate the Soviet economy "was causing economic stagnation, bringing our society to the brink of a crisis, and weakening the Soviet Union's prestige and influence in the international area."[29] In explaining the link between the domestic problems of the Soviet Union and its effectiveness abroad, he adds:

> We must admit that capitalism's ability to adapt to the new historical environment has exceeded our expectations. The prospect of socialist transfor-

mations in the developed capitalist countries has been put off to the in-
definite future. In a number of countries that are socialist in orientation, the
situation remains unstable and fraught with the possibility of backsliding;
communist parties in the capitalist countries and the third world, with few
exceptions, have not been able to . . . gain the support of the majority of
the working class. . . . There are a number of reasons for this, and the
failures, contradictions, crisis phenomena and stagnation phenomena in the
development of the Soviet Union . . . doubtless figure among them.
Socialism has not yet been able to acquire the force of example of which
Lenin spoke.[30]

Without sweeping economic reforms that propel the Soviet Union to the
forefront of the modern technological revolution, Bovin warns, "the
worldwide balance of power could change in favor of capitalism."[31]

The urgency of Gorbachev's calls for sweeping economic reforms designed to boost Soviet efficiency, productivity, and technological dynamism
do not, thus, stem simply from a desire to improve living standards. They also
reflect his awareness that a sluggish economy and lagging technology are incompatible with the degree of global influence to which the Soviet Union
aspires. The sweep and frankness of Gorbachev's criticisms of Soviet
economic practices suggest that he shares the assessments of Western
specialists who conclude that the Soviet model was effective for "heavy industry and growth in the smokestack period of industrialization, but is terri-
ble . . . in the current electronics-computer phase" and that "the Soviet system
is widely seen as a completely ineffective model."[32] He recognizes that
economic weakness threatens to diminish the Soviet Union's future global
status. This is why he asserts that the success or failure of his economic
reforms will determine whether the USSR will operate in the next century "in
a manner worthy of a great power."[33]

The obstacles to thoroughgoing economic reform in the Soviet Union are
several. Central planning agencies and ministries will resist the loss of authority that would follow the alteration of the hypercentralized system of
economic management by devolving more decision-making authority to
managers of farms and factories. Those in the party bureaucracy committed
to ideological orthodoxy will seek to portray any increase in the role of incentives, market forces, and private property as incompatible with socialism. If
changes in economic organization are accompanied by a shift of resources
from the military to the civilian sector, the armed forces must be persuaded
to yield their privileged status in budgetary politics. While some sectors of
Soviet society (e.g., the literati) may welcome and benefit from the greater intellectual freedom accompanying reform, others, such as industrial workers,
may be alienated if measures taken to promote efficiency bring diminished job
security, a greater stress on quality and discipline at work sites, and increased
prices for basic commodities long governed by subsidies judged now to be too

costly. If these separate strands of opposition to radical economic change coalesce, Gorbachev will find it difficult to build the political consensus necessary to implement reform. And, as Stephen White argues in his chapter on the Soviet leadership, changes in the post-Stalin political system have diminished the general secretary's ability to command change and have increased the importance of skillfully building support for programs by winning the backing of increasingly powerful institutional interests.

Martha Olcott's chapter on Soviet Central Asia identifies another barrier to reform: the opposition of party leaders in Central Asia to changes in economic management that threaten to reduce their authority, autonomy, and control of local resources. Analyses of Soviet Central Asia usually focus on two potential problems. The first is the implication for unity and political stability posed by the region's population growth rates, which exceed those of the Slavic-Baltic republics, and the sense of cultural separateness engendered by Islam, even though it is not thriving as a religion. The second is the effect that ethnic tensions in the Soviet armed forces could have on morale and unity in wartime. In the perspective of the seventy years since the Bolshevik Revolution, however, what is striking is how well both problems have been managed. Despite the Soviet Union's kaleidoscopic ethnic diversity and evidence of disunity—occasional riots, the grievances of non-Russian nationalities expressed in *samizdat* (underground dissident writings), and reports of ethnic animosity in the armed forces—the Soviet leaders, through policies involving a combination of rewards and repression, cajoling, and co-optation have kept a multinational system intact. In the military, the proportion of recruits from Central Asia has grown from 13 percent in 1970 to 24 percent in 1985.[34] Their lower technical skills and lack of mastery of Russian, the command language, may affect military *efficiency,* but the problems of military *loyalty* have been managed much more effectively than is often supposed.[35] Olcott's chapter on Central Asia focuses on an equally important matter bearing upon the prospects for Soviet power: the opposition in Central Asia to economic reforms proposed by Gorbachev. As noted earlier, their success or failure of these reforms will decide the future status of the Soviet Union as a global power.

Economic weakness will limit general Soviet influence in the world. But perhaps more worrisome for the Soviet leaders is the possibility that it may also diminish the Soviet strong suit, military power. The actual and potential application of microelectronics, robotics, sensors, and lasers to weaponry, and the rapid rate of change in modern technology pose an especially great problem for the Soviet Union that, as David Holloway has observed, faces the challenge "of a basically non-innovative system to cope with revolutionary technological change, which has been generated primarily by the Soviet Union's potential enemies."[36] The relationship between economic and military power has not escaped the Soviet leaders. The writings of Marx,

Engels, and Lenin show that the view of economic and technological dynamism as the foundation for effective military power is part of the Soviet ideological heritage.[37]

But could it be that the Soviet defense sector (the privileged recipient of resources and technical expertise, and a top priority for the Kremlin leaders) does not suffer from the foibles of the civilian economy? Although there are several problems in answering this question, not the least of which is the difficulty of obtaining reliable information, Holloway's conclusion is that, in the Soviet Union, "the processes of innovation are more effective in the defense sector than in civilian industry, but [this] does not support the view that the defense sector turns out technology of a qualitatively different level." In the military field, he adds, the level of Soviet achievement "is not as high as in the advanced capitalist countries, when measured in terms of major technological innovations and their diffusion through the stock of weapons."[38]

This suggests that, in the Soviet Union, there are not two economies—a lethargic civilian sector unable to match the technological standards set by Japan and the West, and a military production complex that (by virtue of its importance in the leadership's hierarchy of goals and consequent access to raw materials, investment funds, and technical personnel on favored terms) has been immunized from the ills plaguing the civil economy. Judith Thornton's chapter discusses the many reasons why the Soviet system has failed to generate the kind of technological dynamism achieved in Japan, the United States, and Western Europe. She even alludes to the possibility that this weakness could hinder the Soviet effort to remain competitive in the sphere of modern military technology.

In fact, however, the impressive growth of Soviet military power notwithstanding, there is evidence to suggest that this is a problem of the past and present, not just one for the future. This conclusion is suggested by various pieces of information on Soviet weapons technology. A comparison of the two superpowers' achievements in 20 basic technologies with military application "in the next 10 to 20 years" made by the U.S. Department of Defense in 1986 showed the United States leading in 14, equality in 6, and the Soviets leading in none.[39]

The Soviet lag in weapons technology is suggested by other evidence as well.[40] When a defecting Soviet pilot, Viktor Belenko, flew his MiG-25 to Japan in 1976, some surprising information was revealed about his plane, which many in the West regarded as exemplifying Soviet prowess in military technology and which had set world records for speed and altitude. It was found to have vacuum-tube–based electronics, a much shorter range than had been supposed, and an engine unable to withstand more than one flight at maximum speed. Similarly, in both submarine-launched and land-based strategic ballistic missiles, the Soviet Union was unable to quickly introduce solid-fuel propellants despite the well-known hazards, logistical problems, and lower readiness levels of liquid-fueled systems. Although its latest strategic ballistic missiles (the SS-24, SS-25, and SS-N-20) incorporate this feature, over 80 percent of Soviet sea-based and land-based strategic nuclear missiles are still liquid-fueled. The United States began deploying solid-fueled missiles in 1960, almost a decade before the Soviets. As a final example, the frequent breakdowns and greater noise levels of Soviet submarines help explain why fewer than 20 percent, in comparison to over 50 percent for the United States, are at open sea and why, although the era of counterforce strategic missiles has increased the vulnerability of ICBMs, fewer than a third of Soviet strategic nuclear warheads are deployed on submarines.

The military implications of the Soviets' inability to stay abreast of the West and Japan in what might be termed "cutting-edge" technologies can be illustrated by considering the apprehension evoked in the Soviet Union by the Strategic Defense Initiative.[41] The Soviet concern about the SDI can be explained in different ways. Ever conscious of the technological gap between the two superpowers and respectful of U.S. abilities, the Soviet leaders may fear a worst-case scenario: the United States and its allies pool their scientific-technological resources in a sustained effort and succeed in creating a defensive shield against ballistic missiles, thus rendering the Soviet Union vulnerable to nuclear attack by reducing, or even eliminating, U.S. vulnerability to Soviet retaliation. Although the Soviets are by now well aware both of the various countermeasures that could be taken against a deployed ballistic missile defense system and of the political circumstances that make a U.S. nuclear attack extremely unlikely, the possibility that the Soviet Union really worries about this contingency should not be dismissed. This ignores the effect that over four decades of the U.S.–Soviet ideological and military competition have had on images of the opponent.

Another worry—and one that is more plausible—involves the unanticipated military side effects of a massive, sustained program of research and development on behalf of the SDI. Even if the vision of a fully reliable defense against ballistic missiles proves to be a pipe dream, its technological spinoffs could yield discoveries that could improve vastly the capabilities of the *conventional* weapons of the United States and its allies. The writings of the former chief of the Soviet General Staff, Marshal Nikolai Ogarkov, and other Soviet authorities display concern about the advent of "smart" precision-guided conventional missiles capable of homing in on the advancing columns and rear echelons of armed forces.[42] As Louis Lavoie, an analyst at Honeywell's Defense Systems Division, points out, the integration of such weapons into the arsenals and combat tactics of NATO and Japan would pose a major challenge to the faith placed in Soviet military doctrine on a rapid offensive by numerous tank and motor rifle divisions supported by strikes launched from aircraft.[43]

The economic implications of a full-scale competition with the United States to develop ballistic missile defenses are also apt to disturb the Soviet leaders. Whether or not an effective shield against nuclear weapons proves possible, the Soviet Union will have no choice but to follow if the United States proves determined to try. This would mean embarking on an enormously expensive effort in an area where the level of U.S. technology and the wealth and scientific abilities of U.S. allies put the Soviet Union at an inherent disadvantage. Moreover, this would place additional strain on an already problem-ridden Soviet economy. The cost of the program and the accentuation of national-security concerns that would accompany this new aspect of military competition with the United States would complicate both the reallocation of investment funds and the process of moving economic reforms from theory to practice.

The availability of countermeasures, the difficulties that the United States will face in pursuing a staggeringly expensive program amid vast budget deficits, and the numerous technological complexities involved in constructing an effective defense against ballistic missiles make SDI a long-term and less worrisome *military* problem for the Soviet Union than it seemed when the program was first announced. But as a new and potentially costly facet of the arms race that could become a major claimant on important funds needed elsewhere, it is a continuing problem. The incompatibility between reassigning investment and promoting economic reform on the one hand and the acceleration of defense expenditures on the other is not merely a hypothesis unrelated to Soviet reality. It has, for example, been considered at length in *Pravda* by Yevgeni Primakov, director of the Institute for World Economy and International Relations and advisor to Gorbachev, in discussing the notion of "reasonable sufficiency" in military spending and deployment.[44]

A final source of worry, although not voiced directly in Soviet writings, may be that the SDI has appeared at a time when both superpowers have been deploying counterforce strategic missiles. The combination of a deployed missile defense system and counterforce strategic systems that put the other side's retaliatory forces at risk would weaken deterrence from the standpoint of the side that had yet to erect defenses. This is of particular concern to the Soviet Union because 61 percent of its strategic nuclear warheads (as compared to 19 percent for the United States) are on land and thus are more susceptible to a first strike than those deployed on submarines. Moreover, generally the United States has been the first to develop and deploy new systems in the nuclear-arms competition. The Soviet leaders have good reason to fear that this would be true of a race to deploy ballistic missile defenses as well.

A possible solution—and one that the Soviets have adopted in the 1980s—involves shifting to a greater reliance on submarine-launched warheads. But such restructuring is costly. It is also made less attractive by the relative shortcomings of the Soviet submarine force in avoiding both breakdowns and detection. Another, less expensive, option to reduce the vulnerability of Soviet land-based missiles is the construction of mobile ICBMs. The deployment of the new, mobile SS-24 and SS-25 ICBMs indicates a Soviet decision to make such a choice.[45]

The common denominator in each of these challenges posed by the SDI is that the Soviet Union must reckon with a United States that has a more sophisticated technological base and is thus likely to deploy new weapons first, with the added advantage of having allies whose technological level is higher than that of the Soviet Union and its Warsaw Pact partners.[46]

The Limits of Military Power

My emphasis on the weakness of the nonmilitary components of Soviet power could be faulted for not recognizing that military power is the great equalizer, which either compensates for or begets other forms of power. Lasswell and Kaplan seem to provide the basis for such a critique by arguing that "Forms of power are agglutinative: those with some forms acquire other forms too."[47] Yet this generalization is not valid for the Soviet Union. Few would deny that there has been a great expansion of Soviet military power since 1945: a plethora of charts, graphs, and statistics, presented in countless publications, attest to this.[48] It has hardly been true, however, that a corresponding and commensurate surge has occurred in other forms of Soviet power. Indeed, the preoccupation with, and expenditures on, military might largely explains the one-dimensional nature of Soviet power.

On the economic front, Soviet optimism of the Khrushchev era about besting the United States in economic competition now appears quixotic as evidence mounts—much of it from Soviet sources—about the weaknesses of the Soviet economy. Not only is the United States well ahead in the economic-technological race, but Japan has pulled alongside the Soviet Union and stands ready to surpass it in the value of industrial output. On the ideological-cultural front, polycentrism is a permanent reality, the appeal of Soviet Marxism and its economic model has diminished, and the fads and fashions of the world emanate from Western Europe, Japan, and the United States. Prowess in the military domain has not translated into effectiveness in other spheres.

Indeed, military power, far from being fungible enough to be applied in the quest for influence on nonmilitary issues, has on occasion proven counterproductive—especially if one evaluates it using Bertrand Russell's criterion of producing "intended effects." Thus the Soviet military preponderance over the states of East Asia, the expansion of Soviet conventional and nuclear forces in that region since the mid-1960s, and Moscow's unyielding position on the Kurile Islands dispute have together limited Japan's willingness to engage in economic cooperation in Siberia on the scale hoped for by the Soviets.[49]

Similarly, the buildup of Soviet forces along the Sino-Soviet border from the same period did not elicit the Chinese leaders' deference; it intensified their suspicion and sense of vulnerability to the point that, by the late 1970s, evidence appeared of a trend that the Kremlin leaders feared: strategic cooperation between the United States and China.[50] Indeed Soviet efforts at détente with China since 1982 amount to a recognition of the failure of a strategy of intimidation.

As regards U.S.–Soviet relations, the role of Soviet military power in Angola, Ethiopia, and Afghanistan contributed to the withering of détente by the late 1970s. The Soviets failed to reap the economic benefits—chiefly access to advanced technology through expanding economic transactions—expected from détente. And there occurred a hardening of U.S. attitudes toward the Soviet Union at once symbolized and intensified by the election of Ronald Reagan as president. This is now well understood by the Soviets. An article appearing in *Literaturnaya gazeta* in 1988 noted the harm that Soviet military activity in the Third World had done to détente, blaming "the miscalculations and incompetent approach to the Brezhnev leadership." It was blamed for ignoring the USSR's "true national state interests" and pursuing "petty and essentially formal gains associated with leadership coups in certain developing countries." This, it was argued, brought about the deterioration of U.S.–Soviet relations and spurred a major military buildup by the Reagan administration that made Soviet foreign policy "exceptionally costly."[51]

The theoretical generalization, then, could be stated thus: although it is not without utility, military power can be counterproductive; moreover, it does not compensate for weaknesses in other forms of power. This certainly has been the Soviet experience.

One would expect the limits of military power to be well understood by now. Yet, in a survey and critique of the literature on power analysis published in 1979, David Baldwin noted: "Two of the most important weaknesses in traditional theorizing about international politics have been the tendency to exaggerate the effectiveness of military power resources and the tendency to treat military power as the ultimate measuring rod to which other forms of power should be compared."[53]

These flaws are quite prominent in analyses of Soviet foreign policy. They exist for a number of reasons: the great effort and resources invested by the Kremlin leaders in weaponry, the Soviet–U.S. arms competition, and the mistrust and hostility that the two superpowers display toward each other. These factors have combined to produce a natural and understandable tendency to focus on the *military* aspects of Soviet power. States, however, pursue not only military objectives, but political, ideological, and economic ones as well. In the first of these, the armed forces of the USSR have been a potent instrument; it would be folly to deny this. But a valuable insight offered by power analyses is that military power cannot be used as an effective tool in other realms. As Baldwin notes:

Power resources (or assets) in one policy-contingency framework may not only lose their effectiveness in another context; they may actually become liabilities rather than assets. . . . Money, tanks, information and allies, are often called "power resources"; but one can easily imagine plausible policy-contingency frameworks within which each . . . becomes a liability.[53]

Whether a particular form of power is liable to be useful in producing "intended effects" can only be assessed by answering two prior questions: power over whom and power in what realms of policy?[54] Efforts in the 1980s to show that Soviet effectiveness in world politics suffers from the reliance chiefly on military power are a promising beginning and a needed corrective to the still-dominant tendency to focus principally on the military components of Soviet power and to gloss over the significance of their being nontransferable.[55]

Not only is power composed of various elements, even military power is multifaceted. As Klaus Knorr has pointed out:

Military forces are not a homogeneous entity with which different states are endowed in varying amounts. . . . [S]tates may have forces more suitable for some modes and theaters of war than for others. For example, a state may possess a strong capability to deter a nuclear attack . . . but lack strong forces for waging conventional combat. Or its forces may be strong for the defense of its territory but lack the logistical capacity for large-scale operations in far away places. . . . In general, the armed forces of great military powers have large size, more versatility, wider geographical reach, and are capable of more varied expansion. . . . But sheer scarcity of resources places limitations even on the capabilities of great and wealthy military powers.[56]

Knorr's point is well demonstrated by Michael Klare's chapter in this book. Klare shows that—although the Soviet Union has impressive conventional forces for Eurasian military operations plus a large nuclear arsenal—reports suggesting that Soviet power-projection capabilities are vast and rapidly expanding are incorrect. Moreover, a major buildup in Soviet interventionary forces is unlikely. Aircraft carriers, amphibious ships, and transport aircraft are expensive items. The USSR will be hard-pressed to acquire them amid an economic slowdown and the sizable expenditures needed for the maintenance and modernization of strategic nuclear forces and conventional armaments for Eurasian contingencies.

Klare recognizes that the constraints on the Soviet capacity for distant intervention need not be a hindrance when military force is to be applied against a weak and proximate state, such as Afghanistan. As Melvin Goodman's chapter indicates, however, in important respects the invasion of neighboring Afghanistan has involved costs for the Soviets: it has been a key obstacle to improved relations with China and Iran; it has prompted another neighboring state, Pakistan, to expand security ties with the United States and China; and it is certain to make other states who have signed security treaties with the USSR suspicious. After all, the invasion of Afghanistan was justified by Moscow in terms of the 1978 Soviet–Afghan friendship treaty.

It is, of course, legitimate to ask why the Soviets took over eight years to withdraw from Afghanistan if indeed the invasion involved significant costs. The answer involves a paradox. As the war in Afghanistan proceeded, the costs for the Soviets mounted; the number of soldiers killed or maimed increased. Soviet press reports began openly to speak of the travails of war against Afghan resistance.[57] At one level, this disillusionment should have increased the Soviets' frustration and thus their eagerness to leave Afghanistan. But the passage of time, the money spent, and soldiers killed, at another level, made Moscow determined to prevail and reluctant to withdraw. Disengagement, it was feared, would have led to the certain collapse of the regime supported by the Soviets and the victory of the *mujahedeen*. This would have been a colossal symbol of failure and a confession of error by the Brezhnev leadership. Much time and effort were expended in the Afghan war. Afghanistan is a bordering state whose political orientation is seen as directly relevant to Soviet security. For both of these reasons, the continuation of the war was for long preferable to any withdrawal involving the collapse of the Soviet-supported regime.[58]

Soon after Gorbachev became general secretary in March 1985, the Soviet leadership undertook a reassessment of its policy in Afghanistan. At the 27th Party Congress in February 1986, Gorbachev spoke of Afghanistan as a "bleeding wound," thus betraying his frustration at a long, costly, and bloody campaign that was manifestly failing to achieve Soviet objectives.[59] Yet withdrawal was not Gorbachev's first impulse. Efforts were made to devise a more effective strategy. To this end, PDPA leader Babrak Karmal was replaced by Najibullah in May 1986 and the Kabul regime was urged to broaden its base of support by, among other measures, seeking a dialogue with the opposition aimed at "national reconciliation" and the sharing of power. Changes were also made in Soviet military tactics to wage war more effectively against the numerous guerrilla bands fighting tenaciously and using the advantages of Afghanistan's formidable terrain.

Withdrawal through the Geneva Accords was decided upon only when the failure of these measures became apparent. The decision was facilitated by Gorbachev's lack of involvement in the original decision—made in 1979—to invade. The exit from Afghanistan was thus not a symbol of failure on his part. The war could be depicted as yet another Brezhnev-era blunder that needed to be rectified. Moreover, by 1988, it was apparent to the Soviet leadership that the *mujahedeen* were not being defeated. On the contrary, the U.S. decision to supply them with *Stinger* antiaircraft missiles from the fall of 1986 made air strikes against guerrilla strongholds, a principal feature of

Soviet strategy, much more dangerous and costly. Gorbachev also understood that the Afghan war was hampering the progress of his key objectives: arms control, expanded East–West economic relations, and rapprochement with China.

The war in Afghanistan raises another point relevant to power analysis. Purely quantitative comparisons would suggest that, in war, the side with greater wealth, superior technology, and more weaponry will prevail. The Afghan war, like the Vietnam war, demonstrates, however, the significant role that can be played by intangible, nonquantifiable factors: morale, the nature of the terrain, and so on. Moreover, elements that ordinarily might be seen as liabilities—scattered *mujahedeen* units fighting without a central command, primitive communications, relatively backward weapons—actually emerged in Afghanistan as advantages. They reduced the resistance's vulnerability and the prospects for a quick Soviet victory. Due to disunited guerrilla bands, it was impossible for Soviet forces to seek victory by destroying a central command headquarters; rudimentary communications were less easily disrupted; and simple weaponry was more easily mastered, maintained, and transported. The lessons on the importance of intangible elements in war and the advantages of technological backwardness may appear simple and obvious.[60] But history offers many examples of attackers being swayed by their superiority in the quantifiable elements of power and the hubris engendered by technological advantage.[61]

Conclusion

The analysis in this chapter suggests that commonplace questions such as "How powerful is the Soviet Union?" and "Is Soviet power growing?" are virtually without meaning. Power is composed of diverse elements; means appropriate to affecting outcome in one realm may be inappropriate, even counterproductive, in another. To make judgments or comparisons about power without stating the goals toward which it is to be used is to ignore the multifaceted character of power. The growth of Soviet power in the military sphere is striking and deserves attention. An equally important topic for analysis is the causes of the one-dimensional character of Soviet power and its implications for the USSR's future status in world politics.

Gorbachev's reforms are nothing less than an effort to remedy the imbalances among the components of Soviet power. Will he succeed? Parallels between his efforts and those of Khrushchev have led many experts to voice pessimism. Further, *perestroika* (Gorbachev's proposal for economic restructuring) calls for new modes of thinking, stricter standards of performance, and economic sacrifices in the short term from Soviet citizens, while its benefits will be realized only in the long term. The changes it proposes threaten the power, privileges, and resources of important institutions. But as long as there does not emerge a leader with a strong base of support within the party capable of offering a well-developed conservative critique of *perestroika* that both offers solutions to the problems plaguing the Soviet system *and* mobilizes the various segments of Soviet society who are opposed to thoroughgoing reforms, the political survival of Gorbachev is assured. What is far more uncertain is whether the Gorbachev reforms can be implemented. The success or failure of *perestroika* will decide whether the one-dimensionality of Soviet power is overcome. This will decide the status and efficacy of the Soviet Union in world politics in the next century.

Notes

1. Harold D. Lasswell and Abraham Kaplan, *Power and Society* (New Haven: Yale University Press, 1950), pp. 74–77.

2. Bertrand Russell, *Power,* quoted in ibid., p. 75. The label "causal conception" of power appears in David A. Baldwin, "Power Analysis and World Politics: New Trends versus Old Tendencies," *World Politics,* 31, no. 2 (1979): 161.

3. Lasswell and Kaplan, *Power and Society,* p. 76.

4. Ibid., pp. 76–77, 83–84, 85–93.

5. The distinction between these two forms of power is drawn in Rajan Menon, *Soviet Power and the Third World* (New Haven: Yale University Press, 1986), pp. 214–15 and derives from Alvin Z. Rubinstein's introductory chapter in Rubinstein, ed., *Soviet and Chinese Influence in the Third World* (New York: Praeger, 1975).

6. Carl J. Friedrich, *Constitutional Government and Democracy: Theory and Practice in Europe and America* (Boston: Little, Brown, 1941), pp. 589–90; idem., *Man and His Government: An Empirical Theory of Politics* (New York: McGraw-Hill, 1963), ch. 2. The manifestation of power in this form is also recognized in Terence Ball, "Power, Causation and Explanation," *Polity,* 8, no. 2 (winter 1975): 196–203; Peter Bachrach and Morton Baratz, "Two Faces of Power," in Roderick Bell, David V. Edwards, and R. Harrison Wagner, eds., *Political Power: A Reader in Theory and Research* (New York: Free Press, 1969), pp. 95–96; Robert Dahl, *Modern Political Analysis* (Englewood Cliffs, N.J.: Prentice-Hall, 1970), p. 31; and Jack H. Nagel, "Some Questions about the Concept of Power," *Behavioral Science,* 13, no. 2 (March 1968): 146. For a critique of this conception of power, see James March, "An Introduction to the Theory and Measurement of Power" in Bell et al., eds., *Political Power,* pp. 166–94.

7. On the tendency and consequences of conceptualizing power in this way, see James Lee Ray, *Global Politics,* 3rd ed. (Boston: Houghton Mifflin, 1987), pp. 181–83.

8. See Jerry F. Hough, *The Struggle for the Third World* (Washington, D.C.: Brookings Institution, 1986), pp. 238–41, 253.

9. For the text of Gorbachev's speech, see Current Digest of the Soviet Press (CDSP), *Current Soviet Policies IX* (Columbus, Ohio: CDSP 1986), pp. 10–46.

10. *Christian Science Monitor,* April 7, 1987, pp. 1, 8.

11. Rosanne Klass, "Afghanistan: The Accords," *Foreign Affairs,* 66, no. 5 (summer 1988): 922–45. In April 1988 I was part of a delegation of private Americans— assembled by the International Center for Development Policy (ICDP)—that traveled to Moscow and Afghanistan for discussions with Soviet scholars and leaders of the PDPA government on the future of Afghanistan in the wake of the Geneva Accords. See Rajan Menon (in conjunction with the staff of the ICDP Commission on U.S.-Soviet Relations), *Afghanistan after the Geneva Accords: A Report by the International Center for Development Policy on Its April, 1988 Fact-finding Mission to the USSR and Afghanistan* (Washington, D.C.: ICDP, May 26, 1988); and Rajan Menon, "Only Afghans Can Decide Afghanistan's Fate," *Newsday,* May 17, 1988, p. 61.

12. *Christian Science Monitor,* March 5, 1987, p. 14. Also, Dina R. Spechler and Martin C. Spechler, "Economic Constraints and External Behavior: Soviet Involvement in the Third World," paper presented at the 1987 Annual Meeting of the American Political Science Association, Chicago, September 3–6, 1987.

13. See Melvin A. Goodman, "The Soviet Union and the Third World: The Military Dimension," in Andrzej Korbonski and Francis Fukuyama, eds., *The Soviet Union and the Third World* (Ithaca, N.Y.: Cornell University Press, 1987), pp. 50–53; and Edward Gonzalez, "Cuba, the Third World, and the Soviet Union," in ibid., p. 139.

14. Jyotirmoy Banerjee, "Moscow's Indian Alliance," *Problems of Communism,* 36, no. 1 (January-February 1987): 1–2.

15. During Shevardnadze's visit to Argentina in September 1987, a former Argentine foreign-ministry official remarked: "The possibilities of the Soviets supporting Latin America in their urgent needs such as foreign debt [relief], new investment, and credit are really limited. They're not in a position to give us a penny." *Christian Science Monitor,* September 28, 1987, p. 9.

16. On Romania, see Ronald H. Linden, *Bears and Foxes* (Boulder, Col.: East European Quarterly, 1979), pp. 177–217. On Cuba, see Raymond Duncan, *The Soviet Union and Cuba: Interests and Influence* (New York: Praeger, 1985).

17. This point is made with reference to Poland in Walter Z. Laqueur, "What Poland Means," in Steven L. Spiegel, ed., *At Issue,* 4th ed. (New York: St. Martin's, 1984), pp. 290–91.

18. Soviet military writings stress the need for soldiers in multinational armies to believe in the justness of a war, because it is believed that the stresses of war can breed disunity by exacerbating the tensions that may have existed in societies before the outbreak of hostilities. See Christopher D. Jones, "Soviet Hegemony in Eastern Europe: The Dynamics of Political Autonomy and Military Intervention," *World Politics,* 29, no. 2 (January 1977): 238. On the question of the Warsaw Pact's reliability in war, see Daniel N. Nelson, ed., *Soviet Allies: The Warsaw Pact and the Issue of Reliability* (Boulder, Colo.: Westview, 1984); and David Holloway, "The Warsaw Pact in Transition," in Holloway and Jane M.O. Sharp, eds., *The Warsaw Pact* (Ithaca, Cornell University Press, 1984), pp. 29–31.

19. In 1984 current U.S. dollars. U.S. Arms Control and Disarmament Agency (ACDA), *World Military Expenditures and Arms Transfers 1986* (Washington, D.C.: ACDA, 1987), pp. 93–94.

20. On the costs to the USSR of aid to allies and clients, see Charles Wolf, Jr., K.C. Yeh, Edmund Branner, Jr., Aaron Gurwitz, and Marilee Lawrence, *The Costs of the Soviet Empire,* R-3073/I-NA (Santa Monica, Calif.: Rand Corporation, September 1983); Abraham S. Becker, *The Soviet Union and the Third World: The Economic Dimension,* OPS-005 (Rand Corporation, March 1986); and Spechler and Spechler, "Economic Constraints and External Behavior."

21. For the shift in Soviet foreign-aid policy and estimates of the economic burden of Soviet aid to the Third World, see Spechler and Spechler, "Economic Constraints and External Behavior," pp. 9, 13, 22–28.

22. An influential statement of this view is Robert O. Keohane and Joseph S. Nye, Jr., *Power and Interdependence* (Boston: Little, Brown, 1977).

23. This is a major theme in Robert Gilpin, *The Political Economy of International Relations* (Princeton, N.J.: Princeton University Press, 1987).

24. For example, the USSR does not belong to the IMF, World Bank, or GATT. Its share of the value of world trade is less than 4 percent; its foreign-aid program is about the size of those of the Netherlands, Belgium, Norway, and Denmark. Developed countries conduct less than 2 percent of their trade with the USSR and less than 4 percent with the entire Soviet bloc, while the Third World depends on the USSR and Eastern Europe for less than 4 percent of its trade. Information drawn from Paul Dibb, *The Soviet Union: The Incomplete Superpower* (Urbana: University of Illinois Press, 1986), pp. 216–20.

25. This example is presented and the argument developed in Jerry F. Hough, "Gorbachev's Strategy," *Foreign Affairs,* 64, no. 1 (fall 1985): 40.

26. Dibb, *The Soviet Union.*

27. David Holloway, *The Soviet Union and the Arms Race* (New Haven: Yale University Press, 1983), p. 82; John Lenczowski, *Soviet Perceptions of U.S. Foreign Policy* (Ithaca, N.Y.: Cornell University Press, 1982), pp. 51–53; Menon, *Soviet Power,* pp. 22–33, 51–53.

28. Yu. S. Novopashin, "The Influence of Real Socialism on the World Revolutionary Process," *Voprosy filosofii,* no. 8 (August 1982): 3–16; tr. in CDSP, *Soviet Foreign Policy Today,* 2nd ed. (Columbus, Ohio: CDSP, 1986), p. 126.

29. Alexander Bovin, "Restructuring and the Fate of Socialism," *Izvestia,* July 11, 1987, p. 6; tr. in *CDSP,* 39, no. 28 (August 12, 1987): 5–6.

30. Ibid., p. 6.

31. Ibid.

32. Hough, "Gorbachev's Strategy," pp. 39–40. On Gorbachev's recognition of the implications of the Soviet economic and technological lag, see Peter G. Peterson, "Gorbachev's Bottom Line," *New York Review of Books,* 34, no. 11 (June 25, 1987): 29.

33. Gorbachev quoted in Gail W. Lapidus, "Gorbachev and the Reform of the Soviet System," *Daedalus,* 116, no. 2 (spring 1987): 1.

34. Ellen Jones, *Red Army and Society* (London: Allen & Unwin, 1985), p. 188.

35. For the view that neither efficiency nor loyalty is seriously threatened by the increased number of Central Asian recruits, see ibid., pp. 188–95. For the argument that both have been, and will be, adversely affected, see Alexander Alexiev and S. Enders Wimbush, *The Ethnic Factor in the Soviet Armed Forces,* R-2930/1 (Santa

Monica, Calif.: Rand Corporation, August 1983). My view that the problems of efficiency—deriving from a lack of thorough knowledge of Russian and lower technical skills among Central Asian recruits—remain strong while military morale and loyalty have not been seriously impaired is based on discussions with Martha Olcott.

36. Holloway, *The Soviet Union,* p. 148. On the Soviet economy's basic weakness being its noninnovative character, see Marshall I. Goldman, "Gorbachev and Economic Reform," *Foreign Affairs,* 64, no. 1 (fall 1985): 57; and Kendall E. Bailes, "Science and Technology in the Soviet Union: Historical Background and Contemporary Problems," in Alexander Dallin and Condoleeze Rice, eds., *The Gorbachev Era* (Stanford, Calif.: Stanford Alumni Association, 1986), pp. 67–71.

37. Holloway, *The Soviet Union,* pp. 131–32, 170.

38. Ibid., p. 137.

39. U.S. Department of Defense, *The FY 1987 Department of Defense Program for Research and Development,* statement by the undersecretary of defense, research and engineering to the 99th Congress, 2nd sess., 1986 (n.p.:n.d.), table II-3. Table II-4, pp. 11–12, compares the United States and USSR with respect to 29 *deployed* military systems. It finds the United States leading in 16 (with a trend toward parity in 7), equality in 9, and a Soviet lead in 4 (with a move toward parity in 1). The systems in which the USSR leads are antisatellite technology (ASAT), artillery, chemical warfare, and mines.

40. I have drawn these from Louis Lavoie, "The Limits of Soviet Technology," *Technology Review* (November-December 1985): 71–73; and Andrew Cockburn, *The Threat: Inside the Soviet Military Machine* (New York: Random House, 1983), pp. 13–15, 199, 256–57, 262–63, and passim.

41. For Soviet views of the SDI, see, for example, Bruce Parrott, "The Soviet Debate on Missile Defense," *Bulletin of Atomic Scientists,* 43, no. 3 (April 1987): 9–12; David Holloway, "The Strategic Defense Initiative and the Soviet Union," *Daedalus,* 114, no. 3 (summer 1985), esp. pp. 265–77; Benjamin S. Lambeth, "Soviet Perspectives on the SDI," in Samuel F. Wells, Jr., and Robert S. Litwak, eds., *Strategic Defenses and Soviet–American Relations* (Cambridge, Mass.: Ballinger, 1987), pp. 37–77; and Benjamin Lambeth and Kevin Lewis, "The Kremlin and SDI," *Foreign Affairs,* 66, no. 4 (spring 1988): 755–70.

42. Hough, "Gorbachev's Strategy," p. 40; and Dibb, *The Soviet Union,* pp. 19–20. See also Condoleeza Rice, "Soviet Military Policy under Gorbachev," talk given at the Kennan Institute for Advanced Russian Studies, (Washington, D.C., May 13, 1987, as summarized in the Institute's *Meeting Report* (undated); and Jack Snyder, "Limiting Offensive Conventional Forces: Soviet Proposals and Western Options," *International Security,* 12, no. 4 (spring 1988): 54–57.

43. Lavoie, "The Limits," p. 75. Also, David R. Jones, "The Two Faces of Soviet Military Power," *Current History,* 86, no. 522 (October 1986): 337.

44. Yevgeni Primakov, "A New Philosophy of Foreign Policy," *Pravda,* July 10, 1987, p. 4; tr. in *CDSP,* 39, no. 28 (August 12, 1987): 1–4.

45. Stephen J. Flanigan, "SALT II," in Albert Carnesale and Richard N. Haas, eds., *Superpower Arms Control: Setting the Record Straight* (Cambridge, Mass.: Ballinger, 1987), p. 122; *Christian Science Monitor,* August 10, 1987, p. 2, and August 12, 1987, p. 2. On Soviet reliance on the land-based leg of the strategic triad in the era of counterforce strategic nuclear weapons, see Jones, "Two Faces," pp. 314–15.

46. The Soviets have been particularly concerned with U.S. efforts to involve its allies in SDI research and have also criticized the 1983 Japanese decision to institute a change in policy and begin selling technology with military applications to the United States and later to participate in the SDI research program. On the latter issue, see, for example, *Pravda,* July 23, 1987, p. 4.

47. Lasswell and Kaplan, *Power and Society,* p. 97.

48. These appear in the U.S. Department of Defense's annual publication, *Soviet Military Power.*

49. Edward A. Hewett and Herbert S. Levine, "The Soviet Union's Economic Relations in Asia," in Donald S. Zagoria, ed., *Soviet Policy in East Asia* (New Haven: Yale University Press, 1982), pp. 221–22.

50. In the 1980s, Soviet apprehension about such a trend has been reduced by China's decision to adopt a more balanced, independent policy vis-à-vis the super-powers and by the growth in economic and political contacts between China and the Soviet Union.

51. Professor Vyacheslav Dashichev, "East–West: Quest for New Relations. On the Priorities of the Soviet State's Foreign Policy," *Literaturnaya gazeta,* May 18, 1988, p. 14; trs. in Foreign Broadcast Information Service," *Daily Report—Soviet Union,* FBIS-SOV-88-098, May 20, 1988, pp. 7–8.

52. Baldwin, "Power Analysis," p. 180.

53. Ibid., pp. 166–67.

54. Ibid., p. 163; and Lasswell and Kaplan, *Power and Society,* pp. 76–78.

55. The best of such efforts is Dibb, *The Soviet Union.*

56. Klaus Knorr, *Military Power and Potential* (Lexington, Mass.: D.C. Heath, 1970), p. 4.

57. *Christian Science Monitor,* July 21, 1987, p. 10.

58. On the tendency of military operations to be continued despite the lack of success and rising costs, when "emotions and institutional interest" make disengagement difficult, see Edward N. Luttwak, *Strategy* (Cambridge, Mass.: Belknap Press of Harvard University Press, 1987), pp. 47–49, 58–59.

59. CDSP, *Current Soviet Policies IX,* p. 35.

60. On the importance of intangible factors—factors difficult to measure—in war, see Luttwak, *Strategy,* pp. 82–89. Luttwak makes the point in the context of a future war in Europe between NATO and Warsaw Pact forces.

61. In his acclaimed study of the Vietnam war, Col. Harry Summers notes that "by every quantifiable measurement there was simply no contest between the United States, the most powerful nation on the face of the earth, and a tenth-rate backward nation like North Vietnam. Yet there was one thing that did not fit into the computer—national will, what Clausewitz calls the moral factor." He adds: "Neither our civilian nor our military leaders dreamed that a tenth-rate underdeveloped country could defeat the United States, the world's dominant military and industrial power." Col. Harry G. Summers, Jr., *On Strategy* (New York: Dell, 1982), pp. 42–43, 167.

Part I
Internal Constraints

1
The Economic Burden of the Soviet Empire: Estimates and Reestimates

Dina R. Spechler
Martin C. Spechler

F or some years, commentators have been referring to the economic "burden" of the Soviet empire—the mounting costs borne by the USSR to sustain its allies in exchange for more and more uncertain political and strategic benefits. Once a zone of exploitation, Eastern Europe and other Communist countries, such as Cuba and Vietnam, have allegedly become a drag on Soviet resources.[1]

It is true that Soviet representatives have pressed for reform of the Council for Mutual Economic Assistance (COMECON) institutions and practices so that the USSR will receive a better return from its aid, especially in the form of technological innovations and higher-quality imports.[2] At the same time, many Soviet foreign-policy specialists appear to be growing skeptical of the value of involvement in the Third World.[3] There is evidence that Kremlin policymakers have sought to limit the growth of Soviet expenditures on aid to developing countries. A number of requests for economic and military assistance from loyal or potentially loyal clients have been declined.

We believe, however, that it is seriously misleading to speak of a large and rising burden of the Soviet empire or to assume (as many scholars and policymakers do) that the Soviet Union will be less able or less determined to maintain its position in Eastern Europe or the Third World as a result of economic stringency. After a critical reexamination of the main studies that have shown a rising economic cost of "empire,"[4] we present a new set of calculations that establish that the current cost of Soviet external empire is fairly small and certainly tolerable. Since the mid-1980s, at least, costs of empire have not risen, and the resources available to the USSR or the entire Soviet European empire for maintaining the integrity and power of that em-

The authors acknowledge the support of the Russian and East European Institute, the assistance of Bob Clough, and helpful suggestions of Michael Marrese, Paul Marer, and other members of the Centrally Planned Economies workshop at Indiana University–Bloomington.

pire are not scarcer than before. During the 1980s the burden (cost relative to resources) of the external empire has been stable or even declining, owing in part to successful efforts by the Soviets to economize.

The "Burden" of Earlier Literature

The most influential quantitative studies showing the cost to the USSR of its imperial satellites undoubtedly have been those of Jan Vanous and Michael Marrese.[5] Around 1980, these two specialists on Eastern Europe called attention to the enormous implicit trade subsidies that the USSR had been allowing its COMECON clients for nearly a decade.

Implicit trade subsidies occur when the USSR or Eastern Europe sells exports to other CMEA members for less than the best available price or buys goods more expensively than it could on the world market. Such subsidies to foreigners do not appear in balance-of-trade statistics. They arise within the Soviet empire because the USSR and its allies have agreed to trade at "world prices" held stable for a period of years, although bid/offered prices in the outside spot market change more frequently.

Moreover, since no unambiguous world price exists for manufactured capital goods and some consumer goods of the standard and quality usually traded within COMECON, intrabloc prices and payment conditions must be negotiated. Apparently the negotiated ruble price tends to be generous relative to the price obtainable in the West.[6] This differential may arise because capitalist countries discriminate against the Soviet bloc by means of Common Market or most-favored–nation preferences not extended to the CMEA. Alternatively, prices obtainable by Soviet-bloc countries in Western markets may be low because the CMEA countries have not developed the quality and marketing skills required in this market. Whatever the reasons, it seems undeniable that the typical machine or vehicle that passes in COMECON trade would not be salable at full price in the West. This situation favors the Eastern European partners in COMECON because they typically sell the USSR manufactured goods, while importing fuels and raw materials in return.

While trade subsidies have existed for a long time, they became much larger in the mid-1970s. At that time, the world spot price for petroleum suddenly quadrupled, while the Soviet Union was still obliged under the Bucharest formula (later amended at Moscow) to provide nearly all Eastern European needs at the average world price for the previous five years. By the calculations of Marrese and Vanous, the six Eastern European CMEA countries benefited from Soviet subsidies of about $6 billion yearly from 1974 through 1978. These rose to a peak of $21.7 billion in 1980 before subsiding gradually in the early 1980s. Adding in subsidies to Cuba raises the peak figure to $23.7 billion; with Vietnam and Mongolia, the grand total of implicit trade subsidies provided by the USSR in the peak year might well have exceeded $25 billion.

While economically meaningful and politically salient, these implicit trade subsidies are only a putative opportunity cost, not an out-of-pocket expense. Subsidies that arise from external price increases do not reduce the resources left to the donor; they only reduce the maximum material welfare that might be obtained if the windfall were fully utilized. Still, Soviet experts understood that the price concession given to COMECON did reduce their potential trading profits, although less than believed in the West.[7] Subsequently, as we shall see shortly, the Soviets made vigorous diplomatic efforts in COMECON councils to reduce the implicit subsidy by limiting the volume of planned and above-plan shipments at the subsidized price as well as by demanding compensation in investments and better-quality imports.

The Marrese-Vanous estimates have been subject to sharp criticism, some justified.[8] Perhaps the entire effort was too ambitious considering existing data. Using foreign-trade unit-values as proxies for prices is tricky, even when trade amounts and volumes are regularly published.[9] (The necessary data are not regularly published by COMECON, even for fungible commodities.) Manufactured goods are heterogeneous within the most detailed Standard International Trade Commission (SITC) classifications. Therefore, the observed, aggregate ruble unit-volume may reflect the particular mix of types (not to speak of qualities) being traded in any year. The mix may change from year to year without the underlying prices having been altered.

As for quality, Marrese and Vanous were forced to make an arbitrary adjustment of 50 percent to allow for inferior COMECON machinery. That is, if the observed West-to-West price was $100 and the observed East-to-East price was 100 transferable rubles for a nominally similar item, Marrese and Vanous assumed than an *identical* article would yield the Eastern seller only $50 on Western markets.[10] Hence, they reasoned, for $50 in Western markets the Soviets could have bought a machine equivalent to the COMECON type they in fact bought in the East at twice its world value. In other words, the West-to-East price would have been $50 because the East-to-West price was $50. Several critics felt this adjustment was too drastic, because the discount for COMECON machinery on Western markets also reflects discrimination—chiefly, absence of most-favored–nation tariff treatment. The reported East-to-West price was so low because the Eastern exporter had to pay an unusually high tariff to gain access to the large Western market; hence, the net price received was lower than it might have been without discriminatory tariffs on Eastern-bloc goods. What is more, as Marer and Poznanski have emphasized, Eastern European types may be worth more to the USSR than to Western European customers, because the Eastern Europeans have adopted Soviet standards and specifications. Moreover, the Eastern Europeans undoubtedly have improved their export quality since the underlying price data were assembled.[11] On the other hand, Soviet and Eastern European exports to the West usually are prepared specially and may be worth more than their shipments of the same items to bloc customers. To this extent, the Marrese-Vanous discount may have been understated.

These criticisms do not affect the bulk of implicit Soviet trade subsidies provided for petroleum and other fuels, as well as for imported commodities, for which world prices can be ascertained with some accuracy.[12] Those huge implicit petroleum subsidies apparently ceased in 1984; all that remain are the inflated prices paid mostly for Cuban sugar and nickel.[13] What OPEC wrought, its decline undid. Vanous, now president of PlanEcon, no longer computes the subsidies; as he admits, they are no longer very interesting.

One constructive alternative to Marrese and Vanous's procedures has been offered by Kazimierz Poznanski. Poznanski proposes to compare the terms of trade the USSR received in its oil/nonoil trade with the oil/nonoil terms of trade *paid* by the Federal Republic of Germany during the same years.[14] During the two oil shocks of 1973–74 and 1979, the Soviet terms of trade improved less rapidly than they might have in the open market, judging by the (inverse) West German trade prices. But within about two years of the initial shocks, the terms of trade (relative to 1970) of the USSR and FRG converged, and then for a time the Soviet returns were even somewhat greater than those of the average West German supplier. Poznanski uses the West German benchmark as a way of telling what the Soviets could have done with the oil they sold to Eastern Europe at subsidized prices. Doing so reduces the estimated wealth transferred to Eastern Europe during 1970–83 from about $80 billion in the Marrese-Vanous calculations to only $40 billion.

While the details of Poznanski's methods are not yet published, the crucial result seems to depend on a virtual elimination of the manufactured import subsidy (some 44 percent of the total implicit subsidy in the late 1970s). This occurs, Poznanski believes, because, contrary to the Marrese-Vanous assumption, the Soviet Union could not have obtained goods in the West at the "world-market" price, adjusted for quality desired, paying with the money that they might have earned from increased hard-currency sales of oil. Based on a sample of thirty-three West German exports, Poznanski found that Eastern Europe paid between 45 and 68 percent more for the same items than Western customers paid in 1978 and 1982. The larger markup was apparently a compensation for the credit and buyback provisions of West German contracts with COMECON customers. Evidently the West does discriminate against the East on the export side as well as on imports. Allowing for an average 55 percent surcharge, the cost of COMECON-standard machinery in the West, adjusted for a 20–30 percent quality difference, would not be very different from the "subsidized" COMECON prices. Therefore, buying machinery in the East, Poznanski concludes, is not nearly so disadvantageous for the USSR as previously believed.

To the extent that this adjustment is responsible for the halving of the Marrese-Vanous estimate of implicit trade subsidies, it seems questionable. Had the Soviets sold more oil on world markets, they could have paid cash for much of the imports and not insisted on buyback or credit provisions often demanded by cash-poor Eastern Europeans. Hence, the cash price to the USSR might have been considerably lower, and the opportunity cost of trade subsidies to Eastern Europe correspondingly higher. We do concur with Poznanski (and Rand), however, that the total trade subsidies computed by Marrese and Vanous were somewhat exaggerated.

The Rand study by Charles Wolf, Jr., and his collaborators derived almost all of its quantitative impact from the Marrese-Vanous trade subsidies, though the Rand authors did adjust the quality discount down somewhat. In addition to implicit trade subsidies, Rand's "cost of Soviet empire" (CSE) also included military and foreign aid, the incremental cost of the Afghanistan operation, and diplomatic personnel and covert operations abroad, all estimated in both dollars and rubles. In constant 1981 dollars, their CSE rose from $13.6–21.8 billion in 1971 to $35.9–46.5 billion by 1980—a remarkable, and obviously unsustainable, 8.7 percent annual rise. By 1980, Rand's estimated CSE, which excluded defense of the Soviet Union itself, represented 2.3–3.0 percent of Soviet GNP. In ruble terms, the Rand team calculated that direct costs to the Soviet Union of maintaining the entire "external empire" rose from 8.6 billion 1980 rubles in 1971 to 42.2 billion rubles by 1980—an annual growth rate of 16.3 percent.[15] By 1980, their ruble figure represented 6–7 percent of Soviet GNP.

This burden, when measured in rubles, seemed to the Rand authors to transcend "the bounds that have been acceptable to imperial powers in the past."[16] Wolf himself even conceived a U.S. strategy of containing the Soviet Union by raising the cost of empire to even more intolerable levels.[17]

The Rand study has now been extended to 1983 without changing the methods and without substantially revising the data for 1971–80.[18] In constant prices of 1981, the Rand revised series shows a rapid fall from 1981 on, with some two-thirds of the decrease owing to the collapse of petroleum subsidies and the rest chiefly to reduced military aid.[19] The Rand authors now argue that the sharp reversal of trend in their CSE proves that they were right all along in thinking that the excessive and rising cost of empire had to be controlled on account of "serious stringencies in the Soviet economy." Further, "lagging Soviet growth probably led to action by the Soviet leadership to reduce these costs; absent such reductions, economic growth would probably have been still lower."[20]

Implicit price subsidies and military aid are hardly the things to cut if the purpose is to divert resources to the domestic economy. Subsidies, if reduced because of falling prices, do not divert resources at all; military aid, as we shall argue, has low opportunity cost. A more natural explanation of the pattern, in our opinion, would be that the Soviet authorities allowed implicit price subsidies to rise during the late 1970s because it was impractical to collect the full price increase from the Eastern Europeans immediately. After 1981, as oil prices began to fall, the Bucharest formula would indicate a declining obligation to provide subsidies. Moreover, Eastern Europe's need for such assistance was also declining. Military aid fell (along with military sales generally) because the Soviets perceived the disappointing *benefits* from this aid, which goes mainly to noncommunist LDCs. What is more, they realized that military adventures would meet Western resistance.[21]

We would argue that, in concept and in application, the Rand measure is misleading for the purpose of evaluating Soviet foreign policy. First, the Rand use of the Marrese-Vanous subsidies—which constitute 65–70 percent of the ruble CSE in 1980, but only 14–26 percent in 1970—imparts an exaggerated, and temporary, dynamic to the ruble measure, which is critical in the Rand conclusion.[22] By concentrating originally on the years 1970–80, the Wolf team showed a sharply rising cost. This increase in real and foregone costs was feasible owing to the improved terms of trade the Soviets enjoyed in energy trade with the outside world.[23] As a political matter, the trade subsidies were tolerable in 1974–77 and 1979–81 largely because the Soviets coincidentally enjoyed an improvement in their actual terms of trade with both Eastern Europe and the West and could afford not to press imperial clients for the full price at once.

Second, we believe that CSE is exaggerated because the original dollar estimates of the subsidies are translated back into rubles at the average domestic value of hard-currency imports, using Treml's input-output data.[24] Because the USSR trades so little, this average ruble value of a dollar of imports (which would exceed the desirable, but unknown, *marginal* value) is quite high. Although such a valuation of external trade may be appropriate for certain purposes, it is not appropriate for valuing the *burden* of trade subsidies—which Rand puts at 4–5 percent of Soviet GNP in 1980—because demand for imports artificially is restricted to high-priority items, for which the willingness to pay is enhanced. The equilibrium exchange rate for the ruble would put a lower ruble value on dollar imports. Another reasons Rand's ruble estimate of the burden is exaggerated is that the corresponding GNP (the denominator in the burden ratio) has not been measured at these same prices, but rather at stable values that do not reflect the run-up of petroleum prices.[25] Trade subsidies do not deduct 4–5 percent from the Soviet GNP, as measured in rubles; the residual remaining for other domestic uses is unchanged by higher or lower implicit trade subsidies when the change comes from outside the economy. To use as an indicator of a drain on resources available for civilian production, as Rand does, is therefore incorrect.

To some degree, this stricture applies also to the dollar estimates because there, too, as far as we know, the dollar GNP used in the denominator of the burden ratio has not been recalculated to reflect higher petroleum prices. Had this been done, the burden might not have risen at all, though the current dollar cost of trade subsidies would naturally have done so.

There are some other, albeit smaller, sources of exaggeration in the Rand study. Because both trade credits, measured by the Soviet trade surplus, and aid delivered by the USSR are included in CSE, there would appear to be substantial double-counting in the totals. The cost of Soviet technicians in the CSE are normally financed in the economic aid packages, if not compensated in hard currency. Might including them therefore be called "triple-counting"? Military personnel costs in CSE are too high because the Rand team divided the total size of the Red Army into *total* defense expenditures, which obviously include strategic deterrence and R&D not properly assigned to the cost of empire, as defined by Wolf and his coauthors. We try to avoid these pitfalls in our estimates that follow.

While the Rand team does mention certain offsets to the cost of empire that could not be estimated—such as Vietnamese[26] and Eastern European guest workers paid less than their marginal products—other offsets were left out. Realizing the expensive assistance they were providing the Eastern Europeans by holding oil prices steady, the Soviets successfully demanded extra payment in dollars and net projects (the $16 billion Yamburg complex, for example) to compensate them from the debts built up. Some of these deals came too recently to be included in the original study. However, the Rand team overlooked the fact that the concessions granted Eastern Europe during 1974–82 on oil prices were in part repayment for *previous* commercial credits,[27] joint projects (such as the Orenberg gas pipeline and nonferrous metals mines), and ordinary trade surpluses in 1970–74. The Eastern Europeans had also done the Soviets the incalculable favor of redirecting industrial development to the needs of the Soviet military-industrial complex, reliably supplying the Soviet Union, and accepting otherwise unsalable Soviet goods.[28]

Reestimated Cost and Burden of External Empire

Although we feel Rand's cost of external empire is exaggerated, there is definitely merit in aggregating all costs of foreign involvement to see whether the burden has been rising or declining and from what levels. We reestimate the Rand's CSE by somewhat different methods and with more recent and suitable data. Some of the results from these revisions are, we think, strikingly different. These results are summarized in table 1–1 and explained shortly.

Our estimates (which, like Rand's, must be considered quite approximate) are to be read as upper bounds. Because we think the conventional

Table 1–1
The Burden of Soviet Empire, 1971–84

		1971	1972	1973
Economic aid				
To all Non-Communist Less Developed Countries (NC LDC) net	mn $ current	161	237	265
To Communist LDC	mn $ current	731	584	807
Multilateral aid	mn $ current	4	5	5
Total to LDCs	mn $ current	896	826	1077
Deflated	mn $ 1985	2304.76	1936.22	2096.3
Aid and subsidies to Eastern Europe	mn $ 1985	900.29	−164.09	1498.75
Credit subsidies	mn $ 1985	0	0	0
Total ec aid, all recipients	mn $ 1985	3205.05	1772.13	3595.05
Students hosted—				
cost ($5,000 per student)	mn $ 1985	223.63	189.03	220.73
Military aid				
To NC LDCs	mn $ 1985	2225.01	2848.06	6102.05
To Communist LDCs	mn $ 1985	900.29	1453.33	768.84
Total mil aid, all recipients	mn $ 1985	3125.31	4301.4	6870.89
Military technicians	thousands	5	5	5
Cost ($10,059 per technician)	mn $ 1985	50.29	50.29	50.29
Military operations (Afghanistan)	mn $ current	—	—	—
	mn $ 1985	—	—	—
Political activities, incl.	mn $ current	2060	2170	2277
covert operations	mn $ 1985	5298.88	5086.67	4432.02
Total costs	mn $ 1985	11903.17	11399.52	15168.98
Less excess military costs	—	—	—	—
Over 2% "normal" level	mn $ current	5849.36	5562.69	5590.28
	mn $ 1985	15046.13	13039.42	10881.08
Over 1% "normal" level	mn $ current	8823.74	8677.56	8859.84
	mn $ 1985	22697.04	20340.95	17245.05
Equals net cost—2% normal	mn $ 1985	−3142.96	−1639.9	4287.91
—1% normal	mn $ 1985	−10793.88	−8941.44	−2076.07
Soviet Gross National Product (GNP)	bn $ 1985	1452	1477	1583
Burden: cost/GNP (2% normal)	mn $ 1985	−0.22	−0.11	0.27
(1 % normal)		−0.74	−0.61	−0.13
Cf. Rand's Cost of Soviet Empire (CSE)/GNP	current $	1.37	1.21	1.55
	current $	0.86	0.68	1.03

1974	1975	1976	1977	1978	1979	1980	1981
85	79	11	134	149	199	449	385
799	2058	2629	3170	3772	4223	4215	5026
5	5	6	6	6	7	7	6
889	2142	2646	3310	3927	4429	4671	5417
1389.26	3007.77	3685.8	4269.7	4488	4383.75	4073.11	4910.21
8188.67	5883.54	6073.35	5778.93	4137.14	6433.6	14283.36	12780.87
0	966.67	966.67	1365.57	876.98	1295.54	2710.67	3816.87
9577.94	9857.99	10755.73	11413.94	9502.13	12112.9	21067.15	21507.95
175.24	161	231.68	177.16	198.72	209.52	188.98	197.59
3477.06	2850.5	4332.14	6211.07	6942.86	8254.8	7085	410.19
398.49	280.84	285.56	264.44	577.14	2360.64	1621.92	1347.88
3875.56	3131.34	4617.7	6475.5	7520	10615.44	8706.92	8758.07
6.2	8.1	9.4	10.7	12.3	15.9	16.1	16.3
62.37	81.48	94.5	107.53	123.73	159.94	161.95	163.96
—	—	—	—	—	—	1200	1450
—	—	—	—	—	—	1046.40	1314.35
2390	2507	2631	2760	2897	3040	3190	3263
3734.91	3520.3	3664.91	3560.24	3310.86	3008.94	2781.68	2957.73
17426.01	16752.1	19364.51	21734.47	20655.43	26106.73	33953.08	34899.65
6024.68	6013.39	5691.57	5910.46	5715.41	5873.5	6724.86	7957.14
9414.91	8443.92	7928.19	7624.15	6531.9	5813.5	5864.08	7212.71
9442.27	9572.22	9322.52	9648.2	9543.56	9722.85	10572.66	11761.36
14755.66	13441.18	12986	12448.02	10906.93	9623.53	9219.36	10661.02
8011.1	8308.18	11436.32	14110.33	14123.53	20293.23	28089	27686.94
2670.36	3310.92	6378.52	9291.45	9748.5	16483.2	24733.71	24238.63
1643	1660.5	1732	1828	1840	1860.2	1885.5	
0.49	0.5	0.79	0.77	1.1	1.51	1.47	
0.16	0.2	0.37	0.52	0.53	0.9	1.33	1.29
2.02	1.63	1.81	1.82	1.75	2.61	3.2	2.99
1.53	1.17	1.37	1.39	1.28	2.03	2.52	2.43

Table 1-1 (Continued)

		1982	1983	1984
Economic aid				
To all Non-Communist Less Developed Countries (NC LDC) net	mn $ current	332	494	499
To Communist LDC	mn $ current	5612	5329	5577
Multilateral aid	mn $ current	4	4	4
Total to LDC's	mn $ current	5948	5827	6080
Deflated	mn $ 1985	5583.05	5658.29	6059.15
Aid and subsidies to Eastern Europe	mn $ 1985	8447.79	3689.98	2790.4
Credit subsidies	mn $ 1985	3109.3	1963.25	1963.25
Total ec aid, all recipients	mn $ 1985	17140.15	11311.51	10812.8
Students hosted—cost ($5000 per student)	mn $ 1985	206.97	250.82	278.76
Military aid				
To NC LDCs	mn $ 1985	8128.65	7278	7180.3
To Communist LDCs	mn $ 1985	1911.08	1412.87	1435.06
Total mil aid, all recipients	mn $ 1985	10039.73	8690.87	8615.36
Military technicians	thousands	17.2	18.1	19.1
Cost ($10,059 per technician)	mn $ 1985	173.01	182.07	192.13
Military operations (Afghanistan)	mn $ current	1620	1790	2000
	mn $ 1985	1520.6	1738.17	1993.14
Political activities, incl.	mn $ current	3401	3540	3689
Covert operations	mn $ 1985	3192.33	3437.51	3676.35
Total costs	mn $ 1985	32272.8	25610.95	25568.54
Less excess military costs				
Over 2% "normal" level	mn $ current	6411.36	5750.9	6050.86
	mn $ 1985	6017.99	5584.39	6030.11
Over 1% "normal" level	mn $ current	10240.78	9649.87	10059.63
	mn $ 1985	9612.45	9370.47	10025.14
Equals net cost—2% normal	mn $ 1985	26254.81	20026.56	19538.43
—1% normal	mn $ 1985	22660.35	16240.48	15543.4
Soviet Gross National Product (GNP)	bn $ 1985	1927.4	1970.1	2028
Burden: cost/GNP (2% normal)	mn $ 1985	1.36	1.02	0.96
(1 % normal)		1.18	0.82	0.77
Cf. Rand's Cost of Soviet Empire (CSE)/GNP	current $	2.34	1.85	
	current $	1.8	1.33	

Sources: Economic aid: OECD, *Development Cooperation* (Paris, 1987 and previous years); to Eastern Europe, CIA, *Handbook of Economic Statistics* (Washington, D.C.: U.S. Government Printing Office, 1986 and previous years), using the latest revision for each year reported excluding Romania.

Deflator: International Monetary Fund, *International Financial Statistics,* various issues, using dollar export values for industrialized countries.

Credit subsidies to Eastern Europe: Keith Crane, *The Soviet Economic Dilemma of Eastern Europe* (Santa Monica, Calif.: Rand, 1986.

Military aid: CIA, *Handbook of Economic Statistics;* Arms Control and Disarmament Agency, *World Military Expenditures and Arms Transfers, 1985,* for Communist LDCs, using the share of Soviet and Eastern European arms to a given country for a five-year period applied to the total imports for the given year.

Students hosted: *Development Cooperation,* 1987, table 26.

Military technicians: U.S. Department of State, *Warsaw Pact Economic Aid to Non-Communist LDCs, 1984* (Bureau of Intelligence and Research, no. 9345, May 1986); cost per military technician using ruble estimate of CIA in *Allocation of Resources in the Soviet Union and China—1985* (Washington, D.C.: U.S. Government Printing Office, 1986), p. 156.

Military operations (Afghanistan): Upper end of range reported in Charles Wolf, Jr., et al., *The Costs and Benefits of the Soviet Empire, 1981–1983* (Santa Monica, Calif.: Rand, 1986), based on extrapolation of estimate of General Eugene F. Tighe, Jr., in *Allocation of Resources in the Soviet Union and China—1980* (Joint Economic Committee, 1980), p. 26, based on troop presence from Joseph J. Collins, *The Soviet Invasion of Afghanistan* (Lexington, Mass.: Lexington Books, 1986), p. 151, and U.S. Department of Defense, *Soviet Military Power* (1987 and previous years).

Political activities: 75 percent (to adjust for activities in the industrialized West) of estimates by Edmund Brunner, appendix 1, in Charles Wolf, Jr., et al., *The Costs of the Soviet Empire* (Santa Monica, Calif.: Rand, 1983).

Military expenditures in Eastern Europe: Thad Alton, E. Bass, Z. Badach, and G. Lazarcik, *East European GNP—Originated and Domestic Final Uses of Gross Product, 1970–84* (New York: L.W. International Financial Research, 1985).

GNP and adjusted purchasing power parity conversion rates: Paul Marer, *Dollar GNPs of the U.S.S.R and Eastern Europe* (Baltimore: Johns Hopkins University Press for the World Bank, 1985), tables 1–1, 3–1, and 3–18).

Rand's Cost of Soviet Empire: Upper and lower bounds as estimated by Wolf et al., *Costs,* (1983), table 2, for earlier years; and Wolf et al., *Costs and Benefits* (1986), table 4, for 1978–83.

appraisal of the burden is exaggerated, we aim to show that it is small and declining, even when uncertain elements are included at generous dimensions.

In contrast with Rand, we estimate net economic aid directly, using the continuous OECD series, which alone includes major repayments. In 1984, the last year (as of 1988) with complete figures, the net Soviet aid cost was $6,059 million—about 92 percent allocated to CMEA developing countries, and a mere 8 percent to other LDCs.[29] To this is added the implicit trade subsidy figure computed for the 1970s by Rand and extended by using the roughly equivalent CIA series for aid to Eastern Europe. At most, the 1984 subsidy figure was $2,790 million, expressed in 1985 prices. (This 1984 figure will probably be revised downward in 1988, and later years' figures will be much lower.)

With respect to credit subsidies, which have accrued because Eastern European countries have accumulated trade deficits with the USSR financed at interest rates far below the market, we employ Keith Crane's series, published by Rand. We do this even though we think the Crane figures are too high because he failed to deduct invisible earnings from the apparent trade deficit in cumulating Eastern European debt since 1973 and because the comparable Western interest rate would be the one in an inflation-free environment, such as that of Switzerland. Swiss interest rates are similar to those within COMECON. Ignoring recent repayments, the credit subsidy could have amounted to $1,963 million in 1984. It is to be remembered that implicit credit subsidies are also an opportunity cost, not an out-of-pocket expense. When they are included nevertheless, the total expenditure on economic aid to Eastern Europe and the LDCs was $10.8 billion in 1984.

Student scholarships for study in the Soviet Union add about $278 million to the civilian aid cost. We prefer this figure, based on a student count and estimated yearly cost, to the OECD figure of $250 million, which is unexplained. Manifestly the two are quite similar. Rand omits this item.

On the military side, we employ a CIA series published by Joan Zoeter to estimate military aid. This series supposedly excludes sales for cash or credit, though this adjustment must be considered arbitrary absent any published explanation. Military aid was $8,615 million in 1984, about five-sixths to the noncommunist developing countries. Although some deliveries to COMECON clients may be left out, we believe the military aid figures are higher than their *incremental* cost to the USSR to the extent that obsolescent arms are supplied at conventional prices, not at their alternative cost. Moreover, had the Soviets sold those arms via the world arms bazaar, it is reasonable to suppose their price would have fallen. Suppose, for example, that the Soviets are already selling the maximum *value* of arms to the world's cash customers; then any additional arms diverted from aid recipients or from Red Army reserves would have negligible real market value. An x percent increase in market sales would cut the price by the same x percent.

Military-aid totals, unlike economic-aid agreements, probably do not include the cost of support personnel provided by the Soviet armed forces to their allies. On the assumption that military technicians posted abroad are paid the average Soviet military cost, as computed from CIA estimates of the Soviet military budget, they add about $192 million to our 1984 figure. This counts each technician as present for a full year, though the original U.S. government series does not certify this. Again, we deliberately make our estimate too high. With the exception of Afghanistan operations beginning in 1980, we assume that all military personnel sent to Ethiopia, Syria, and other war theaters are included as "technicians" in these data.

Total costs for 1984, both economic and military, would be $25,568 million, just over one percent of Soviet GNP in that year, as estimated by the CIA series—a third to a quarter less than the burden estimated by Rand for the last year of their revised study and, of course, only about one-third of the level Rand showed for 1980.[30]

Finally, we take account of certain offsets that are not considered in the previous literature. In estimating the cost to the Soviet Union of the external empire, it would be proper to net out any material benefits to the USSR itself from that empire.[31] The chief offset is the Eastern European contribution to Soviet defense. It is probably true that the thirty-three Soviet divisions in

Eastern Europe and the roughly 60,000 troops on the Mongolian-Chinese border are Soviet-supported.[32] As the USSR has the option of stationing those troops at home—at much less cost, one would suppose—evidently their forward positions do afford a military advantage, not to mention political intimidation throughout Central Europe. In rebellions such as that of August 1968, these troops may also serve to keep Eastern Europeans in line, but such uses of troops have not occurred since the beginning of the period considered in this chapter. Thus, the excess cost of forward stationing Soviet troops reflects a benefit to the defense of the USSR, not its external empire.

Moreover, the five Eastern European satellites of the Soviet Union that are active in the Warsaw Pact Treaty Organization (WTO) spend much more on defense than they probably would if they withdrew from the WTO. Proof of this is the fact that Romania has spent a much smaller, and continually declining share, of its GNP on defense since withdrawing from active WTO participation. We therefore posit that if the Eastern European countries were to assume the same posture as the Romanians toward the Soviet Union, their military expenditures would be 2 percent of GNP at most. Were Eastern Europe to be "Finlandized" or neutralized on the Austrian model, military expenditures could be even lower—about 1 percent, aside from police functions. Because the Eastern Europeans in fact spend from 3 to 5 percent of their products—based on minimal estimates by Crane of Rand and Alton and his team at L.W. Financial Research, Inc.—the extra margin can fairly be credited to defense of the Soviet European empire. This excess would be between $6 and $10 billion in 1984, depending on the contrafactual assumption made.[33] Accordingly, the net costs of Soviet external empire were $15.54 billion to $19.54 billion in 1984, depending on one's assumption about normal military expenditures in Eastern Europe. Both figures are estimated upper bounds—we believe the true amount to be less.

Looking at the trends since 1971 (see figure 1–1), we see that the real costs of Soviet empire have not risen monotonically. Indeed most of the rise—all the rise in Rand's estimates—occurred by 1974! Over the thirteen years, gross costs have doubled from $11.9 billion to $25.6 billion in constant 1985 prices, a compound annual rate of 6.1 percent—considerably below the long-term rate estimated as of 1980. Net costs, excluding excess military costs over the 2 percent level, were negative until 1974 and have averaged 0.76 percent of Soviet GNP over 1971–84. As indicated in the figure, we estimate that these net costs peaked in 1980 at 1.5 percent of GNP and have declined since—probably more than indicated.

Prospects: Will Resources Become Scarcer?

While we have seen that the cost of Soviet empire is small and has increased only moderately since the late 1960s, it might be argued that the Soviets will not be able to bear even this burden in the future. After all, Soviet growth has

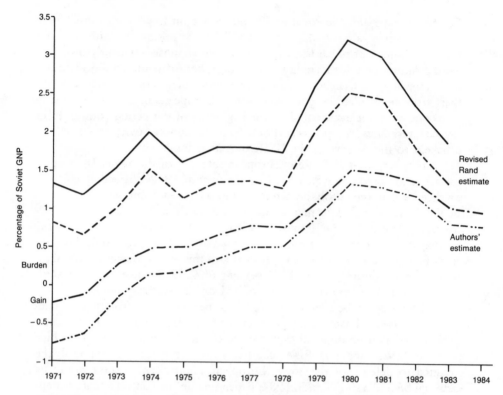

Revised Rand estimate uses upper and lower bounds of dollar estimate provided by Rand.

Figure 1–1. The Burden of Soviet External Empire on the USSR, 1971–84

slowed in recent decades. According to the CIA's most recent (1987) estimate of Soviet GNP (expressed in ruble factor cost prices of 1982), the average annual growth rate during 1981–85 was 2.2 percent. That compares with an average of 2.3 percent during each of the preceding five years and 3.1 percent annually during 1971–75. During the 1950s and 1960s, the quinquennial averages ranged from 3.5 to 7.2 percent.[34]

Western estimates of Soviet GNP describe Soviet economic growth according to Western consumption-oriented standards. The Soviet leadership does not recognize Western concepts for measuring their national product and may even suspect our calculations are biased. Still, annual growth of net material product (NMP), the Marxist concept that excludes certain consumer services, also decelerated in recent years, though the rates remained substantially higher than for GNP. By the NMP standard, USSR growth averaged 3.4 percent during 1981–85, as compared with 4.2 percent during 1976–80 and 5.6 percent during 1971–75.[35]

While growth has continued, surely its slowdown and the inability of the economy to produce the kind of goods desired by the population at large are sources of deep concern. Leading Soviet and Western specialists agree on the nature of the threats to Soviet growth in coming years. There is a labor shortage, particularly in the Slavic areas, caused by low rates of natural increase. Low investment rates during the Tenth Five-Year Plan (about 29 percent annual growth against 41 percent in the prior five years) have also impeded growth of productivity in various sectors.[36] Energy usage is phenomenally wasteful, in part because of the development within the USSR and its Eastern European neighbors of energy-intensive industries and processes. Continued growth even at current rates would exhaust apparent energy-production potential within one or two decades, according to the leading Western expert, unless current use coefficients can be reduced.[37] Some additional reduction of the petroleum available for export seems inevitable, and available exports will be produced at a much greater marginal cost than before owing to harsh conditions in the main West Siberian fields. It seems doubtful that natural-gas exports can make up for this, even in terms of energy equivalents, let alone foreign currency value. Overall Soviet sales to the OECD countries in 1985 were down about $4 billion from their 1981–84 levels, mostly owing to reduced oil revenues.

Nonetheless, most Western forecasts would concede to the Soviets a decent chance to grow at 2 to 2½ percent yearly to the end of the century, as compared with a growth in the available Soviet labor force of only 0.4 percent.[38] As the Soviet population is predicted to continue growing at about 0.9 percent yearly, these aggregate growth forecasts imply real growth per capita of about 1 to 1½ percent. If discretionary spending by the regime on its political and foreign objectives were to continue to grow along with the economy as a whole, how much would be left to reequip and expand the Soviet economic base? In other words, would investment growth be so low as to necessitate eventual cuts in public and private consumption, including defense and the cost of empire?

Let us consider one realistic scenario to illustrate the macroeconomic issues here. It is an arithmetic truism that

$$g = w_c g_c + w_i g_i + w_s g_s$$

where g is the growth rate of national income; g_c, g_i, and g_s are the growth rates of consumption (including general government), investment (including depreciation, inventories, and net foreign investment or net exports), and security (including defense); and w_c, w_i, and w_s are their weights in some base period (about 53.6, 32.6, and 13.6 percent, respectively, for a well-known 1985 projection).[39] Therefore, net investment growth possible emerges as a residual:

$$g_i = \frac{1}{w_i} (g - w_c g_c - w_s g_s)$$

Now suppose that consumption per capita must be allowed to grow at the rate actually achieved during the past ten years (1978–88)—about 1.5 percent. This means that aggregate consumption must grow a little less than 2.5 percent. If the economy were to grow at 2.5 percent overall, it is easy to see that nonconsumption items could also grow at rate a bit above 2.5 percent. Continuing defense spending on a 2 percent yearly increase, as estimated by the CIA, would allow gross investments to rise more than 15 percent during the five-year plan.

But suppose, more pessimistically for the Soviets, that aggregate growth turned out to be only 2 percent yearly to the end of the century. Then nonconsumption could grow at only 1.4 percent per annum. With defense growth continuing at 2 percent yearly, as the CIA presumes, this would not permit gross investment to grow more than 7 percent over the quinquennium. Capital intensity would hardly rise, not considering increased write-offs of obsolete equipment. These are two possible scenarios—bleak, certainly, but hardly a crisis of such proportions as to require major cuts in expenditure on empire.

Most important, Soviet leaders are not all convinced there is such a crisis. Using preferred Soviet statistical concepts, the planned growth rate for NMP for 1986 is 4½ percent with projected acceleration to the end of the century based upon higher investment rates and greater labor productivity gains. Even at 4 percent yearly, a calculation similar to the preceding one reveals that continued defense buildup and growth in consumption per capita allow a five-year growth of investment of 26 percent, the high end of the planned range for the Tenth Five-Year Plan, when calculated in Soviet terms. From the Soviet leaders' point of view, then, the immediate future is not altogether discouraging, and there are many measures to try before taking any steps that might undermine their position in Eastern Europe or the Third World.

The situation is even more sanguine when it is remembered that security expenditures are to be weighed in comparison with Western expenditures and capabilities. While it is true that since about 1979, the United States has increased its spending dramatically in real terms, the NATO partners have not met their targets for a 3 percent yearly increase and Soviet conventional war capacity in the European theater remains superior. What is more, Western economic growth has slowed no less than the Soviet bloc's since the 1960s, especially if one excludes Southeast Asian countries that do little as yet in defense of the noncommunist world. OECD-European and U.S. real growth rates since 1973 have been averaging less than 3 percent yearly with considerable variation from year to year.[40] The current economic recovery has not reversed this secular slowdown; productivity growth rates continue to be unusually low throughout NATO. The median expenditure on defense among the NATO countries was still 3 percent of GNP in 1986. Only Britain (and the United States, at 6½ percent in 1986) among the major Western allies spent more than 4 percent.[41] Hence, the Soviets can still feel, as they indicate in their statistical publications, that Warsaw Pact growth is comparable to or possibly exceeds that of the NATO countries as of 1987 and that there is no need to increase the share of GNP devoted to defense spending.[42]

Our view is that as of late 1987 the dominant faction in the Soviet leadership, including Gorbachev himself, considers the economic situation serious, eventually requiring radical reform. But the situation is not critical enough to force immediate radical changes in face of conservatives' warnings that reforms must be carefully prepared. Thus, the leadership has preferred to temporize by concentrating on the mobilization of "hidden reserves" of materials and human effort, redirecting investment to reequipment and away from new construction, and some adjustment in bonus indicators. More radical steps, for which price reform is a necessary prerequisite, have been postponed until the early 1990s.

Part of this two-track policy of vigorous, but not radical, efforts to increase productivity alongside deliberate preparation of pragmatic, but possibly radical, reforms may turn out to be efforts to cut the cost of external commitments. These possible cuts, however, are likely to be small and would not be made if there were any risk of losing major clients or appearing to surrender to U.S. pressure. Eastern Europe would appear to be a logical candidate for increased pressure to produce. We are skeptical of the argument, frequently heard from Eastern Europeanists, that the Soviet Union cannot squeeze any harder lest the Eastern European subject populations rebel. Perhaps it is true, as Valerie Bunce has written, that the sources of loyalty on the part of Eastern European intellectuals have been exhausted. Their increased employment prospects and prestige, as well as their pride in the industrial and egalitarian achievements of their regimes, are now things of the past. Knowledge of Western living standards is widespread, and many see the remaining gap as a central failure of their own political system.[43] Yet cynicism does not mean rebellion. From 1945 to 1988, there have been several political protests in the area; they have never been directly associated with poor economic performance. Rather, dashed hopes would seem to be the immediately prior condition.[44]

It would be even easier politically for the Soviets to reduce the cost of their efforts in the Third World, and they have already done so. Major demonstration projects in the Third World have nearly ceased, and the real cost of aid has fallen since the mid-1970s. Military sales, often of low-tech, even out-of-date equipment, have been on a pay-as-you-fight basis—very few Soviet clients get modern arms free of charge these days. But again, it must be emphasized that the cost of the USSR's Third World involvement is so small that further cuts in this area can accomplish little in economic terms. At present, the most costly Soviet intervention, Afghanistan, costs less than 1 percent of total defense expenditures. The Afghan war has been an ugly surprise for the Soviets, no doubt, and one they would like to cut short, but it remains tolerable in material terms. Maintaining allies acquired through intervention, their most expensive Third World activity, is very cheap. Aid to Cuba and Vietnam together amount to a percent or two of Soviet defense costs, and the discomfiture to the United States and China make it worthwhile. But the room for belt tightening is limited by the size of the belt. Since, as we have shown, the Third World involvement costs the Soviet Union very little, it cannot be a promising target for cuts. If expenditures on this portion of the Soviet empire are further reduced in years to come, the reason will be altered political priorities and outside pressures, not economic burden.

Conclusion

Growing resource constraints are not irrelevant in explaining recent trends in Soviet foreign policy and predicting Soviet behavior in the future. Economic stringency has led the Soviets to scrutinize all expenditures more carefully and has made them more impatient with allies who are perceived to squander Moscow's resources. This pattern is likely to persist for some time. Nonetheless, the burden of empire is not so great and Soviet resources are not so scarce as to require the USSR to jeopardize highly valued positions on its borders or overseas.

Notes

1. As we shall see, the most influential proponents of this idea have been Jan Vanous, Michael Marrese, Charles Wolf, Jr., and Wolf's collaborators at Rand. See Charles Wolf, Jr., K.C. Yeh, Edmund Brunner, Jr., Aaron Gurwitz, and Marilee Lawrence, *The Costs of the Soviet Empire* (Santa Monica, Calif.: Rand Corporation, R-3073/1-NA, 1983).

The origin of the idea goes back at least to the article by Paul Marer, "The Political Economy of Soviet Relations with Eastern Europe," in Steven J. Rosen and James Kurth, *Testing Theories of Economic Imperialism* (Lexington, Mass.: D.C. Heath, 1974), pp. 231ff. More recent examples of the use of the idea of the burden or liability of Soviet empire include Michael I. Handel, "The Future of Dominant-Subordinate Systems," in Jan Triska, ed., *Dominant Powers and Subordinate States* (Durham, N.C.: Duke University Press, 1986), pp. 423–39; and Valerie Bunce, "The Empire Strikes Back: The Evolution of the Eastern Bloc from a Soviet Asset to a Soviet Liability," *International Organization,* 39 (winter 1985): 1–46.

2. COMECON is another name for the Council on Mutual Economic Assistance (CMEA), the Soviet-bloc council for negotiating trade and some aid decisions.

3. Elizabeth Valkenier, *The Soviet Union and the Third World: An Economic Bind* (New York: Praeger, 1983); Francis Fukuyama, *Moscow's Post-Brezhnev Reassessment of the Third World* (Santa Monica, Calif. Rand Corporation, R-3337-USDP, 1986), based on an original idea by S. Sestanovich. Apparently Soviet experts began to question the value of certain Third World involvements under Andropov and even Brezhnev. We have examined the evidence on retrenchment in the Third World and find that it is highly selective, as some Third World activities have lately been expanded. See our "Economic Constraints and External Behavior: Soviet Involvement in the Third World," presented to the meeting of the American Political Science Association, Chicago, September 5, 1987.

4. Especially Charles Wolf, Jr., et al., *The Costs of Empire*.

5. Michael Marrese and Jan Vanous, *Soviet Subsidization of Trade with Eastern Europe: A Soviet Perspective* (Berkeley, Calif.: Institute of International Studies, 1983), though preliminary results appeared in working papers and the national press in 1980. Revised estimates and some answers to critics were published in Michael Marrese, "CMEA: Effective but Cumbersome Political Economy," *International Organization*, 40 (spring 1986): 287–327.

6. Hungarian sources report they pay 2.2 times the comparable world price for CMEA imports of equipment, twice the world-market price for consumer goods, but only 1.3 times the world price for food, which is more easily appraised. That COMECON unit price appears high—in all directions and for most goods—is a fact established long ago in the debate between Franklyn Holzman and Horst Menderhausen; it can be explained by bilateral bargaining insulated from the outside world market. Franklyn D. Holzman, *Foreign Trade under Central Planning* (Cambridge, Mass.: Harvard University Press, 1974), ch. 12. The original debate was published in the *Review of Economics and Statistics* between 1959 and 1962.

7. The Soviets estimate the windfall losses given up to Eastern Europe at some $18 billion for these years, considerably less than the approximately $50 billion cumulative total estimated by Marrese and Vanous and by Ed Hewitt. The source was Radio Moscow. APA, "Ost-Handel," November 11, 1980, cited by Raimund Dietz, "Advantages and Disadvantages in Soviet Trade with Eastern Europe: The Pricing Dimension," U.S. Congress, Joint Economic Committee, *East European Economies: Slow Growth in the 1980's,* vol. 2 (Washington, D.C.: U.S. Government Printing Office, 1986), p. 283.

8. Paul Marer, "The Political Economy of Soviet Relations with Eastern Europe," in Sarah M. Terry, ed., *Soviet Policy in Eastern Europe* (New Haven: Yale University Press, 1984), pp. 155–88; A. Koves, " 'Implicit Subsidies' and Some Issues of Economic Relations within the CMEA," *Acta Oeconomica*, 31, nos. 1–2 (1983): 125–36; Raimund Dietz, loc. cit., pp. 263ff. The main disagreements concern the opportunity cost or price of Eastern European manufacturers actually exported to the USSR and the exchange rates to be used in the calculations. The present authors believe that Marrese and Vanous make a good case for their procedure, but that lack of up-to-date figures make any adjustment highly uncertain. In any case, the adjust-

ments made by Marer or by Rand do not change the relative levels or pattern of the trade subsidies to Eastern Europe, and there is little disagreement about the proper treatment of the CMEA developing countries.

9. Foreign-trade unit-values are computed by dividing the value of trade for the narrowest possible commodity group by the volume traded of the same group, given in tons, units, and so on.

10. Assuming, for the sake of a simple example, that $1 = 1 TR.

11. Examples are Polish ships, Hungarian buses, and Czechoslovakian nuclear-power plants. Paul Marer and Kazimierz Poznanski, "The Costs of Domination, Benefits of Subordination," in Triska, op, cit., pp. 371ff.

12. With respect to oil, for which the Soviets have not published unit-value data since 1977, there is one further difficulty. Marrese and Vanous seem to assume that if the Soviets sold their oil in the open market, there would be no price response. Such a price response would come from increased spot supply, since the Eastern Europeans would probably not have been able to afford to replace their Soviet purchases with an equal volume of oil purchased on the open market for hard currency.

13. Cf. criticism of CIA estimates of these sugar subsidies by Andrew Zimbalist, "Soviet Aid, U.S. Blockage, and the Cuban Economy," *ACES Bulletin* (now *Comparative Economic Studies,* 24, no. 4 (Winter 1985): 137–46. Since the world price (around $0.09 per pound in 1987) fluctuates greatly, the difference between that price and the sum $0.44 paid by the Soviets fluctuates too.

14. Paul Marer and Kazimierz Poznanski, "The Costs of Domination," in Triska, op. cit., pp. 394–95. The calculations and approach are Poznanski's.

15. Wolf, et al., p. viii.

16. Ibid., p. 50.

17. Charles Wolf, "Beyond Containment: Redesigning American Policies," *Washington Quarterly* (winter 1983), and a fuller version published by the California Seminar on International Security and Foreign Policy. Cited in Wolf et al., *Costs of Soviet Empire,* p. 54, n. 3.

18. Charles Wolf, Jr., Keith Crane, K.C. Yeh, Susan Anderson, and Edmund Brunner, *The Costs and Benefits of the Soviet Empire, 1981–83* (Santa Monica, Calif.: Rand, 1986).

19. Ibid., p. 7.

20. Ibid., pp. 44–45. No other evidence is presented for this interpretation. Based on examination of available series for GNP growth and changes in costs of empire, we do not believe there is a general, positive relationship between "prosperity" and external spending. If we may be guided by historical parallels, it would seem that major initiatives by the Soviet Union in the Third World have not followed prosperity, nor have economic difficulties conspicuously restrained them. The major increase Soviet aid in 1954–55 *preceded* the economic successes of Nikita Khrushchev's middle period. More aid to the Third World came at the same time as competing initiatives in the Virgin Lands and with respect to consumer goods. Involvement in the Middle East has come in both prosperous and straitened circumstances, while the commitments of the 1970s and 1980s in Afghanistan and southern Africa hardly were made from full pockets.

21. For a full account of the change in Soviet foreign policy, see our "Economic Constraints and External Behavior." We argue, in particular, that Soviet economic failures were not fully recognized by the leadership before 1983.

22. Without the trade subsidies, the ruble estimate of burden, which is the theoretic ideal for measuring internal opportunity cost, would rise only about 10 percent a year, rather than 16 percent.

23. Even with the five-year moving-average formula adhered to by the USSR in its energy trade with the CMEA, its terms of trade improved 48 percent from 1972 through 1982.

24. V. Treml and B. Kostinsky, "Domestic Value of Soviet Foreign Trade: Exports and Imports in the 1972 Input-Output Table," *Foreign Economic Report* no. 20 (Washington, D.C.: U.S. Department of Commerce, 1982).

25. Ordinarily, ruble evaluations of Soviet GNP reflect the opportunity or factor cost of current production. Aside from a long-term rise in Soviet extraction costs for fuels, the ruble factor cost of petroleum, however disposed of, would not rise and, hence, a ton of petroleum sent to Eastern Europe and Cuba would not constitute a growing burden to the USSR in ruble terms.

26. Estimated at 100,000 for COMECON as a whole. *Economist,* April 20, 1985.

27. Granted by the Czechoslovak Socialist Republic (CSSR) in 1966 and the German Democratic Republic (GDR) in 1967 against Soviet obligations for five million tons of petroleum each.

28. Morris Bornstein, "Soviet Economic Growth and Foreign Policy," in S. Bialer, *The Domestic Context of Soviet Foreign Policy* (Boulder, Colo.: Westview, 1981), pp. 227–55; Paul Marer, Statement before the House Subcommittee on Europe and the Middle East, Committee on Foreign Affairs, October 7, 1985. One might add that Eastern Europe supplies certain invisible services, such as transportation, health, and tourist accommodation, to the Soviet Union in partial settlement of the visible trade imbalance. The exact magnitudes are at present unknown. So are dollar settlements for certain Soviet "hard" exports and the foreign-currency cost of inputs for Eastern Europe goods required by the Soviet Union. For an extensive calculation of the burden of Eastern Europe upon the USSR, see our "Is the Soviet Empire Really Declining?" presented to the Centrally Planned Economy Workshop, Indiana University-Bloomington, September 11, 1987.

29. All text figures are expressed in 1985 dollar prices, deflated by the OECD index of dollar export prices for industrial countries. We choose this index over a purely U.S. index because the Soviet Union buys manufactured goods, the assumed marginal purchase, mostly in Western Europe.

30. Wolf et al., *Costs and Benefits,* table 5, p. 16, using the midpoint of the 1983 dollar estimates. It is to be remembered that the present estimates represent an upper bound; therefore, the gap between them and those presented by Rand is deliberately underestimated.

31. But not such things as Cuban military surrogates fighting in Angola and Ethiopia or Eastern European paramilitary advisors in Mozambique. This support for Soviet aims in the external empire would properly be excluded when considering the cost of Soviet involvement in one or another *part* of the empire.

32. Conversation with Keith Crane.

33. We discuss these assumptions more fully in our paper "Is the Soviet Empire Really Declining?" cited previously.

34. Central Intelligence Agency and Defense Intelligence Agency, "The Soviet Economy under a New Leader," paper submitted to the Subcommittee on Economic

Resources, Competitiveness, and Security Economics of the Joint Economic Committee, Congress of the United States, March 19, 1986, mimeo, table A–1.

35. "1986 Panel on the Soviet Economic Outlook," *Soviet Economy*, 2, no. 1 (1986): 8. Soviet net material product rose by 4.1 percent in 1986, as against 3.5 percent in 1985. PlanEcon also sees an acceleration, but growth in both 1985 and 1986 was less than 2 percent if reduced taxes on vodka sales are allowed for.

36. Boris Rumer, "Realities of Gorbachev's Economic Program," *Problems of Communism* (May-June 1986): 20ff.

37. Robert C. Campbell, "The Economy," in Robert Byrnes, ed., *After Brezhnev* (Bloomington, Ind.: Indiana University Press, 1983), pp. 68–124.

38. Wharton has recently predicted 2½ to 3 percent growth through 1990.

39. Daniel L. Bond and Herbert Levine, "An Overview," in Abram Bergson and Herbert S. Levine, eds., *The Soviet Economy: Toward the Year 2000* (London: Allen & Unwin, 1983), table 1.6. So long as growth is nearly balanced, these weights would not change within the decade or two foreseeable.

40. Martin C. Spechler, "Social Influences on Growth and Productivity in the West, 1965–1984," in Benjamin Gilad and Stanley Kaish, eds., *Handbook of Behavioral Economics,* vol. B (Greenwich, Conn.: JAI Press, 1986), pp. 163–200; *OECD Historical Statistics,* various issues.

41. *NATO Review,* as cited in *Economist,* June 13, 1987.

42. According to the Soviet statistical handbook, *Narodnoe khoziaistvo 1985* (Moscow: Finansy i Statistika 1986), p. 580, the CMEA countries grew in national income by 3.3 percent annually from 1981 to 1985 while the capitalist countries were growing at only 2.2 percent annually. Soviet growth was 3.6 percent, versus 2.5 percent for the United States. Oddly, the handbook shows a slight slippage in the Soviets' relative standing—to 66 percent of U.S. national income.

43. Bunce, loc. cit.

44. Martin C. Spechler, "The Bankrupt Successes of Eastern Europe," *Soviet and Slavic Series,* 5, nos. 1–2 (1980): 30–38; J. Michael Montias, "Economic Conditions and Political Instability in Communist Countries: Observations on Strikes, Riots, and Other Disturbances," *Studies in Comparative Communism,* 13 (winter 1980): 283–95.

2

The Soviet Political Leadership and Soviet Power

Stephen White

T he Soviet Union is conventionally regarded as a state whose politics is dominated by a single party, within which the leadership and the general secretary in particular enjoy close to a monopoly of decision-making authority. For the theorists of totalitarianism, it was axiomatic that a political system of this type was characterized by a "single mass party typically led by one man," the "dictator," whose power was all but absolute and who in turn depended upon coercion and mass persuasion to maintain his position.[1] More contemporary students of Soviet politics, while generally wary of the totalitarian label, have nonetheless substantially agreed upon the mechanisms that ensure that a political system of the Soviet type is an authoritarian one in which power is very highly centralized. These key mechanisms include "democratic centralism" and the "ban on factions," which help to ensure dominance of the leadership within the party. Further, the principle of the party's "leading role" is intended to ensure that the party monopolizes political initiative and determines the main parameters of political, social, and economic development for the society as a whole.

Party policies, moreover, are supposedly guided, at least in principle, by an official ideology, Marxism-Leninism. Such an official ideology does not change from one general secretary to another, and it prescribes a definite long-term goal: the achievement of full communism both in the USSR itself and internationally. The current version of the official ideology is set out most authoritatively in the Party Program, a new and substantially revised version of which was adopted by the 27th Congress of the Communist Party of the Soviet Union (CPSU) in March 1986. The program makes clear that the party's "ultimate goal" remains the achievement of full communism on a global scale, and it defines the present epoch as one of the "transition from capitalism

The research reported in this chapter was carried out with the aid of a grant (E0023 2238) from the UK Economic and Social Research Council, whose support is gratefully acknowledged.

to socialism and communism," an "inevitable" and "irreversible" process initiated by the October revolution of 1917.

In line with this ideological charter, Soviet foreign and domestic policy
consistently emphasized a number of key priorities: at home, rapid
socioeconomic development led by heavy industry, and broad, the
maintenance of the socialist community together with support for "progressive" movements and regimes as against the "imperialism" of the United
States and other nations.[2] The clarity and coherence of these goals and the
steadfastness of the authorities in pursuing them have often combined to give
the impression of a regime able to "plan" its environment to a greater extent
than others and able to adjust its tactics with little regard to domestic opinion
or other circumstances.

This was probably always an exaggerated view of the consistency of
Soviet objectives and of the ability of the leadership to seek to achieve them.
Even in the Stalin period, it has been shown, bureaucratic and ministerial interests placed some limits upon the unconstrained use of executive power.[3]
Matters have now become considerably more complicated. The ideology has
become more qualified and ambiguous in response, among other things, to
the Polish crisis of the early 1980s;[4] the leadership has become more
"representative" in its composition, accommodating to an increasing degree
the varied interests of leading institutions and regions rather than the personal
choices of the general secretary; the role of associational and lobby groups has
expanded considerably; and public opinion is more openly expressed and
(arguably) more influential than in earlier periods of Soviet history. Beyond
Soviet borders, the complex and unpredictably course of world events, particularly in the Third World (as discussed by Mel Goodman in this book), has
forced unwelcome choices upon the leadership and has compelled some
reconceptualization of international politics.[5]

Although it would certainly be going too far to equate the pressures upon
a Soviet general secretary with those that bear upon political leaders in the
Western liberal democracies,[6] it has nonetheless been the constraints upon
executive action, rather than the opportunities for such action, that have
become more apparent over recent decades. In the remainder of this chapter,
I shall consider three of the most important of these constraints so far as
Soviet domestic politics in the 1980s are concerned: leadership constraints,
institutional or bureaucratic constraints, and popular constraints upon
executive action.[7] In a brief concluding section, I shall attempt to relate these
various "limits on power" to the field of foreign policy with which this book
as a whole is primarily concerned.

The Soviet Leadership and the Limits of Power

The first group of constraints to be considered concern the position of the
general secretary within the leadership as a whole. In the totalitarian concep-

tualization, systems of the Soviet type were seen as essentially Führerist in type, dominated by a single leader who exercised ideological as well as political authority. Current, more widely accepted, models generally suggest that the general secretary is typically at least *primus inter pares* within the leadership. Some scholars have argued further that the accession of a new and relatively youthful general secretary in Mikhail Gorbachev may lead to the reemergence of a leader-centered Soviet system of a kind that the decrepit Brezhnev and then his short-lived successors did not make possible.[8] At least one reason for the gradual accumulation of power in the hands of the general secretary is the "circular flow of power" by which each successive party leader uses his influence to promote supporters who will in turn support him and promote the continued expansion of his authority.[9] Each successive general secretary, on this basis, will feel obliged to retain his position in order to defend his "clients" and may fear for his reputation, if not his physical security, if he should ever leave office. Each group of clients, in their turn, will feel compelled to maintain the position of their patron since their own political fortunes will largely depend upon the extent of his success.[10]

The structural dynamics of the Soviet leadership and the position of the general secretary in particular are still the subject of scholarly debate, and only a limited consensus has so far emerged.[11] It is nonetheless clear that the picture so far presented is at least an incomplete one. In the first place, it neglects the structural differentiation of the Soviet leadership that has occurred since the death of Stalin and that has placed significant constraints upon the power of the general secretary. To some extent, this has been a function of the separation of key posts. Stalin, during the latter part of his rule, was prime minister, minister of defense, and commander in chief as well as party leader. Khrushchev succeeded him as party leader and (from 1958) as prime minister, also becoming chairman of the Defense Council of the USSR (a post that has now become automatically attached to that of the party general secretaryship). Brezhnev combined the state presidency (chairmanship of the Presidium of the USSR Supreme Soviet) with the party leadership from 1977 until his death. Following Khrushchev's resignation in 1964, however, the Central Committee adopted a resolution providing that, in order to guard against the excessive concentration of power in the hands of a single person, the party leadership and prime ministership should in the future be held by different people.[12] This important principle has been observed up to the present.

Both Andropov and Chernenko, following Brezhnev, combined the state presidency with the party leadership. Gorbachev, proposing Chernenko for the presidency in April 1984, observed that the Central Committee had considered it "essential" that the general secretary should also hold the post of chairman of the Supreme Soviet Presidium; this reflected the leading role of the party in the wider society and had "great significance" for the conduct of Soviet foreign policy.[13] In July 1985, however, rather against expectations, it was the veteran foreign minister, Andrei Gromyko, rather than Gorbachev himself, who was elevated to the presidency. Gorbachev, proposing Gromyko for the post, this time explained that although previous circumstances had justified the combination of the party leadership with the state presidency, the Central Committee now took the view that the tasks facing the country were such that the general secretary should concentrate his entire attentions upon the party's own activities.[14] Gorbachev was himself elected an ordinary member of the Supreme Soviet Presidium, a position that may be felt to allow him to represent the USSR as a whole and not just the CPSU. Although this arrangement may not prove permanent (in many other communist states, the party leader is also president for diplomatic and ceremonial purposes), it does at least for the present represent a further extension of the "separation of powers" within the leadership, removing a further (admittedly largely symbolic) set of functions from the disposition of the party leader.

A second trend that has also tended to limit the power of the general secretary has been the increasingly "institutionalized" composition of the Politburo and of leading party bodies. Rather than a collection of influential individuals, the Politburo may perhaps better be seen as a collection of important posts, the holders of which are in practice entitled to full or candidate Politburo membership by virtue of office.[15] By the late 1980s, the Politburo appeared to have become a combination of three distinct groupings, many members of which appeared to enjoy Politburo membership as of right: first, three or four senior members of the party Secretariat, led by the general secretary; second, key party leaders from the country as a whole, including the Moscow city and Leningrad regional first secretaries together with the Ukrainian, Belorussian, Georgian and Uzbek republican first secretaries for most of the 1970s and 1980s; and third, key members of the state apparatus, including, for most of the same period, the president and prime minister together with the ministers of defense and foreign affairs, the chairman of the KGB, and the prime minister of the Russian Soviet Federated Socialist Republic (RSFSR) (by far the largest of the USSR's fifteen union republics).

The evidence of the 1980s was that the "institutionalization" of Politburo membership upon this basis was gaining ground, although the changes associated with the accession of Gorbachev made the trends less apparent than would otherwise have been the case. Throughout the 1970s and 1980s, for instance, the president and prime minister were full members of the Politburo, together with (as full or candidate members) the ministers of defense and foreign affairs (from 1973) and the RSFSR prime minister. Successive Ukrainian party first secretaries (Shelest and Shcherbitsky) and Belorussian party first secretaries (Masherov, Kisilev, and, until his movement to the secretariat in 1987, Slyunkov) have been full or candidate members, respectively. Yuri Solovev, who succeeded Georgy Romanov as Leningrad regional party leader in 1985, followed him into the Politburo in 1986; similarly, the new Moscow party leader, Boris Yeltsin, took Viktor Grishin's place in the

Politburo (as a candidate) in 1986, and the new defense minister, General Yazov, took Marshal Sokolov's Politburo seat within a month of his appointment in May 1987. A similar process of "creeping institutionalization" has been taking place at the same time in other party bodies, such as the Central Committee.[16] The greater the extent to which leading officials owe their positions to the importance of the posts they occupy, rather than to the personal favor of the general secretary, the greater the extent to which they can afford to diverge from the general secretary on policy matters and the greater the extent to which he must earn their support rather than assume it.

The general secretary, admittedly, may have helped to secure the appointment, and later the Politburo membership, of other members of the leadership in the first place. This is, however, no guarantee of future loyalty. T.H. Rigby has identified four separate factors underlying patronage relations: (1) shared loyalties and attitudes arising from common ethnic, local, religious, organizational, or professional backgrounds, (2) bonds formed through work together, (3) shared policies or ideas, and (4) the act of appointment itself, in the absence of any previous bonds. The last of these, the act of appointment itself, is in Rigby's view the weakest of all such bases of support.[17] Khrushchev, for instance, was deposed by a Politburo almost all members of which had been appointed under his own first secretaryship; and Brezhnev's position began to crumble, toward the end of his general secretaryship, although broadly the same was true. The available evidence suggests rather that Politburo members tend to identify themselves with the particular interest they represent at least as much as with the general secretary responsible for their original appointment. When Vyacheslav Molotov, for instance, was put in charge of the railway system, he "tried to get everything he could for the railways," according to Khrushchev's memoirs.[18] Pyotr Shelest, the Ukrainian party leader who joined the Politburo under Brezhnev's dispensation, used his position similarly to advance the claims of his own republic as against others. Party membership within the Ukraine increased disproportionately under his leadership, increasing the pool of local eligibles for leading positions, and Shelest also argued quite openly for greater investment in the republic, telling delegates to the 24th Party Congress in 1971, for instance, that it was "incorrect" to divert funds from the coal mines of the Ukraine to the production of oil and natural gas in Siberia. He is reported to have insisted privately that the Ukraine was being exploited economically by the other republics.[19]

An interpretation of this kind is certainly consistent with what we know of the Politburo and its mode of operation. In Stalin's time, according to Khrushchev, the party leader "did everything himself, bypassing the Central Committee and using the Politburo as little more than a rubber stamp." Stalin "rarely bothered to ask the opinion of Politburo members about a given measure. He would just make a decision and issue a decree."[20] By the Brezhnev period, rather different practices obtained: the Politburo operated,

Brezhnev explained in an interview with the Western press, on a consensual basis; votes were rare, and if serious disagreements occurred, they were referred to a subcommittee that would come back later with an agreed recommendation.[21] By the 1980s, some of these practices had emerged publicly: the Politburo met weekly, usually on a Thursday (a brief report of its meetings began to appear from late 1982), and it had spawned quite an elaborate system of subcommittees, including, at least in the earlier part of the decade, commissions on educational reform, on consumer goods and services, and on the reform of economic management.[22] The Politburo, as before, might be attended by nonmembers, and it might be chaired, in his absence, by someone other than the general secretary.[23] These were all indications of an institutionalized, consensual system of decision making, very different from the personalized forms of rule of earlier decades.

Put simply, by the 1980s, there was an agreed separation of leading functions, an increasingly institutionalized pattern of membership, and well-established, consensual procedures. There was also, in the early years of the Gorbachev general secretaryship, some evidence that the leadership contained differences on substantive matters of policy with which the general secretary had no alternative but to reconcile himself. In the immediate aftermath of the Chernobyl nuclear explosion, it has been reported that Gorbachev was himself in favor of making the whole truth known at once, but found himself with only two supporters (RSFSR premier Vorotnikov and KGB chairman Chebrikov) in the Politburo. A full statement of the official position, in the event, took some time to emerge, and Gorbachev's first public comment on the event (a television address on May 14) took place more than two weeks after the explosion had occurred.[24] The revision of the Party Rules, which took place at the 27th Party Congress in 1986, may also have represented a defeat for Gorbachev's own position. In the debate that took place before the Congress, based upon a draft version of the new Rules that had been published in November 1985, suggestions for reform were put forward in party journals (and therefore almost certainly with Gorbachev's support), which included the introduction of retirement ages and limited tenure for party officials and compulsory turnover rules for elected party bodies. In the event, none of these proposed amendments was incorporated in the final version of the Rules, which the Party Congress approved on March 1, 1986.[25]

There was also evidence, albeit of a Kremlinological character, that the Gorbachev Politburo was by no means united on all the issues that it confronted. The former Moscow party leader Boris Yeltsin, for instance, was very clearly on the reformist wing. His speech to the Party Congress, in which he spoke openly about privileges and other shortcomings, was the most outspoken of all that were delivered to an unusually plain-speaking assembly; his speeches to party activists in Moscow itself, according to unpublished accounts, have dealt with social problems such as crime, drugs, and the abuse of power in an open and forthright way.[26] Indeed, Yeltsin's outspoken manner led to his ultimate dismissal, in November 1987, as leader of the Moscow party organization. Eduard Shevardnadze, formerly the Georgian party secretary and now minister of foreign affairs, was reponsible for pioneering many social experiments in his own republic[27] and has since then associated himself publicly (most notably in his Lenin anniversary address of April 1986) with further "democratization," electoral reform, the election of factory management, greater social justice, and economic reform generally.[28] At the other extreme, Yegor Ligachev, effectively the party's second-ranking secretary, criticized *Pravda* at the Party Congress for (in effect) allowing a discussion of the privileges and self-interest of party and state leaders, and he is on record as declaring that there would be "no movement towards the market or private enterprise." In a speech in June 1987, he warned that the "class enemy" was hoping that *perestroika* would undermine the influence of Marxist-Leninist ideology in the USSR and had been making use of it to spread "irresponsible demagogy, hostile to the interests of the toilers."[29]

Prime Minister Nikolai Ryzhkov, who was also a Gorbachev Politburo appointee, took a similar line at the Party Congress. He told delegates there would be no retreat from centralized guidance of the economy, which was the "fundamental advantage of socialism," and promised that the hopes of "bourgeois apologists" to this effect would not be justified.[30] President Andrei Gromyko similarly warned that "no-one should be allowed, under the pretext of encouraging the healthy and necessary cause of criticism and self-criticism . . . to resort to fabrications alleging that there are rifts in our Party and in Soviet society."[31] It was presumably because of differences of this kind that the January 1987 Central Committee plenum, on Gorbachev's admission, had to be postponed three times and required a threat of his own resignation before it could take place. The plenum itself, according to the testimony of participants, was a stormy one that gave clear expression to "conflicts" at leading levels.[32] It would seem reasonable to assume that at least those members of the present leadership who have been mentioned, together with remaining Brezhnev appointees and perhaps others, occupied a more "conservative" position within the spectrum of leadership opinion and that the Gorbachev Politburo (like its predecessors) was a coalition of interests and opinions within which the general secretary fell far short of unanimous and unconditional support.

Institutional and Bureaucratic Constraints on Executive Action

Opposition within the leadership, however significant, is in a sense the least of the general secretary's problems. Far more important, at least from the point of view of executive action, are the formidable obstacles to change that are located within the bureaucratic apparatus. The checks upon executive action that exist at this level have been dubbed "bureaucratic pluralism," "centralized pluralism," or "pluralism of elites,"[33] although not all scholars were happy to apply a "pluralist" label, however qualified, to a political system of the Soviet type.[34] There has been little disagreement, however, that phenomena such as "narrow departmentalism," "usurpation" (*podmena*), "parallelism," and "localism" are a very real feature of Soviet institutional life and that they deserve attention whatever labels were chosen to apply to them. In circumstances in which a political leadership is attempting a far-reaching strategy of "acceleration" and "restructuring," these bureaucratic protection mechanisms offer a good deal of scope for noncompliance with or even open opposition to centrally determined priorities.

Gorbachev himself has certainly been in no doubt that the party and state apparatuses, both in Moscow and in the localities, represent perhaps the most serious obstacles to his reformist intentions. In a speech to media officials just after the 27th Party Congress, Gorbachev reminded them that it would be necessary to "fight, literally fight" for every line of the Congress resolutions.[35] At the Central Committee plenum the following June, he warned that restructuring was "still proceeding slowly" and that "inertia was still strong." Some executives, he pointed out, were "generous in their declarations about openness, correctly speak about the roles of the collective, about the development of democratic principles in life, but the trouble is that it all ends there. Thus the illusion of restructuring is created: in words all is fine, but there are no real changes." Despite the fact that the top-heavy administrative apparatus itself represented an obstacle to change, leading officials had been very reluctant to delegate any of their powers and some had even proposed new organs of government and additional staff. Several republics had made similar proposals, apparently believing that they should copy the elaborate structure of the central government in their own area.[36]

Speaking later in the year to party activists in Krasnodar, Gorbachev dealt more particularly with the Ministry of Heavy and Transport Machine-Building. Although it had been conducting its activities on an experimental basis for three years, Gorbachev noted, the forces of conservatism were still strong. Ministry officials did all they could to retain powers that should properly have been delegated to other bodies, even though these bodies in fact determined whether the plan was fulfilled or not. Staffing levels had apparently fallen, but the volume of correspondence was just the same, and the ministry continued to employ success indicators that were not required under the terms of the experiment. The role of cost accounting within enterprises attached to the ministry remained "practically unchanged," and many of the responsible executives had either no knowledge at all or else a very poor knowledge of the new methods of management and economic stimulation. All of this was in a ministry that had supposedly been working for three years under experimental conditions and that was headed by a minister who was known to be experienced and capable.

Nor was this situation in any way atypical. Other ministries also post-poned urgent tasks, revised party and government directives in whose for-mulation they had themselves taken part, or else proposed amendments before the ink on the original directive had had a chance to dry. Ministries, in sum, were changing very slowly, as also were the bodies such as the State Committee on Science and Technology that were nominally responsible for monitoring them.[37]

Although, consistent with the doctrine of democratic centralism, there can be no direct refusal by lower levels of party and government to implement the decisions of policymakers at higher levels, central and local officials have many means at their disposal for resisting the pressures that may be placed upon them. One of the most widely practiced of such stratagems is foot-dragging or passive noncompliance. Many officials, as Ligachev told a meeting in the Tatar Republic in May 1986, appeared to believe that, now that the Party Congress had taken place, "the storm had passed" and they could sit it out quietly until the next congress.[38] A Central Committee con-ference meeting in late September 1986 complained more generally that the policy of restructuring was being carried out "without sufficient dynamism" and that it was encountering sociopsychological and organizational obstacles. In particular, the conference cited the "egotistical opposition" of the ap-paratus as a source of delays, together with "bureaucratic distortions" and the "inertia" of ministries and other state bodies, which abandoned old ways of working with great reluctance, refusing to delegate responsibilities directly to enterprises and continuing to send out huge quantities of circulars in order to create the appearance of practical activity while at the same time failing to deal with their proper responsibilities within the appointed time.[39] Officials of this kind, as Ligachev put it at the Party Congress, confused "acceleration" with the more rapid circulation of bureaucratic paperwork.[40]

Perhaps more common than passive noncompliance is "formalism," purely verbal compliance with party and government directives. This was the approach adopted by those officials, as Gorbachev put in in Krasnodar, who were "able quickly to adapt to a changing situation." They were a "capable people, even resourceful." Their main concern was to

> preserve the old, outmoded ways, to preserve their privileges, even though this is not in accordance with our principles, laws and morality or with our current policy. We see now . . . how they are shouting—from every rostrum and louder than anyone else—about restructuring, although in fact they are delaying its implementation under all sorts of pretexts, including some very specious ones.[41]

The bureaucrat was particularly dangerous in current circumstances, Shevardnadze explained in his address on the Lenin anniversary, because the bureaucrat of today was "more educated, if you wish—more qualified, better able to adapt himself, more easily capable of changing his outward appearance and therefore more seriously harmful to the [party's] cause."[42] Bureaucrats of this kind, Gorbachev explained in his address to the Central Committee in January 1987, acknowledged criticisms to be valid, "even thank you for them," but made no serious effort to eliminate the shortcomings that had been identified.[43]

"Formalism" overlaps in Soviet practice with "campaignism" or, in other words, short-lived and perfunctory compliance with central directives. One example of campaignism in action, reported in *Pravda* in December 1986, concerned the antialcoholism campaign to which the leadership has attached much importance since its inception in May 1985. The place in question was a mining village in the Ukraine that had been declared a "sobriety zone" and in which there had indeed been a reduction in the amount of alcohol sold over the past year or so. However, it emerged that no less alcohol had actually been consumed over the same period. (Much had evidently been home-brewed). Of sixty-five weddings held in the locality, only one had been nonalcoholic; the local library was open only between 11 A.M. and 7 P.M., which was convenient for librarians but hardly for workers seeking an alternative use for their free time; there were no antialcohol films showing in the local cinema, and the local House of Culture was empty. The struggle against alcohol abuse, it appeared, had effectively ended the year before: a few shops had been closed, a commission or two had come into existence at least on paper, and then the whole thing had been forgotten. Drunkenness, already above the regional average, had not declined, and street crime had actually increased. Furthermore, an "unbelievable incident" had occurred in which a collective drinking bout had taken place at a young people's evening in the local discotheque, with the local Komsomol secretary and his deputy both in attendance. Good results, the paper concluded, were likely to be forthcoming only when the necessary measures were undertaken, "not for the sake of form," but on a more serious basis.[44]

Official policies may also be sabotaged by local officials, who often act in collusion with other local notables in such matters. (Soviet sources refer to such alliances as "family circles.") An "outrageous instance" of this kind was reported by Gorbachev in his speech to the Central Committee in June 1986. The case concerned an engineer, A.I. Chabanov, who worked as director of a research institute under the Ministry of the Electrical Equipment Industry in the town of Cherkassy in the Ukraine. Chabanov's institute developed new types of machine tools and control systems for application within the industry, which won international recognition and foreign and domestic orders. The factory attached to the same ministry within Cherkassy itself, however,

"stubbornly ignored the new equipment." Chabanov was appointed temporary director of the factory as well as of the institute in July 1985, and he began to organize production of the new equipment without waiting for its specification to be confirmed. Some employees complained to the ministry and to local party officials that the new director was deviating from his instructions. "It cannot be said," Gorbachev went on, "that they acted in an innovative way." The director was removed from his post, and the matter was placed in the hands of the police. In the event, no crimes or even improprieties were discovered. Chabanov was nonetheless expelled from the CPSU, and when local party members sent a letter to Moscow to inform them of the circumstances, it was simply removed from the post by local officials.[45] The case, exceptional but hardly unique, recalls the frustrated inventor of Dudintsev's *Not by Bread Alone* published thirty years earlier.

Local officials, moreover, can engage in the "suppression of criticism" and in the victimization of individual critics if they judge it necessary, notwithstanding party and state regulations to the contrary. Current policies in favor of greater "openness" (*glasnost*) have admittedly encouraged all sections of the media to discuss social ills such as prostitution, drug taking, and violent crime. At the local level, however, officials have been less willing to allow their actions to be critically evaluated in publications that they themselves control, and even at the center there have been some notable violations of spirit of the new directives.

In February 1986, for instance, the Central Committee severely criticized the ministries of civil aviation and the waterways for suppressing criticism in the two journals they sponsored, *Air Transport* and *Water Transport*.[46] A more remarkable, even "unprecedented" case occurred when the whole of a local paper in the Pskov region was destroyed because it had unwisely printed criticism of the efforts of local officials to create a false impression when delegates from an all-Russian seminar on public catering visited the area. In classic Potemkin-village style, shops overflowed with goods that had not been seen for a long time, the bakery was baking only high-quality bread, and buildings had been freshly painted. The truth about this expensive farce was revealed in the local paper, *Za kommunizm*. Party officials, however, decided that now that the Congress was over, the time for criticism had passed, so the whole print run of the newspaper was held up. Then a substitute edition, minus the offending article, was printed in its place.[47]

In this and other ways, party and state officials both at the center and in the localities have considerable resources at their disposal if they wish to thwart the wishes of the leadership. They can provide reports to the center that suit their own interests or exaggerate successes; they can delay implementing central directives, implement them in a wholly formal manner, or even (in extreme cases) attempt to undermine them, enrolling the support of other local notables and (if necessary) repressing those who bring the facts to the attention of higher bodies or the press. Strategies of this kind are of course common currency in studies of Western bureaucracies, and terms derived from this context such as *authority leakage, information distortion,* and *turf battles* have a good deal of relevance to political systems of the Soviet type. They suggest, in turn, that even a united and determined political leadership may find it difficult to achieve its objectives if those objectives fail to accord with the priorities of the central and local bureaucrats who will bear the most direct responsibility for implementing them.

Popular Constraints upon Executive Action

The Soviet system is obviously not one in which popular constraints upon executive action are as extensive and significant as in the liberal democracies. There is no choice of candidate in national elections (although there was a modest move in this direction at the local level in 1987); associational and civic groups may come into legal existence only if they acknowledge the party's leading role and refrain from direct opposition to official policies; and the press is subject to a strict and unaccountable censorship, despite modest moves under Gorbachev in the direction of openness or *glasnost.* Finally, freedom of assembly, meetings, street processions, and demonstrations, although nominally available to all citizens under article 50 of the Constitution, are qualified by the provision that the exercise of these rights must be "in accordance with the interests of the people and . . . the socialist system." In the Soviet view, only the party may be the legitimate judge of matters of this kind, and in practice the exercise of the rights detailed in article 50 has been restricted to approved and pro-regime groups and organizations.

It has nonetheless become apparent, particularly since the late 1970s or so, that public opinion is not a factor that the Soviet leadership can readily ignore. In the first place, the Soviet public has a great variety of means—from letter writing to contacts with deputies, TV phone-ins, and influence exerted through bodies such as the trade unions and environmental associations—to make their views known and often to insert them directly into the policy-making process through the elaborate framework of organized consultation that has come into existence under party and state auspices. If approved forms of political action prove ineffectual, moreover, a second form of influence is available: "unconventional political participation" or, in other words, riots, demonstrations, strikes, and even (in exceptional circumstances) political violence. When official policy offends some deeply held public sentiment, such forms of action come to the fore. (Perhaps not coincidentally, the 27th Party Congress was the first in modern times in which three very senior speakers, including Gorbachev himself, warned that the political stability of the USSR could not be taken for granted.)[48]

Many studies have already shown the manner in which public opinion may be taken into account through proper or approved channels, particularly in social or environmental questions such as the pollution of Lake Baikal.[49] More recent instances of the same kind have included the cancellation of plans to divert the Siberian rivers toward the south. (The Politburo noted in August 1986 that "broad segments of the public" had urged further study of the social and ecological consequences of such a change.) At the same meeting, the Politburo decided to halt the construction of a large and unlovely war memorial in the immediate outskirts of Moscow, having "taken into account the results of the extensive discussion of the project design and the observations and suggestions advanced by the public." An open competition was to be held to decide upon a suitable replacement.[50] Less widely publicized "victories" for public opinion in recent years have included the restoration of historic inner-city areas rather than their comprehensive redevelopment and the reversion to older and more historic place names in many urban areas.[51] The adoption of a law on referenda ("all-people's discussions"), promised by Gorbachev in his speech to the 27th Party Congress and approved by the USSR Supreme Soviet in June 1987, may extend such principles of consultation further.[52]

Public pressure, particularly on issues of this kind, is exercised by a variety of civic groups and associations as well as by journalists and other concerned individuals. Associations of this kind are often larger and more influential than is commonly supposed. The recently formed All-Union Voluntary Society for the Struggle for Sobriety, for instance, was reported in early 1987 to have as many as 13 million members organized in 450,000 separate branches.[53] Older established bodies such as the Soviet Peace Committee and the Soviet Women's Committee have memberships running into tens of millions and substantial publishing, international, and other forms of activity.[54]

More important and interesting for our present purposes are the environmental organizations that have come into existence since the 1960s, with substantial memberships, publications, and demonstrated influence upon official policy within their areas of interest. One of the first such organizations was the *Rodina* (Homeland) Club, established in 1964 for the purpose of promoting the study of ancient monuments. The following year, the All-Russian Society for the Preservation of Historical and Cultural Monuments (VOOPIK) came into existence; by 1977, it had more than 12 million members, almost 10 percent of the population of the Russian Republic. Comparable societies have come into existence elsewhere in the USSR. VOOPIK appears to have been founded chiefly by the efforts of citizens; it has been able to canvass public support through lectures for publications and has repeatedly come into conflict with local authorities who have taken a negligent attitude toward the churches and other historic buildings for which they are responsible. The All-Russian Society for the Preservation of Nature, with about 19 million members in the 1970s, exercised a similar influence on behalf of the environment.[55]

If public pressures through official channels are ignored, the danger from the authorities' point of view is that opposition will make itself apparent in other ways. This is by no means a hypothetical risk. One of the most substantial demonstrations in recent years, for instance, occurred in Tbilisi, the capital of the Georgian Republic, in April 1978, following the publication of a draft constitution omitting the clause stipulating that Georgian was the republic's official language. On the day the new constitution was to be adopted, a demonstration of such proportions took place in central Tbilisi that the draft was altered and Georgian was reinserted as the official state language.[56] Similar disturbances took place at the end of 1986 when Dinmukhamed Kunaev, a native Kazakh, was replaced as republican party leader by Gennadi V. Kolbin, a Russian national. As *Literaturnaya gazeta* subsequently reported, the news provoked "inexperienced and politically illiterate youths" to take to the streets, who were later joined by "hooligans, drunks and other antisocial types"; nationalist slogans were chanted, and the crowd, armed with metal posts, sticks, and stones, proceeded to beat up local citizens, overturned cars and set them on fire, and smashed the windows of shops and other public buildings.[57] Western press reports suggested that at least 7 policemen and up to 15 demonstrators had been killed; at least 200 citizens were seriously injured and hospitalized, and there were over 1,000 arrests.[58]

Popular discontent on social and economic issues has flared up in the same way on several occasions. In May 1980, for instance, it was reported that workers in the giant Togliattigrad car works in central Russia had walked out in protest against poor meat and dairy supplies. The walkout, believed to have been the largest in recent Soviet history, closed down the plant and involved more than 170,000 workers. It ended only when the authorities took steps to improve the local food supply.[59] Shortly afterward, a group of paint-sprayers was reported to have held unscheduled "on-the-jobs 'discussions' about working conditions" in the nearby Gorky car and truck plant.[60] In late 1986, a potentially more serious disturbance occurred at the giant KamAZ factory in the city of Brezhnev in the Tatar republic. According to the government newspaper *Izvestia*, "stormy protests" erupted at the plant in opposition to the introduction of new quality-control procedures, which are an integral part of the new leadership's restructuring objectives. In general, the introduction of new procedures of this kind, involving independent monitoring of the quality of production, could "not be said to be proceeding smoothly," *Izvestia* reported.[61] Soviet industrial relations, based upon relatively low levels of pay combined with job security and relatively easy-going discipline, will evidently not easily be replaced by arrangements that deliberately widen wage differentials and offer bonuses and other rewards only for hard and high-quality work. Another example involves protests in 1988 by Armenians seeking, without success, to have the Armenian-populated enclave of Nagorno-Karabakh transferred to Armenia from neighboring Azerbaijan.

Active resistance to changes in public policy represent no more than the public face of the political leverage of public opinion, especially of organized labor; the other side of this power is the effective veto maintained over changes in existing policies that are perceived as favorable to working-class interests. One of the most important of these is the subsidies from public funds that hold down the price of housing, transport, and particularly foodstuffs. Originally, under Stalin, substantial government revenues were raised from the population through the sale of food at prices greater than those paid to producers. From Khrushchev onward, this situation began to reverse itself. By the late 1980s, it had changed to such an extent that government food subsidies accounted for about 12 percent of total budgetary expenditure (or more than one and a half times the official defense budget). Subsidies on meat, milk, and dairy products alone amounted to over 48 percent of total retail expenditure on these items.[62] However economically irrational they were (bread, for instance, was being fed to animals in the late 1970s although harvests were well below target), there appeared to be considerable popular resistance to any change in these arrangements. The authorities, for instance, were compelled to make extensive purchases on the international grain market to make good domestic deficiencies, and in 1982 a much-vaunted Food Program was introduced in response at least in part to a flood of angry letters from members of the public in this connection.[63] It appeared unlikely, in the late 1980s, that the Gorbachev leadership will be able to persuade Soviet working people to abandon their attachment to below-cost foodstuffs or to public subsidies of other kinds or, more generally, to surrender their security of employment and relaxed pace of work despite the fact that these sacrifices are central to the leadership's program of restructuring.

Domestic Politics and Foreign-Policy Limits

The "limits to Soviet power" from abroad are discussed more directly in other chapters in this book, and have themselves been the subject of an extensive secondary literature.[64] It may nevertheless be helpful, in conclusion, to point up some of the more obvious respects in which the domestic constraints upon executive action discussed in this chapter impinge upon the conduct of Soviet foreign policy. Within the leadership itself, according to those best placed to judge, there are no significant differences so far at least as the objectives of Soviet foreign policy are concerned. Some of its members—typically the representatives of the Central Committee apparatus and the military—may incline toward the use of direct force, while others—typically the representatives of Foreign Ministry and economic interests—may favor the use of more orthodox political instrumentalities. There appear, however, to be no significant differences—certainly not any that would seriously constrain the general secretary—so far as the ultimate goals or basic principles of Soviet foreign policy are concerned.[65] At least one study of Soviet foreign policy quite deliberately uses the term *the leadership* throughout in order to avoid speculative and probably misleading judgments about high-level differences about such matters.[66] Other studies deal with such questions with great circumspection and often in the light of single case studies such as the Soviet-led intervention in Czechoslovakia in 1968.[67]

Constraints upon executive action, however, may nonetheless apply at the level of bureaucratic or institutional interests. The military, for instance, explicitly conceded that the moratorium on nuclear testing, introduced in August 1985, was directly prejudicial to Soviet security interests. This may have played some part in the Soviet decision to suspend the ban in early 1987 following the continuation by the United States of such tests.[68] The Foreign Ministry and Foreign Trade Ministry have been among the institutions most directly affected by Gorbachev's restructuring. The Foreign Ministry received as minister a republican party leader with no real diplomatic experience in 1985, presumably as a means of strengthening party guidance of that institution. Both ministries also took part in a two-day seminar in the early summer of 1986 at which Gorbachev called for significant changes in working practices and for the elimination of corruption in the Foreign Trade Ministry in particular.[69] The Foreign Ministry, Gorbachev told the Central Committee plenum in January 1987, was being "restructured" both at home and abroad, with extensive changes in organization and in the Soviet diplomatic corps itself. (New ambassadors to the United Nations, United States, United Kingdom, and other NATO nations have been an important part of this process.) Restructuring of this kind, Gorbachev indicated, would continue to be pursued in the future.[70]

It is in the area of popular constraints, however, that Soviet executive action abroad is perhaps most significantly limited. Studies of Soviet political culture, the testimony of visitors and emigrés, and the experience of Russian history all suggest that the authorities will receive unqualified popular support in any actions that are seen as defending the legitimate interests and, above all, the territorial integrity of historically Russian domains.

There will be no such support, however, for any efforts made to extend Soviet power abroad, especially where Soviet lives are lost. The war in Afghanistan appears to be regarded in this light. Already, it is estimated, well over ten thousand Soviet lives have been lost and over twenty thousand have been wounded in a war for which there is no obvious justification in terms of the defense of Soviet territory or vital interests. Letters in the Soviet press have criticized the Soviet media's glamorized treatment of the war and official explanations of the manner in which the USSR became involved in the conflict. There has been particular criticism of the manner in which (it is believed) officials' children have been allowed to avoid direct participation in the hostilities.[71] Gorbachev's declaration to the 27th Party Congress that he intended to seek a political settlement in Afghanistan will undoubtedly be welcomed, together with the troop withdrawals that have followed in 1988. The more he seeks to build domestic support for his program of restructuring and to engage the "human factor," the more he is likely to give attention to the strong feeling that exists at the popular level in favor of a strong, secure, but not necessarily expansionist USSR.

Notes

1. Carl J. Friedrich and Zbigniew K. Brzezinski, *Totalitarian Dictatorship and Autocracy,* 2nd ed. (Cambridge, Mass.: Harvard University Press, 1965), p. 22 and ch. 3 generally.

2. *Materialy XXVII s"ezda KPSS* (Moscow: Politizdat, 1986), part 1.

3. See, for instance, Timothy Dunmore, *Soviet Politics, 1945–53* (London: Macmillan, 1984).

4. See the discussion in Alfred B. Evans, "The Polish Crisis in the 1980s and Adaptations in Soviet Ideology,' *Journal of Communist Studies,* 2, no. 3 (September 1986): 263–85, and more generally in the same author's "Developed Socialism and the New Programme of the CPSU" in Stephen White and Alex Pravda, eds., *Ideology and Soviet Politics* (London: Macmillan, 1987).

5. See particularly Jerry F. Hough, *The Struggle for the Third World* (Washington, D.C.: Brookings Institution, 1986); and Rajan Menon, *Soviet Power and the Third World* (New Haven: Yale University Press, 1986).

6. Cf. Jerry F. Hough and Merle Fainsod, *How the Soviet Union Is Governed* (Cambridge, Mass.: Harvard University Press, 1979), p. 263.

7. My discussion of these points has been informed by the literature on power in Soviet politics. See particularly Jerry F. Hough, "The Soviet Experience and the Measurement of Power," in his *The Soviet Union and Social Science Theory* (Cambridge, Mass.: Harvard University Press, 1977), ch. 10; and Alexander J. Groth, "USSR: Pluralist Monolith?" *British Journal of Political Science,* 9, no. 4 (October 1979): 445–64.

8. See, for instance, Graeme Gill, "The Future of the General Secretary," *Political Studies,* 34, no. 2 (June 1986): 223–35. A more general account is Archie Brown, "The Power of the General Secretary of the CPSU," in T.H. Rigby et al., eds., *Authority, Power and Policy in the USSR* (London: Macmillan, 1980), pp. 135–57.

9. See, for instance, Hough and Fainsod, *How the Soviet Union Is Governed,* pp. 260–61.

10. For a general discussion of political clientelism in the USSR, see T.H. Rigby and Bohdan Harasymiw, eds., *Leadership Relations and Patron–Client Relations in the USSR and Yugoslavia* (London: Allen & Unwin, 1983).

11. See Gill, "Future," and Brown, "Power," for representative views.

12. P. Rodionov, *Kollektivnost'—vysshii printsip partiinogo rukovodstva* (Moscow, 1967), p. 219, as cited in Gill, "Future," p. 225n.

13. *Pervaya sessiya Verkhovnogo Soveta SSSR (odinnadtsatyi sozyv) 11–12 aprelya 1984g. Stenograficheskii otchet* (Moscow: Izvestia, 1984), p. 38.

14. *Tret'ya sessiya . . . 2–3 iyulya 1985g.* (Moscow: Izvestia, 1985), pp. 5–6.

15. John H. Kress, "Representation of Positions on the CPSU Politburo," *Slavic Review,* 39, no. 2 (June 1980): 218–38, at p. 218. For an influential earlier discussion, see T.H. Rigby's "The Soviet Leadership: Towards a Self-Stabilising Oligarchy?" *Soviet Studies,* 22, no. 2 (October 1970): 167–191; on the "battery of internal checks and balances in order to stabilize and perpetuate the oligarchy," see ibid., p. 188.

16. Robert E. Blackwell's term cited in Kress, "Representation," p. 236n. See more generally Robert V. Daniels, "Office Hold and Elite Status: The Central Committee of the CPSU," in Paul Cocks et al., eds., *The Dynamics of Soviet Politics* (Cambridge, Mass.: Harvard University Press, 1976), pp. 77–95.

17. T.H. Rigby, "The Soviet Regional Leadership: The Brezhnev Generation," *Slavic Review,* 37, no. 1 (March 1978): 23.

18. Cited in Hough and Fainsod, *How the Soviet Union Is Governed,* p. 476.

19. See Geoffrey Hosking, *A History of the Soviet Union* (London: Fontana, 1986), p. 428–29. Shelest's remarks to the Party Congress are in *Pravda,* April 1, 1971, pp. 3–4.

20. *Khrushchev Remembers,* tr. Strobe Talbott (London: Sphere, 1971), p. 244.

21. *New York Times,* June 15, 1973, p. 3; Brezhnev explained Politburo procedures further to the 26th Party Congress in 1981 (*XXVI s"ezd KPSS 23 fevralya–3 marta 1981. Stenograficheskii otchet,* 3 vols. [Moscow: Politizdat, 1981], vol. 1, p. 88). The fullest available account of the Politburo and its operation is John Lowenhardt, *The Soviet Politburo* (Edinburgh: Canongate, 1982).

22. See Stephen White, "Soviet Politics since Brezhnev," *Journal of Communist Studies,* 1, no. 2 (June 1985): 130, n. 50.

23. Arkady N. Shevchenko, *Breaking with Moscow* (London: Cape, 1985), p. 177. Gorbachev was still on holiday while Politburo meetings were taking place in the late summer of 1986.

24. See RAND Background Report no. 78 (USSR), Santa Monica, Calif.: RAND Corporation June 5, 1986, p. 1.

25. See Stephen White, "The New Programme and Rules of the CPSU," *Journal of Communist Studies,* 1, no. 2 (June 1986): 187–89.

26. See *Pravda,* February 27, 1986, pp. 2–3; and *Detente,* no. 7 (autumn 1986): 2–5.

27. On the "Poti experiment" particularly, see Darrell Slider, "More Power to the Soviets? Reform and Local Government in the Soviet Union," *British Journal of Political Science,* 16, no. 4 (October 1986): 495–511.

28. *Pravda,* April 23, 1986, pp. 1–2.

29. *Pravda,* February 28, 1986, p. 4; *The Economist,* September 7, 1985, p. 61; *Pravda,* June 4, 1987, p. 2.

30. *Pravda,* March 4, 1986, pp. 2–5.

31. Ibid., February 27, 1986, p. 6.

32. Radio Liberty Report RL 82/87, February 20, 1987; M. Ul'yanov in *Kommunist,* no. 5 (1987): 51–57, p. 51, for the plenum. The existence of substantial leadership differences on matters of economic policy during the Brezhnev period is documented on the basis of a content analysis of Politburo members' public statements in Roger A. Blough and Philip D. Stewart, "Political Obstacles to Reform and Innovation in Soviet Economic Policy: Brezhnev's Political Legacy," *Comparative Political Studies,* 20, no. 1 (April 1987): 72–97.

33. These terms belong respectively to Darrell P. Hammer, Alec Nove, and Gordon Skilling. See Hammer, *The USSR: The Politics of Oligarchy,* 2nd ed. (Boulder, Colo.: Westview, 1986), p. 228.

34. See the symposium in *Studies in Comparative Communism,* 12, no. 1 (spring 1979), and the discussion in Susan G. Solomon, ed., *Pluralism in the Soviet Union* (London: Macmillan, 1983).

35. *Pravda,* March 15, 1986, p. 1.

36. *Partiinaya zhizn',* 1986, no. 13, pp. 7–8.

37. *Partiinaya zhizn',* 1986, no. 19, pp. 8–9.

38. *Pravda,* May 22, 1986, p. 2.

39. *Pravda,* October 1, 1986, p. 1.

40. *Pravda,* February 28, 1986, p. 4.

41. *Pravda,* September 20, 1986, pp. 1–2.

42. *Pravda,* April 23, 1986, p. 2.

43. *Sovetskaya Rossiya,* January 28, 1987, p. 3.

44. *Pravda,* December 8, 1986, p. 3.

45. *Pravda,* June 17, 1986, p. 3. Further developments are reported in ibid., August 24, 1986, p. 3.

46. *Pravda,* February 11, 1986, p. 1.

47. *Pravda,* June 13, 1986, pp. 1–2 (which reproduced both editions).

48. This point is noted in Peter Frank, "Gorbachev's Dilemma: Social Justice or Political Instability?" *The World Today* (June 1986): 94.

49. A good review of such matters is available in John Lowenhardt, *Decision Making in Soviet Politics* (London: Macmillan, 1981).

50. *Pravda,* August 16, 1986, p. 1. In the event, none of the proposals submitted was found to be satisfactory (*Pravda,* March 1, 1987, p. 3).

51. See Martin Walker, *The Waking Giant: The Soviet Union under Gorbachev* (London: Michael Joseph, 1986), ch. 10.

52. For the text, see *Vedomosti Verkhovnogo Soveta SSSR,* no. 26 (July 1, 1987), item 387.

53. *Sovetskaya Rossiya,* January 10, 1987, p. 1.

54. See *Yezhegodnik bol'shoi Sovetskoi entsiklopedii 1985* (Moscow: Sovetskaya entsiklopediya, 1985), pp. 21–30.

55. See John B. Dunlop, *The Faces of Contemporary Russian Nationalism* (Princeton, N.J.: Princeton University Press, 1983), ch. 3.

56. Helene Carrere d'Encausse, *The Decline of an Empire* (New York: Newsweek, 1979), pp. 212–13.

57. *Literaturnaya gazeta,* 1987, no. 1 (January): 1.

58. Radio Liberty Research RL 476/86, p. 9; *The Guardian,* December 20, 1986, p. 6.

59. Radio Liberty Research RL 461/86, p. 2.

60. Ibid., pp. 2–3.

61. *Izvestia,* December 4, 1986, p. 1; Radio Liberty Research RL 461/86, p. 1.

62. Alistair McAuley in Archie Brown and Michael Kaser, eds., *Soviet Policy for the 1980s* (London: Macmillan, 1982), pp. 154–55; and Abel Aganbegyan in *The Guardian,* January 26, 1986, p. 14.

63. See Stephen White, "Political Communications in the USSR: Letters to Party, State and the Press," *Political Studies,* 31, no. 1 (January 1983): 43–60, at p. 60.

64. See particularly Seweryn Bialer, ed., *The Domestic Content of Soviet Foreign Policy* (London: Croom Helm, 1981); Paul Dibb, *The Soviet Union: The Incomplete Superpower* (London: Macmillan, 1986); and Menon, *Soviet Power.*

65. Shevchenko, *Breaking with Moscow,* p. 180.

66. Robin Edmonds, *Soviet Foreign Policy: The Brezhnev Years* (Oxford, England: Oxford University Press, 1983).

67. See, for instance, Karen Dawisha, *The Kremlin and the Prague Spring* (Berkeley: University of California Press, 1984).

68. See Radio Liberty Research RL 381/86.

69. *Pravda,* May 24 and 25, 1986.

70. *Sovetskaya Rossiya,* January 28, 1987, p. 5.

71. See *The Guardian,* July 12, 1986, p. 6; and *The Observer,* January 25, 1987, p. 2.

3

Gorbachev's Nationalities Policy and Soviet Central Asia

Martha Brill Olcott

Gorbachev versus the Republic First Secretaries

The post-Brezhnev succession struggle has been a dramatic and protracted one. In the several years before and after Brezhnev's death, the struggle focused on who would replace the general secretary. This drama was played out three separate times, as Brezhnev was replaced, in turn, by two dying men. The length of this protracted power struggle and the physical weakness of three successive general secretaries inevitably changed the way certain key Soviet political institutions functioned. Contenders for power in the Secretariat in Moscow sought to aggrandize their own influence by increasing the residual authority of their positions, while incumbents in the periphery took advantage of the increasing vacuum at the top to advance the interests of their regional or ethnic constituencies.[1]

In the previous chapter of this book, Stephen White discusses Gorbachev's swift elevation to general secretary after Chernenko's death and his efforts to reinvigorate that office. Proceeding slowly, as much by necessity as by choice, Gorbachev has tried to build a strong and stable personal power base within the party and the government, and to portray himself as a man capable of solving the USSR's problems at home and abroad.

The image that he has tried to convey is one of a radical reformer, of someone who is willing to risk total defeat in his effort to reconstruct the economy and to reinvigorate the cultural and political life of the country. Gorbachev has argued that the Soviet Union has very serious economic and social problems that can be remedied only if the party rids itself of corrupt, inefficient leaders and accepts the principles of self-sacrifice. But this message has not been uniformly well received. Instead, many occupants of powerful positions in both the party and state apparatus have seen Gorbachev's statements as personally threatening and have tried to forestall the introduction of his most innovative suggestions.

Although pockets of resistance to Gorbachev's leadership can be found throughout the USSR, probably the most concentrated opposition to Gorbachev's leadership and his policies has come from the party and state bureaucracies in the national republics. Gorbachev's economic and political policies have threatened the vested interests in the national republics in two ways: first, by attempting to eliminate any republic-level discretionary authority over the determination of economic-development priorities and, second, by reducing the republic leadership's autonomy in the appointment and retention of cadres. Both these changes, which are part of Gorbachev's overall strategy of reform, have been further legitimated as part of his nationality policy. Moreover, he has further antagonized the national republic leadership by defining the needs of the USSR as greater than the sum of its parts, meaning that the national minorities are not to be permitted special considerations. But, while Gorbachev has used nationality policy as a tool in his efforts to increase his control over the national republics, the republic first secretaries have also tried to use their own formulations of the "national problem" as a way to defend the perpetuation of the status quo.

Since Khrushchev, every general secretary has advocated increased economic development of the national region. Under Andropov and, more forcefully, under Gorbachev, however, the evaluation of national minority cadres has been directly linked to execution of Moscow's development schemes. Both Gorbachev and Ligachev have firmly stated that only nationalist "deviationists" or corrupt officials would refuse to fulfill Moscow-defined responsibilities.

Throughout the USSR, Gorbachev has used cadre policy to reward and promote those who share his vision. Yet, by linking cadre policy to support for a program designed to enhance the authority of the general secretary and the Secretariat at the expense of the republic first secretaries, the Moscow government has antagonized entrenched interests in regional party organizations and in the national republics. The 1986 Party Program and subsequent party documents have included implicit redefinitions of the authority of the republic in general and the first secretary in particular. Specifically, much of the de facto authority that had devolved to the republic party leadership during the late Brezhnev years has been eliminated. Gorbachev and others such as Ligachev who support this position have made it clear that authority is not vested in the office of republic first secretary, but accrues to the individual who satisfactorily performs Moscow's designated tasks. The predictable opposition of republican political interests to this obvious threat to their authority gave Gorbachev further cause to replace cadres in the national republics. Party and state committees as well as economic enterprises are to be run by rational management techniques, not by old-boy networks, clans, or regional mafias.

Gorbachev needs to eliminate all rival authorities to cement control over the distant parts of the country and to ensure the success of his economic policy. Gorbachev must obtain, however, the support of some alternative group of regional and national minority elites. Lacking such support, the consolidation of his authority—needed for the success of his economic strategy—becomes less certain. The policy of recentralization provides a different set of challenges in the national republics than it does in the party organizations of the Russian Soviet Federated Socialist Republic (RSFSR), where Gorbachev can build on Andropov's substantial efforts to unseat party dynasties and where he and his allies have substantial personal contacts upon which they can draw in the recruitment of replacement cadres. The situation in the national republics is quite different. Unlike in the RSFSR, the party purges of 1982–84 were not wholly successful in Central Asia and in the Caucasus. When Gorbachev took over, he found that not only were many of the cliques still in place, but also that new incumbents were less effective, albeit more honest, than cadres they had replaced. Further, it became clear that potential aspirants for power in these republics share the same values as those slated for replacement, including the conviction that they should help set the economic priorities of their own republics and should retain the privilege of perpetuating patron–client networks.

All the republic party organizations have undergone major changes, although in many cases Gorbachev has simply built on Andropov's earlier efforts. Some of the changes have simply been generational, but most have been designed to alter the styles of leadership and end old patterns of influence. However, Gorbachev's severest criticism of republic party politics has been directed to Central Asia and now increasingly to the Caucasus as well. In all these republics, a model of modern management is likely to encounter substantial resistance from the "old-boy" or ethnically based networks that have long dominated there.

The Central Asian party organizations have been a particular target. Their "reconstruction" was accelerated shortly after Gorbachev took over as general secretary. The tempo was further increased in the last half of 1986 and reached a crescendo with the dismissal in disgrace of Dinmukhamed Kunaev, Politburo member and party boss of Kazakhstan. The leadership in the various Central Asian republics was undoubtedly corrupt, but it also must have mistakenly appeared vulnerable—an easily attainable victory that could strengthen Gorbachev's hand elsewhere. In Central Asia lies a large proportion of the underutilized labor and material resources upon which Gorbachev hopes to draw to achieve a more rational developmental strategy for the USSR. But for this new policy to succeed, the leadership in charge of these republics must share Gorbachev's vision. The Alma Ata riots and the seeming impossibility of identifying capable leadership in Uzbekistan make it clear that this is no easy task.

Time may be on Gorbachev's side insofar as he has demonstrated the ability to dismiss recalcitrant cadres in the national republics. Nevertheless, it is evident that his efforts to introduce political and economic reform and to institute his own "nationality policy" have proceeded neither on course nor smoothly in Central Asia. Support for Gorbachev and his reform efforts has been less than enthusiastic, and local response to what they have defined as his "nationality policy" has been lukewarm at best and violent in the most extreme manifestations. Moreover, it is not clear that Gorbachev will succeed in identifying sufficient numbers of loyal and efficient cadres to ensure the successful introduction of his reform program in either of these areas or that, if introduced, these reform programs will gain sufficient mass support to succeed.

Gorbachev's Nationality Policy

While Gorbachev's economic and political goals for Central Asia (and the national regions more generally) may seem straightforward to the leadership in Moscow, Gorbachev must still justify the wholesale replacement of national minority cadres and the introduction of locally unpopular economic and social policies. Here, potentially, nationality policy could be invoked to offer such a justification. Indeed, the new leadership has tried to restate the goals of the party's nationality policy to make them appear synonymous with the regime's economic, political, and social priorities for the national regions.

On the surface, Gorbachev has tried to demonstrate sensitivity to the aspirations of minorities in his and the party's statements of their goals in the area of nationality relations. However, while leaving many of the old platitudes in place, he has nonetheless tried to create greater coherence between the party's ideological pronouncements on the nature of nationality relations and the economic and social policies that they are following in the national regions.

Gorbachev's nationality policy appears to be similar in premises to the ideas formulated by Yuri Andropov in his address commemorating the sixtieth anniversary of the USSR. In this speech, Andropov described nationality problems in terms of the economic problems associated with the unequal development of national regions. The center's power could not further devolve the national republics, and he explicitly criticized those who sought to apply an arithmetic approach to cadre policy in the national regions. In general, Andropov tried to balance the party's commitment to an ultimate cultural homogenization with a greater receptivity for the sensitivities of the national minorities that are characteristic of the current stage of social development.[2]

Prior to taking over as general secretary, Gorbachev had little personal experience in handling the ideological side of the national problem—although he did have some experience in cadre policy and much more experience in its economic implications, especially those in agriculture. Gorbachev made one brief reference to the problem of nationality relations in his remarks to the December 1984 Central Committee plenum, calling for further economic integration of national regions and nationalities and endorsing a "nationality-blind" cadre policy.[3]

But the need to complete a section on nationality relations for the new party program meant that Gorbachev quickly had to prepare or endorse a more elaborate formulation. There is evidence to suggest disagreement within the Politburo over how to define nationality policy in the months before the new Party Program was published. Geidar Aliev's formulation of nationality policy in the 1985 Lenin Day speech describes the specific economic responsibilities of the nationalities in rather vague terms; he reaffirms the need of all to master Russian, but he goes on to justify their cultural rights as the fulfillment of Marxist-Leninist ideology.[4] In sharp contrast to this were the comments on nationality relations made by Yegor Ligachev in an address given in Erevan, Armenia, in June 1985, when he made it clear that the new regime's acceptance of special needs among national minorities did not connote tolerance of nationalistic "excesses."

Ligachev went on to state the party's immediate goals in the field of national relations as "the fulfillment of shipments to other republics of produce under subcontracting arrangements, interrepublic exchanges of specialists and students, and the mastering of Russian—the language of internation communication."[5] Ligachev's statement seems implicitly to reject Aliev's notion that nationalities have explicit rights. Instead, Ligachev offers a model of nationality rights derived from the fulfillment of their responsibilities.

Ligachev's speech provides a good preview of the nationality section of the draft of the new Party Program, which was published in October 1985.[6] The introductory paragraph of this section unambiguously states that the nationality problem has been solved; nationalities will continue their development but will simultaneously become less distinct, albeit through a voluntary and egalitarian process. The rapprochement of nations is implied to be natural and inevitable, but it is explicitly stated that it cannot be forced. In the end, there will be a complete unity of nations (*polnoe edinstvo natsii*); the goal of fusion (*sliianie*) is not mentioned, because it will not occur before communism, the advent of which is not anticipated during the life of the program. This part of the document is neither new nor surprising.

The section of the party program then goes on to describe three specific tasks, the description and order of which highlight new priorities in the area of nationality relations. The first task, and presumably the most important, is "the comprehensive consolidation and development of the Soviet multinational state." The CPSU will continue to strengthen the "unitary union, multinational state" by opposing all manifestations of parochialism and national insularity, while simultaneously enhancing the role of republics, autonomous oblasts, and autonomous regions as well as the active participation of workers of all nationalities in their administration. The message here is that the responsibility of the republics and smaller national regions will be enhanced to allow them to fulfill the tasks delegated by the center, but that they will not be able to redefine these tasks in the name of national interest. They will have increased authority to see that these tasks are executed and will be held responsible if they are not.

The second task is defined as "the building of the material and spiritual potential of each republic within the framework of a single national economic complex." Only when the initiative of the republics and smaller national regions is combined with management at the center, the program seems to imply, can all resources be used rationally and local features exploited. This requires a better division of labor between republics; the republics must contribute to the development of new regions through sending trained workers and specialists. The notion of an all-union economic complex is not a new one,[7] but unlike earlier formulations,[8] this paragraph unambiguously states that the republics exist to serve the all-union goals and that the national minorities must fulfill these goals even if this means their relocation.

The third task is a more purely ideological one. This task and its description are a repetition of familiar themes: "the development of a single culture of the Soviet people, socialist in content, diverse in its national forms, internationalist in spirit, which is based on the best achievements and unique progressive traditions of the peoples of the USSR." The program then talks in very familiar language about the rapprochement of national cultures through their mutual enrichment.

The next part of the section asserts that all citizens of the USSR will have the right to continue to develop and to use their national languages, but "at the same time mastering, along with the language of their nationality, the Russian language." This formulation seems an effort to help assuage some of the fears of the national minorities that their languages are slated for extinction.

Gorbachev's remarks on nationality issues in the main report to the Congress followed the draft of the Party Program quite closely, as he stressed that the proper contribution of all republics to the development of an integrated national economy must be guaranteed, which could only result from further cooperation between republics. Manifestations of nationalism would not be permitted to impede economic development, and the further consolidation of national cultures must go forward unhampered.[9] Gorbachev also criticized at considerable length the failures of party leadership in a number of Muslim republics, but these remarks are made in the context of delineating the proper Leninist cadre policy and were not tied to problems of nationality relations.[10]

Ligachev, however, did link explicitly the concerns of nationality policy with those of proper management of cadres. He criticized the domination of parochial interests in many national regions, and he stated that the center would continue to reassert its authority by transferring personnel both into and out of all the national regions. Many of his conclusions seemed particularly directed toward the Central Asians:

> To whom is it not clear, comrades, that, in the conditions of our multinational country, tireless concern for the growth of local cadres and for their education in the spirit of internationalism is necessary? Meanwhile, in some places, parochialism and localist attitudes have become prevalent. They prevented the promotion of representatives of all nationalities to positions of leadership, they prevented the interregional exchange of workers, the exchange of experienced workers between republics and the center, between the regions and the cities of the country. In a series of cases this led to self-isolation, stagnating affairs, and other negative phenomena.[11]

The republic first secretaries were fast to recognize the de facto reduction of authority to their offices and to the position of the republics more generally that was implied in the New Party Program and in its interpretation by Gorbachev and the party leadership. Nor were they assuaged by the seeming concessions to national minority sensibilities that were implied by the statements guaranteeing the preservation of national languages. Many of the republic party leaders expressed their displeasure at the 27th Party Congress as well as the republic party congresses that had preceded it.

The various Central Asian first secretaries (three of whom had just been appointed) endorsed the draft Party Program, but each was careful to warn how difficult it would be to achieve these goals in his own republic. Tajik First Secretary K.M. Makhkamov counseled that the low level of Russian-language skills of many Tajiks would impede the economic development of Tajikistan, and he warned that neither the Tajiks nor Tajikistan would soon pull their full economic weight.[12] In his speech before the Kirghiz Party Congress, A.M. Masaliev bemoaned the fact that the number of Kirghiz workers was increasing only slowly, and he said that it would be virtually impossible to send large numbers of trained Kirghiz youth to develop the new economic regions.[13]

Other leaders, including most prominently Kazakh first secretary D.A. Kunaev, quite pointedly blamed many of the republic-level failures on the inability of the all-union ministries to make deliveries on time or sometimes even at all. If the republic-level cadres were to be subject to dismissal on grounds of inefficiency, these first secretaries seemed to imply that cadres based in Moscow must be held accountable to the same standards as well.[14] The three first secretaries who publicly took this stance—Kunaev, Iusupov (Dagestan), and Shakhirov (Bashkiria)—have all been subsequently removed from office.

Then Uzbek first secretary Usmankhodzhaev and Makhkamov both endorsed the interrepublic exchange of cadres, which is not surprising as Central Asia was a particular target of this policy.[15] But others, especially the Caucasian first secretaries, expressed concern that this would reduce their influence in defining the economic priorities of their regions. Both K.M. Bagirov[16] of Azerbaijan and Pastiashivili[17] of Georgia depicted themselves as supporters of a Leninist nationalities policy, but described this policy as the unconditional development of their own national region. Such murmurs of discontent did not appear to influence Gorbachev and his entourage, however, and the final version of the section on nationality relations was quite close to the draft published in October.

Taken as a whole, the legacy of the 27th Party Congress in the field of nationality policy was an uncertain one. The primary tasks that the party set for itself were economic; the fulfillment of these tests in turn demanded that the performance level of party cadres improve substantially as well. But the Party Congress did serve to convey the message that the national republics would be governed by the norms of expected behavior of administrative organs more generally, which meant that they must adequately perform tasks delineated by the center as well as accept the center's direction of the in-migration and out-migration of cadres.

The adjournment of the Party Congress did not end the debate on the proper focus of Soviet nationality policy, and some in the republics continue to express their discontent. In July 1986, G. Yenukidze, a secretary of the Georgian Communist Party, wrote a long article for *Pravda* on "National Education and International Education" in which he praised the enhancement of the role of republics and national regions that would occur for those national units that behave responsibly. But Yenukidze counseled that centralized management without the proper use of local initiative would make it impossible to achieve the desired rates of economic growth. Furthermore, he warned, should Moscow's developmental strategy ignore the specific needs of national republics, a rise in national insularity and exclusivity will be encouraged and not the desired increase in economic efficiency.[18] In a similar fashion, A. Dashdamirov, head of the section of agitation and propaganda of the Azerbaijan Communist Party and a specialist on nationality relations, wrote in a September issue of *Pravda* that no cadre policy can ever truly be "nationality blind." Instead, he maintained, the success of Moscow-inspired development schemes and the interrepublic exchange of cadres both depend on sensitivity being shown to the unique cultural character of each nationality.[19] But warnings such as those of Yenukidze or Dashdamirov were ignored until after the application of Gorbachev's nationality policy led to riots in Alma Ata.

The Alma Ata riots seem to have convinced Gorbachev that his treatment of the non-Russian nationalities requires rethinking, and at the February

Plenum he called for a special meeting of the Central Committee of the CPSU on the nationality question.[20] Official statements and newspaper editorials (that appeared in 1987) on the goals of nationality policy have been conciliatory in tone.[21] Laying part of the blame for the Alma Ata riots on poor socialization, Kazakhstan's Communist Party called for better Russian-language instruction throughout the republic and at the same time pushed for improved Kazakh-language instruction as well. Similar resolutions on improved education in the language of the indigenous nationality have also been introduced in Turkmenistan, in Tajikistan, and in the Baltic republics.

But while Gorbachev has tried to show the Party's commitment to the "flourishing" of nationalities, he has also emphasized that Moscow will remain adamantly opposed to any manifestations of "national exclusivity." Specifically, Moscow has promoted a countrywide campaign to end preferential treatment of indigenous nationalities in education, employment, and appointment to party posts, except where mandated as part of the attainment of economic goals. Thus, the Central Asian nationalities are still being actively recruited to fill places in technical schools and universities and to take technical jobs in industry, but Moscow is closely monitoring the ethnic balance in the humanities departments of universities and pedagogical institutes (the paths to prestigious posts for the younger generation) as well as in the party and government itself. These policies are proving difficult to enforce and unpopular.

Cadre Policy, Moscow's Instrument of Control

Gorbachev appears determined to achieve his economic policy through the use of a nationality policy based on a cadre policy that eliminates holdovers from the past and replaces them with people who share Gorbachev's vision. Here, too, Gorbachev is building upon Andropov's precedent. Numerous party and state officials were dismissed in 1983 throughout the USSR. Then on December 15, 1983, the national republics were singled out for particular scrutiny, when the Central Committee passed a resolution on the work of the Moldavian Communist Party. This resolution was intended to serve as the standard of conduct by which the operation of republic party organizations would be judged. The choice of the Moldavian Party was intended to be instructive, because both Brezhnev and Chernenko had served in Moldavia. The Moldavian Communist Party was criticized for its propensity for paper-shuffling and inertia, for pretentious plans, for passing economic resolutions with no provision for their fulfillment, and for having district and city party committees that had usurped the functions of state organizations and economic enterprises but that had not exercised their own supervisory tasks.[22] Politburo members themselves became vulnerable, when on December 23,

1983, the Central Committee of the Komsomol issued a decree sharply criticizing the past performance of the Kazakh Komsomol, an organization under the indirect supervision of Politburo member and former Brezhnev crony D.A. Kunaev.[23]

Even after Andropov's death, the party continued its drive to weed out weak, corrupt, and inefficient cadres in the RSFSR and, increasingly, in the republic parties as well. The Moldavian, Armenian, Belorussian, and Ukrainian Communist Parties all had higher than average turnovers of personnel, but nowhere was the turnover of personnel greater than in the five Central Asian republics, where in every case literally dozens of senior officials were replaced. Even though Kunaev sat on the Politburo and had not yet been subject to public criticism, nonetheless even the Kazakh party and republic government underwent a major reorganization during 1984 and early 1985.

However, the greatest number of dismissals occurred in Uzbekistan. The effort to restructure the Uzbek party and state apparatuses assumed campaign proportions after the June 1984 (sixteenth) Uzbek Central Committee Plenum, attended by Y.K. Ligachev. Then first secretary Usmankhodzhaev's report to this meeting was the first public discussion of the mismanagement of the Uzbek party and economy. Usmankhodzhaev blamed this mismanagement for the decline in the average annual rate of increase of labor productivity from 3.8 percent in the Ninth Five-Year Plan to 1.1 percent in the eleventh. Crime and corruption were blamed for some of these losses. The most dramatic case was in the cotton-cleaning industry, where dozens of workers had been arrested for theft of state property (for falsifying figures and then reselling the stolen goods) in Dzhizak, Khorezm, Kashka Darya, and Bukhara oblasts.[24] Favoritism was described as widespread, and it was announced that the *obkom* (provincial party committee) first secretaries of Bukhara and Dzhizak had been removed for flagrant abuse of official positions.

After Gorbachev assumed the position of general secretary, the turnover in cadres in all the Central Asian parties was further accelerated, and Russians as well as members of the indigenous nationalities found themselves vulnerable. The Uzbek Party continued to receive "special" attention. The Kazakh party was also under renewed attack. *Pravda* published a highly critical account of the Kazakh Central Committee's March plenum, the first scathing criticism of the Politburo member's own party organization.[25] Kunaev used the forum of the Kazakh Central Committee plenums to defend his actions.[26] With the long-secure Kunaev under attack, the other Central Asian leaders tried even harder to try to disassociate themselves from the failings that had occurred during their stewardships.[27]

In summer of 1985, pressure on the Central Asian leadership intensified.[28] In an article in the August 1985 issue of *Partinaia zhizn'*, Ligachev levied some stern criticism of both the Kazakh and Kirghiz Party organizations. The harshest words were saved for the Kazakhs, but Kunaev remained in office. However, Usubaliev, Gapurov, and Nabiev were all sent into premature retirements in November–December 1985. A.M. Masaliev, who before a six-month transfer to the Central Committee in Moscow had been first secretary of Issyk Kul *obkom,* became first secretary of the Kirghiz Party. S.A. Niazov, who became first secretary of the Turkmen C.P., also served for six months in the Central Committee, returning to his republic as chairman of the Council of Ministers of the Turkmen S.S.R. only days after Gorbachev became general secretary.[29] Only the new Tajik first secretary, K.M. Makhkamov, did not have recent experience working in Moscow. Makhkamov had been chairman of the Tajik Council of Ministers since 1981 and before that a deputy chairman of the Council of Ministers and head of Tajik Gosplan.

Usmankhodzhaev remained as first secretary (until January 1988), but much of the top leadership of the Uzbek party changed during the months preceding the 27th Party Congress. But the dismissals did not mean that new blood was being brought in everywhere. The republic press and especially the Uzbek-language newspapers carried numerous articles about how dismissed senior republic officials were not receiving the proper party punishment.[30] The press also described party meetings at which *raikom* (district party committee) officials had been chastised for failing to punish party offenders and for finding comparable positions for their dismissed friends.[31] The ability of former Uzbek officials to draw on earlier friendships was visibly demonstrated when R. Shermukhamedov, the dismissed minister of education of Uzbekistan, had his comments on the new Party Program published in *Kommunist.*[32]

The failures of the Brezhnev-era leadership was a theme stressed at all five Central Asian Party Congresses, with Moscow's clear orchestration. The Kazakh and Uzbek meetings were the most dramatic. At the Uzbekistan Party Congress for the first time, the late first secretary Sh. Rashidov was publicly blamed for the current poor state of party and economic management in Uzbekistan. Usmankhodzhaev accused Rashidov of fostering a "defective" style of leadership in the Uzbek central committee and in party *obkoms, gorkoms* (city party committee), and *raikoms.* He argued that Rashidov's love of ostentation and self-praise had led to the rise of a "cult of personality." This combined with his disregard for criticism and self-criticism had encouraged the rise of formalism, intrigues, complacency, abuse of position, and even embezzlement. Usmankhodzhaev claimed that the current leadership of the Uzbek party had been "hypnotized" by Rashidov's personality and had been unable to oppose his will.[33]

The themes of Uzmankhodzhaev's speech were reinforced in a number of other addresses as well. Those who like B.F. Satin, the new first secretary of the Tashkent *gorkom* (who had only recently come to the republic), were even more scathing in their criticism. Moscow gave close coverage to the Uzbek party congress. Usmankhodzhaev's recantation was reported at length. For the first time since the Khrushchev years, a former Politburo member was labeled a criminal. The tone of the coverage made clear that both Rashidov and the Uzbek party organization were being made into examples;[34] those who behaved similarly, it was implied, could expect similar punishment.

The Turkmen, Kirghiz, and Tajik meetings, each held a few days before the Uzbek meeting, had served as good preparation. At all three, it was revealed that the former leadership had been ousted; the legacy of each former first secretary was berated before both a republic and an all-union audience. Niazov's congress address blamed Gapurov for Turkmenistan's declining economic growth rates, and he sharply criticized Gapurov for not setting positive models of behavior and for tolerating the incompetent and sometimes even illegal behavior of others.

The Kirghiz Party Congress, which began on January 23, 1986, contained an even more scathing condemnation of the former leadership. First Secretary Masliev placed much of the blame for the republic's economic failures on the faulty leadership of former Kirghiz first secretary T.U. Usubaliev, who (according to Masaliev) encouraged servility and intrigue and compelled party and state officials to juggle their figures in order to record imaginary successes. However, to the outside observer, the link between economic performance and the replacement of cadres appears more tenuous than Masaliev himself explained. The Osh *obkom,* for example, which successfully had completed its five-year plan, nevertheless had its leadership overhauled and was sharply rebuked at the Congress. By contrast, the much-criticized A.D. Dzhumagulov,[35] reputed patron of grandiose and unnecessary construction projects, was promoted to replace Masaliev as Issyk Kul *obkom* first secretary, was elected to candidate membership in the CPSU central committee, and was subsequently made chairman of the Council of Ministers of the republic.[36]

The Tajik Party Congress, which convened one day later, followed what was by then becoming an established form. The newly appointed first secretary, K.M. Makhkamov, blamed the fact that one-fifth of all enterprises in the republic had not managed to fulfill their five-year plans on the failures of leadership of former first and second secretaries R. Nabiev and Iu. Belov, who, he maintained, had condoned careless and unprincipled behavior in their subordinates.[37]

The Kazakh Party Congress seemed to deviate somewhat from Moscow's planned orchestration. This meeting that, with Moscow's clear encouragement, had focused on the failures of Kunaev's leadership and his personal responsibility for the declining economic growth rates that the republic had experienced during much of the Eleventh Five-Year Plan period, nonetheless ended with Kunaev's reelection by a divided party to the post of first secretary.[38] Kunaev then went on to retain his membership in the Politburo at the 27th Party Congress, even though further criticisms were levied against his management of the Kazakh Party during the proceedings in Moscow.[39]

In Kunaev's report to the Kazakh Congress, he admitted that the republic's economic performance in a number of areas merited strong criticism, but he placed much of the blame for this on his subordinates. He noted that five hundred officials occupying posts filled through *nomenklatura* (bureaucratic elite) lists had been removed[40] and described the recent dismissals of first secretaries Askarov and Koychumanov as a demonstration that everyone will be held accountable for his own actions.

In his lengthy report of the state of the republic's economy, Chairman of the Council of Ministers N.A. Nazarbaev strongly attacked the Kazakh Academy of Sciences (headed by Kunaev's half-brother) for inhibiting the development of modern techniques, and he accused D.A. Kunaev of condoning this situation when he said: "Dimash Ahmedovich, we think it is high time to call him to order."[41]

The most striking indictment of D.A. Kunaev's leadership was made by Kzyl Orda *obkom* first secretary E.N. Auel'bekov. He detailed all the malfeasances that had been tolerated in Kzyl Orda by his two predecessors, malfeasances sufficient to cause 159 *obkom* officials on *nomenklatura* to be dismissed in the previous year alone. How could the party Buro have been ignorant of these conditions? Why did they not respond to the state of affairs in Kzyl Orda or in any of the other areas where the corrupt and criminal activities were being tolerated? The impression Auel'bekov left was that the Buro leadership was itself corrupt.[42]

Auel'bekov's speech seemed to have caused quite a stir at the meeting, and Olzhas Suleimenov, the noted poet and first secretary of the Kazakh writers union, delivered a strong condemnation of Auel'bekov in response. Suleimenov urged those assembled to have some perspective in their criticisms and to respect the accomplishment of the party and its leadership. He then upbraided Auel'bekov for not having spoke up six years ago against the very malpractices of his predecessors that he now so enthusiastically critiqued, and he added that he was sure that Auel'bekov would welcome public criticism by his own subordinates.[43] But *Pravda* praised Auel'bekov and criticized the Kazakh secretariat and the central committee for tolerating corrupt practices; the *Pravda* account ended with a query as to how Kunaev (referred to by name) could have been unaware of the criminal activities of his own close associates.[44] At the 27th Party Congress, the attack on Kunaev was renewed. Gorbachev made two critical remarks about the Kazakh party in his political report. Ligachev also made negative reference to Kazakhstan.

The Dilemmas of Governing Central Asia

Following the 27th Party Congress, Moscow continued closely to mind affairs in Central Asia. Pressure to weed out the old anti–reform-minded leadership remained very strong throughout Central Asia, with dozens of *oblast-* (province-) and hundreds of *raion-* (region-) level officials being dismissed for being corrupt, weak, inefficient, or insufficiently committed to the new reform programs. But both the meaning of corruption and the meaning of reform remained ill defined in the Central Asian context during these months.

The new (twelfth) Five-Year Plan set ambitious goals for Central Asia, but failed to provide much more direction than its predecessors about how to achieve them. Most of the economic reforms mentioned throughout 1986 and 1987 had little direct application in Central Asia, where improved economic performance was expected to take the form of increased growth rates, better labor productivity, and less waste. Corruption—be it by pilfering of materials, theft of state funds, or manipulation of accounts—was commonplace and seen by Moscow to be the cause of declining growth rates in the region, which, if the corrected official figures were to be believed, were dropping more rapidly than in most other places in the Soviet Union.

As the purge of cadres continued, growth rates improved slightly but were not uniform within each of the republics. In some areas, the purge of cadres was linked directly to an attack on Islam, as the perpetuation of corrupt practices was said to be yet another manifestation of traditional "feudal-bai" (a term used during the year of the Stalinist purges to refer to landlords opposed to agricultural collectivization) attitudes, which were said to spread with the popularization of the Islamic faith. Certainly Moscow saw the backwardness of Central Asia as in large part the product of its religiously based tradition-bound culture, but the lack of coordination of the attack on religion as in the application of cadre policy more generally throughout 1986 suggests a great deal of discretion was left to local authorities to do Moscow's bidding. The antireligious campaign and the efforts to replace cadres more generally were more chaotic than effective for Central Asia as a whole. The new cadres often resembled the old in every way save for the most important, i.e., that these new officials were tied to those currently in power and not to those who had been dismissed. The economic improvements in which the turnover of cadres resulted were too little to give Moscow much assurance that its policy of reform in either the party or the economy were having the desired effect in Central Asia.

But, while Gorbachev failed to effect the desired economic transformation in Central Asia and his control over these republic party organizations remained tentative at best, his support within the leadership had solidified, allowing him to go after the one Central Asian leader who remained in the Politburo. In December 1986, Moscow announced the "retirement" of Kazakhstan's first secretary, Dinmukhamed Kunaev (a member of the Politburo since 1971) and his replacement by Gennadi Kolbin, the Russian first secretary of Ulianovsk *oblast,* who had never served in Kazakhstan.[45] This event sparked several days of rioting by young Kazakhs, unrest that was publicly explained away by Moscow as a demonstration of the nepotism and chicanery that had dominated Kazakhstan; the rioting youth were said to be protesting the decline in their personal fortunes, which Kunaev's dismissal was said inevitably to foreshadow.

Such explanations belied the complexity of motives that seem to have been behind the Alma Ata riots. In large part, the actions of the rioters seem to have been a statement against what they considered to be a violation of their understanding of nationality policy. Whether or not they should be considered to be nationalists is a semantic problem. They certainly considered themselves to be Kazakh communists, and they were protesting a decision by Moscow to alter the existing social contract. Hitherto, such a social contract had allowed the perpetuation of a fusion of Kazakh nationalism (as defined by the Kazakh party), communism (once again as defined by the Kazakh party), and traditional bureaucratic behavior (what Moscow would certainly call nepotism and corruption). Although others evidently used the riots as an occasion to espouse their own views, including certain inchoate Pan-Islamic sentiments, the thrust of the riots seems to have been to protest the violation of the status quo.

Certainly, many Kazakhs opposed the riots, but their opposition was not so much a product of their support for the CPSU and Moscow as a statement of their alienation from it. Many of the opponents of the riots would also define themselves as Kazakh nationalists, but these people understood their nationalism as derived from the Kazakh past as Kazakh intellectuals (and not party historians) defined it. Such people would obviously see themselves as above the internecine struggles in which Kunaev and his followers—and opponents—all engaged; they were, however, equally unlikely to become party activists in order to enthusiastically throw themselves into the Gorbachev reforms or into any other party activity.

With the possible exception of the territorial disputes between Armenia and Azerbaijan concerning Nagorno-Karabakh,[46] most of the other protests and demonstrations held from late 1986 through early 1988[47] in the national regions of the Soviet Union were by people whose loyalty was already in real question, such as the Baltic nationalists or the Crimean Tatars. What made the Alma Ata riots of critical importance was that they were a violent manifestation of the dissatisfaction of the Central Asian party elite and their children against the course of Moscow's policy. Despite all of Moscow's mollifying statements, the central leadership has yet to identify the scores of loyal communists grateful for the removal of Kunaev and they have yet to identify an alternative party elite from which dependable cadres can be drawn.

The reporting of a few sensational scandals in the first weeks following Kolbin's appointment resulted in some well-publicized dismissals and a few arrests,[48] but a thorough overhaul of the Kazakh party organization has yet to be conducted. Kazakhs recruited to high office in that republic during 1987, the most prominent being Kazakhstan Party Second Secretary S. Kubashev and Chairman of the Kazakhstan Supreme Soviet Z. Kamalidenov,[49] are individuals who held senior appointments under Kunaev and who did not participate in the public baiting of Kunaev occurring prior to his dismissal.

There are similar patterns in appointments made in other Central Asian republics.[50] The highly publicized program for the interrepublic exchange of cadres seems to have suffered a real defeat from the Alma Ata riots. Central Asian cadres are still being dispatched to Moscow, and Russian cadres are being rotated to the Central Asian republics on brief tours of duty. Most of the movement, however, is confined to middle- and lower-level cadres. When U.B. Usmankhodzhaev was dismissed as first secretary of Uzbekistan's Communist Party in 1988, he was replaced by R.N. Nishanov, who had returned to Uzbekistan to fill the post of Uzbekistan's foreign minister after fifteen years of diplomatic service. He then was appointed chairman of the Supreme Soviet of Uzbekistan and managed to impress Moscow. While Nishanov's attenuated local ties were undoubtedly a major reason for his attractiveness as Uzbekistan's first secretary, he did not have the background or the experience of a Kolbin or the type of career pattern that one associates with the cadre policy elaborated by Moscow.

The Push for Ideological Conformity

Gorbachev's drive to increase economic efficiency and end corruption gives us a good sense of how the new general secretary defines modern management. It is not hard to see that the old style of leadership in Central Asia diverges strongly from this model. Gorbachev and, particularly, Ligachev have applied a broad definition of the word *corruption* and have termed the Central Asian parties' traditionally lackadaisical attitude toward enforcing Soviet religious legislation a manifestation of corruption.

Islam is omnipresent in Central Asia if religion is defined in cultural terms. Virtually all Soviets of Muslim extraction practice rites of communal membership such as circumcision and provide religious funerals for their relatives; substantial parts of the community also observe the major Muslim religious festivals and povide religious marriage ceremonies and birth rites for their children.

The Central Asian party leadership certainly recognizes the prevasiveness of Islamic religious practice and the de facto fusion of religion and nationalism in the Muslim regions. The leadership's toleration of religion is politically expedient; to oppose the popular observance of Islamic life-cycle observances is to antagonize the Central Asian masses against the party and Soviet rule. But the identification of the Central Asian leadership with Islam can be more strongly personal, as party leaders often participate in these observances and it is not unknown for them to visit mosques as well.[51]

Gorbachev and Ligachev, however, have identified religion as an impediment to the success of their economic and political goals in Central Asia, and they believe that the linkage of religion with nationalism poses a serious threat to any Moscow-imposed drive to achieve an accelerated rate of economic growth as well as to their goal of obtaining ideological conformity. These ideological goals are particularly important to Ligachev, who seems willing to pursue them even if this antagonizes the party organizations in the predominantly Muslim republics. His December 1985 attack on the Azerbaijani party's harmful tolerance of religious practice was intended for a broader audience. He said that:

> While respecting believers' feelings, it is necessary to assess from a principled Marxist-Leninist standpoint the role of Islam, any religion, and any church, and in the history and cultures of the peoples, and to consistently oppose any attempts to identify, national, spiritual, and ethical values with religious injunctions and to portray religious rituals as popular traditions.[52]

Ligachev has reiterated the message that religion is a source of ideological deviancy on a number of occasions, the most recent one being in his speech at the all-union conference on social science held in Moscow in October, 1986 when he once again spoke out on the illegitimacy of confusing religion with nationalism.[53] However, while Ligachev labeled Islam, Catholicism, and the Ukrainian national church potential sources of deviation, he made no mention of the Russian Orthodox church. Ligachev's distinction among religions, combined with his enumeration of an exclusively Russian list of Soviet national heroes, must have made the national republic leadership uncomfortable. Ligachev's ideological goals, nevertheless, have become accepted as a legitimate part of Moscow's cadre policy, although the attack on Islam plausibly could be seen as motivated by Russian nationalism.

At first, CPSU elites in Moscow were content simply to put increased pressure on party officials throughout the USSR to crack down on the illegal practice of various religious faiths. Central Asian officials responded by spending more time denouncing both the illegal and the legal practice of Islam and by increasing the intensity of antireligious propaganda.[54] Several Central Asian leaders made critical references to the growth of religion among young people, the deleterious influence of religion upon economic growth, and the mistaken fusion of religion and nationalism at the republic Party Congresses.[55]

But in July 1986, it became clear that Moscow had made the goals of the antireligious campaign a part of its cadre policy, when Samarkand *raikom* first secretary, M. Sherkulov, was dismissed for failing to enforce state laws against religion.[56] This dismissal came after an earlier warning from Moscow had been reported in the republic press.[57] Moreover, a speech by a Tashkent *obkom* secretary at the October 1986 plenum of the Uzbek Central Committee maintained that several senior officials in this *obkom* had recently been dismissed on similar charges.[58] How widespread such dismissals are within Uzbekistan and whether they extend to other republics are yet unknown. From late 1986 through 1987, the verbal armor of the antireligious campaign was strengthened. Tajik Party First Secretary K.M. Makhkamov spoke about the widespread practice of religion among party officials in Dushanbe in two reported addresses in 1986; he warned that the virtual nonexistence of antireligious propaganda at the republic's VUZs (higher educational institutions) and the clandestine religious instruction in official institutes would no longer be tolerated, with party officials to be held personally responsible for such malfeasances.[59] However, these harsh words have yet to be followed by the promised dismissals. Even the most forceful verbal admonition is unlikely to produce change, and neither Makhkamov nor any of the other Central Asian first secretaries have shown enthusiasm for using more forceful means to curb party members' observance of Islam.

The degree of party cooperation in religious observance is widespread and unlikely to be contained by any but the most drastic measures. Makhkamov complained that the only way a *raion*-wide observance of the Muslim religious period of Ramadan by high-school–age youth had been detected had been because the *bufetchitsi* (waitresses) did not know how to dispose of massive amounts of uneaten food, after several officials had all turned blind eyes.[60] This indicates the extent of tolerance of religious observances. Corroboration is seen in Usmankhodzhaev's revelation that the now-dismissed first secretary of Dzhizak *obkom* had permitted the construction of a mosque with the use of state funds and materials.[61] It appears that eliminating illegal religious practices by party officials will be impossible.

Also unpopular are some of Gorbachev's cultural policies. *Glasnost* in the cultural sphere is largely confined to the Russian population. While Russians are being given increasing freedom to explore their national pasts, the non-Russians in general, and the Central Asians in particular, are finding new restrictions placed on their publications in the fields of both history and literature. Moscow forcefully maintains that official laxness during the years of *zastoi* (stagnation) allowed nationalist sentiments to take root in the universities and in the artistic unions, and that these negative "manifestations" must be replaced with a proper "scientific" (pro-Russian) socialist outlook. Gorbachev's policy of bureaucratic *demokratia* (democracy) is not only an unpopular policy, but has also been difficult to enforce because most of the unpopular writers and academics have managed to hold onto their posts due to the greater, albeit limited, self-government allowed to the organizations for which they work. Despite the popular support that these individuals enjoy, however, it is unlikely that such bureaucratic stalemates ultimately will be resolved in favor of the Central Asians.

Gorbachev's attitude toward religion is another area of his nationality policy that is causing Moscow problems in Central Asia. While claiming to defend the legal rights of religious practitioners, Moscow has sharply criticized religion when it has served to inflame anti-Soviet nationalist sentiment. Moscow has thus encouraged all the Central Asian party organizations to root out anti-Soviet religious organizations and, even more seriously, to eliminate the observance of Islam by party members themselves. Here, too, *glasnost* has caused problems, because increasingly more frank discussions of the pervasiveness of Islam have dramatized what was in any event a growth in religious identification among the Central Asian population, especially those of the younger generation.

The spread of Islam is a problem requiring a great deal of finesse on Moscow's part. Islam is spreading in the Soviet Union for a number of reasons. There is a return to Islam going on worldwide and Iran's foreign broadcasts undoubtedly are helping to educate Soviet Central Asians as to their own religious background. Central Asians are also rediscovering their faith as part of the process of national-identity formation that accompanies political and economic development. While the Central Asian parties turned a blind eye to Islam, the situation was a relatively stable one in that Islam and communism, as defined in the periphery, were seen as compatible. If Moscow forces the Central Asian party organizations to turn on their own faith and the faith of their people, then the nature of the existing social order will be challenged, with the results sure to further diminish Moscow's popularity. On this issue as well, Gorbachev seems to have allowed himself little flexibility in a reformulation of nationality policy.

Gorbachev and the Future of Central Asia

Gorbachev's nationality policies have exacerbated the tensions that his political and economic reform programs have engendered in Central Asia. He is demanding that the area develop rapidly and in ways that will aid the nation as a whole rather than the local economy, but he is not providing the labor or the material resources necessary to do this. Neither has he found leaders who share this vision and who can effectively communicate these policies to the local population. At the very time that he demands the maximum sacrifice from the local population, he further antagonizes them by pursuing social goals that they perceive as destructive of their traditional cultures. Meanwhile, as a backdrop to life in Central Asia, the Soviet Union has fought an unpopular war in a neighboring Muslim country and now seems likely to pull out and be replaced by an anti-Soviet regime. It is hard to imagine a scenario more likely to produce instability in Central Asia than the one Gorbachev himself has contrived to introduce. What seems the safest course for U.S.

interests is to simply sit on their hands and watch while the drama unfolds, lest the United States inadvertently do anything that might allow Moscow successfully to reassert control.

The protests of the national minorities feed on one another as grievances of one community legitimate the discontent of another. That officials now publicly recognize the existence of national interests among diverse ethnic communities encourages the belief that noncooperation might foster policy changes and the granting of more authority to the nationalities and the national republics.

Although small changes may be introduced, any major shift in the power balances in the national regions would be contrary to the premises of Gorbachev's economic and political reforms, and it would cause him a considerable loss of face. Already, the disturbances in the national regions have given potent new ammunition to Gorbachev's critics within the leadership.

What does this mean for the United States? Most importantly, it must see Gorbachev's authority as seriously weakened by the growing number of outbursts of national interest, and it must take note of this when negotiating with him, as Gorbachev must find ways to demonstrate his credibility as a leader. His critics will have trouble dislodging him if he shows himself to be a world leader of real stature. But, in the Soviet Union, foreign-policy success alone is never sufficient to defeat political enemies. Gorbachev must resolve his domestic problems if he is to remain in power. A resolution to the national problem in Central Asia, however, seems likely to elude him.

Notes

1. For an in-depth discussion of this, see Thane Gustafson and Dawn Mann, "Gorbachev's First Year: Building Power and Authority," *Problems of Communism* (May-June 1986): 1–19.

2. Iu. V. Andropov, "Shest'desiat let SSSR," *Kommunist,* no. 1 (1983): 6–8. For a further discussion of Andropov's nationality policy, see Martha Brill Olcott, "Yuri Andropov and the National Question," *Soviet Studies,* 36, no. 1 (January 1985): 103–17.

3. M.S. Gorbachev, *Zhivoe tvorchestvo narodov* (Moscow, 1984), p. 31.

4. *Pravda,* April 23, 1985, pp. 1–3.

5. From *Kommunist* (Erevan), June 2, 1985, pp. 1–2, as quoted by FBIS (Foreign Broadcast Information Service), *USSR Daily Report,* June 20, 1985, pp. R18–19.

6. *Pravda,* October 25, 1986, p. 6.

7. V. Pavlechenko, "V edinom narodnokhoziastvennom kompleks," *Kommunist,* no. 9 (1972): 65–75.

8. Brezhnev's address to the 26th Party Congress also mentions the specialization and proportional development of the national republics in "an all-union economic complex," but he does not mandate the achievement of this by a shift in the power rela-

tions between center and periphery. *Materialy XXVI s'ezda KPSS* (Moscow, 1981), pp. 184–85.

9. Although neither in Gorbachev's speech nor in anyone else's remarks were guidelines set down for distinguishing progressive national features from reactionary ones.

10. *Pravda,* February 26, 1986, pp. 1–10.

11. *Pravda,* February 28, 1986, p. 4.

12. *Kommunist Tadzhikistan,* January 25, 1986, pp. 2–5.

13. *Sovetskaia Kirghizia,* January 21, 1986, pp. 1–5.

14. *Pravda,* February 28, 1986, p. 4. Others who discussed inadequate central support included M. Yusupov, first secretary of Dagestan (*Pravda,* March 5, 1986, p. 7), who criticized Gosplan and the USSR Ministry of Irrigation and Land Reclamation.

15. *Pravda,* March 1, 1986, p. 4.

16. *Pravda,* March 1, 1986, pp. 2–3.

17. *Pravda,* February 27, 1986, p. 2.

18. *Pravda,* July 4, 1986, pp. 2–3.

19. *Pravda,* September 26, 1986, pp. 2–3.

20. *Pravda,* February 19, 1988.

21. For a good example, see the article by E. Bagramov, *Pravda,* August 14, 1987, p. 2.

22. *Pravda,* December 15, 1983, p. 1.

23. *Komsomol' skaia Pravda,* December 30, 1986, p. 1.

24. Although the full scale of the scandal was not revealed until Usmankhod-zhaev's own dismissal. *Pravda Vostoka,* January 23, 1988.

25. *Pravda,* March 29, 1985, p. 2.

26. JPRS (Joint Publications Research Service), *USSR Political and Social Affairs,* UPS 85-045, pp. 110–26; and FBIS *USSR Daily Report,* June 13, 1985, P.R. 14.

27. For Gapurov's effort, see JPRS, *USSR Political and Social Affairs,* UPS 85-045, pp. 102–5. For Nabiev's, see JPRS, *USSR Political and Social Affairs,* UPS 85-047, pp. 118–23, and his interview in *Pravda,* April 20, 1985, p. 2. For Usubaliev's, see JPRS, *USSR Political and Social Affairs,* UPS 85-045, pp. 127–60, and his interview in *Pravda,* June 7, 1985, p. 2.

28. Some evidence of this appears in Second Secretary Iu. P. Belov's stern address to the special plenum of the Tajik Communist Party in July 1985. JPRS, *USSR Political and Social Affairs,* UPS 85-076, pp. 5–6.

29. The dismissals of at least Gapurov and Usubaliev seem to have been planned for a while as Niazov had been dispatched to Moscow in September 1984 and Masaliev in June 1985.

30. *Sovet Ozbekistani,* November 30, 1985, p. 2, as quoted in JPRS, *USSR Political and Social Affairs,* UPS 86-023, pp. 35–37.

31. *Sovet Ozbekistani,* November 30, 1985, p. 2, as quoted in JPRS, *USSR Political and Social Affairs,* UPS 86-023, pp. 35–37.

32. R. Shermukhamedov, *Kommunist,* no. 2 (1986), pp. 69–70.

33. *Pravda Vostoka,* January 31, 1986, pp. 2–6.

34. *Pravda,* February 2, 1986.

35. *Pravda,* January 27, 1986.

36. *Sovetskaia Kirghizia,* January 24, 1986, pp. 1–5.

37. *Kommunist Tadzhikistan,* January 25, 1986, pp. 2–5.

38. There is no evidence to suggest that Gorbachev thought Kunaev would be ousted during the Congress (although the man on the street certainly did—as I realized when I was in the USSR just before the meeting began), but there is strong evidence that Gorbachev would have like Kunaev ousted.

39. But as if in attestation to Kunaev's other prominant supporters, a self-defensive statement of the good and bad of the Kazakh Communist Party, written by Second Secretary O.S. Miroshkin, appeared in the March issue of *Voprosy istorii KPSS.*

40. Kunaev took credit for purging the party in this address, whereas the *Pravda* account of February accredited Moscow for these dismissals.

41. *Kazakhstanskaia Pravda,* February 9, 1986, pp. 2–4.

42. *Kazakhstanskaia Pravda,* February 8, 1986, p. 6.

43. *Kazakhstanskaia Pravda,* February 10, 1986, p. 4.

44. *Pravda,* February 9, 1986, p. 2.

45. According to the 1979 census, Russians make up nearly 40 percent of the population of Kazakhstan, a higher percentage than the Kazakhs. Data gathered between censuses show the percentage of Kazakhs in the republic exceeding that of the Russians. The criticism of Kolbin's appointment was not that he was a Russian, which certainly disturbed many Kazakhs, but that he was from outside of the republic as well.

46. Over whether the Nagorno Karabakh autonomous region, more than 80 percent Armenian in population, should be moved from the Azerbaijani republic to the Armenian one.

47. There were large demonstrations on August 23 held in all three Baltic capital cities, and another set of demonstrations was held in November. There have also been a series of demonstrations held by the Crimean Tatars, both in Moscow and in Tashkent.

48. These dismissals and arrests were of the Kazakhs and Russians in Kunaev's personal retinue.

49. Kamalidenov was formerly a close protégé of Kunaev, the first Kazakh to head the KGB in modern times, and more recently secretary for ideology in the Kazakh buro.

50. This despite a CPSU Central Committee resolution on the failures of the Tashkent Oblast party organization that was expected to be a model for republic party organizations everywhere.

51. Makhkamov chastised the Dushanbe Party organization for this in a speech published in *Kommunist Tadzhikistan,* April 20, 1986, pp. 2–3.

52. *Bakinskii rabochii,* December 22, 1985, as quoted in FBIS, *USSR Daily Report,* January 2, 1986, p. R.16.

53. *Pravda,* October 2, 1986, pp. 2–3.

54. For some examples, see *Kommunist Tadzhikistan,* July 8, 1986, p. 5; *Komsomol'skaia Pravda,* June 4, 1986, p. 3; *Leninskaia smena,* July 11, 1986, p. 2; and *Pravda Vostoka,* June 28, 1986, p. 3.

55. This point was made particularly forcefully in Uzbekistan (*Pravda Vostoka,* January 31, 1986, pp. 2–5) and Tajikistan (*Kommunist Tadzhikistan,* January 28, 1986, p. 3).

56. *Sovet Ozbekistani,* August 6, 1986, p. 3.
57. *Pravda Vostoka,* June 14, 1986, p. 1.
58. *Pravda Vostoka,* October 7, 1986, p. 2.
59. *Kommunist Tadzhikistan,* September 4, 1986, pp. 2–3.
60. *Kommunist Tadzhikistan,* September 4, 1986, p. 3.
61. *Komsomolets Uzbekistana,* October 7, 1986, p. 2.

4
The Technological Limits to Soviet Power

Judith Ann Thornton

T he persistence of technological lags in many Soviet industries is documented by Western estimates of input productivities and by specific case studies of innovation.[1] Amann, Cooper, and Davies reached the conclusion that, with a few exceptions, Soviet technological performance was inferior to performance of the Western industrialized countries and showed little tendency to catch up. Detailed case studies in their book show that technological lags are shortest at the stages of basic and applied research and widen as Soviet equipment is finally introduced into general production.

The new leadership in the Soviet Union under General Secretary Gorbachev feels urgent concern about the unsatisfactory technological performance of the Soviet economy. The 27th Party Congress in February 1986 and the subsequent Twelfth Five-Year Plan announced by Chairman of the Council of Ministers Ryzhkov in June 1986 make "a radical acceleration of scientific and technical progress" the key task of economic planners for the next decade. Reporting to a CPSU Central Committee conference on June 11, 1985, Gorbachev complained:

> It must be admitted that the quality and the technical and economic level of manufactured articles remains a vulnerable spot in the economy, a source of many difficulties and problems. All this is causing serious social, economic, moral, and political damage. It is totally impermissible when newly developed equipment turns out to be obsolescent while still in the design stage and falls below the best indices in terms of reliability, service life, and economy of operation. Even products that, in terms of their parameters, are assigned to the highest category sometimes bear no comparison to the best world models.[2]

The Twelfth Five-Year Plan, ending in 1990, provides technocratic administrative measures to shift a larger share of resources into the develop-

---

Interviews with Soviet emigré design engineers mentioned in this chapter were supported by the Soviet Interview Project.

ment of new technology and to lower the bureaucratic barriers impeding technology transfer from abroad and modernization of equipment domestically. Moreover, the June 1987 party plenum spells out the basic features of a proposed economic reform intended to foster technological development. The measures proposed in two documents ("The Principal Guidelines for a Radical Reorganization of Economic Management" and "The Law on the State Enterprise") could serve as the basis for a genuine reorganization of Soviet economic institutions.[3] But there are still many questions as to how proposed changes will be implemented and whether they will, in fact, increase the productivity of Soviet resources. One measure already in place, the establishment of state acceptance procedures by USSR *Gosstandart* (State Committee for Standards) to monitor output quality at some fifteen hundred enterprises, led to initial disruptions of production and to a decline in the growth of output during the first quarter of 1987, when state inspectors began to reject a significant share of output that failed to meet specifications. So the fundamental question facing the Soviet leadership is whether they can actually implement the sort of "radical restructuring" of economic institutions and incentives that will allow them gradually to close the technological gaps that separate the USSR from the Western industrial economies as well as from some of the newly industrializing economies of Asia.

The Economic Base of Soviet Power

Rapid growth in the 1950s and sixties at rates exceeding 5 percent per year for GNP, with rates falling gradually from 10 to 6 percent for industry, built an economic base for the Soviet Union second only to that of the United States. While U.S. government estimates published in 1979 valued Soviet GNP at roughly 50–60 percent of U.S. GNP, the Soviet investment effort exceeded U.S. levels. In the late 1970s, the level of Soviet investment was estimated to be 107.6–122.9 percent of U.S. investment.[4] If that investment effort had been yielding fruit, the Soviet economy should have been catching up with the U.S. economy, but it was not.

In the 1970s and early 1980s, the Soviet leaders faced steadily declining rates of economic growth. Western estimates of real growth of GNP, summarized in table 4–1, showed a decline to 3 percent for 1971–75, 2.3 percent for 1976–80, and 1.9 percent for 1981–85. As growth slowed, the Soviet leadership seemed unable to understand what should be done or why the good performance of the early postwar years was not continuing.

Historically, the process of growth in the Soviet Union has differed from the pattern of Western growth. In the West, about half of long-run growth of output can be attributed to increase in the stock of productive inputs in use—increases in acres sown, in numbers of workers and machines, and in

Table 4–1
Growth of Soviet Output and Input Productivity, 1966–86

Growth Rates (Average Annual % Change)	1966–70	1971–75	1976–80	1981	1982	1983	1984	1985	Prelim. 1986
Gross national product	5.1	3.0	2.3	1.4	2.6	3.2	1.4	2.2	4.2
Output per unit of input	0.9	-1.1	-1.1	-1.6	-0.4	0.3	-1.3	-1.4	1.7
Work-hour productivity	3.0	1.3	1.1	0.5	1.6	2.5	0.9	0.7	3.6
Capital productivity	-2.2	-4.6	-4.3	-4.7	-3.4	-2.9	-4.6	-4.5	-1.2
Land productivity	5.0	2.9	2.5	1.5	2.7	3.1	1.5	1.8	4.2
Industrial output	6.2	5.5	2.7	1.3	0.8	2.7	2.6	2.7	3.6
Output per unit of input	-0.2	-0.2	-1.9	-3.0	-3.2	-1.1	-1.1	-0.9	-0.2
Work-hour productivity	3.1	3.9	1.3	0.6	0.0	2.2	2.1	2.2	3.1
Capital productivity	-2.3	-3.0	-4.7	-6.1	-5.9	-4.0	-3.9	-3.7	-2.4

Source: Richard Kaufman, "Industrial Modernization and Defense in the Soviet Union." Paper presented to the NATO Colloquium, April 1–3, 1987, pp. 4, 6.

other traditional inputs. But only about half of the growth of output can be explained in this way. Economists attribute the rest to "technological change," an aggregate measure of the growth of output per unit of aggregated inputs that they believe reflects the average improvement in the qualitative attributes of traditional inputs.

In the Soviet Union, on the other hand, the leadership brought their high rates of growth of GNP through rapid increases in labor participation and unprecedently high levels of capital investment. Most of the high Soviet rates of growth could be attributed to simple increases in traditional inputs. The growth of output attributable to technological improvements was meager, at best. Indeed, beginning in the 1970s, CIA-DIA estimates of total factor productivity in the Soviet economy, presented in table 4–1, showed an actual decline of more than 1 percent per year, while estimates of capital productivity showed falls of 3–5 percent per year. Some of the poor productivity performance may be a consequence of Soviet accounting procedures that sometimes treat qualitative improvements in capital goods as if they were quantitative increases in the number of units. Still, Soviet inability to increase input productivity clearly was a factor in declining growth rates. The warning signs of poor technological performance were clear more than a decade before the leadership sounded the alarm in 1985. With relatively little growth in output per unit of input, a slowdown in the growth of traditional inputs of labor and capital necessarily meant lower growth of total GNP. The rising cost of Siberian energy and natural resources and the inability of planners to adjust the structure of industrial production to a changing world economy all contributed to the declines in measured productivity. So the fundamental problem that the leadership confronted in 1985 was a backward technological base embodied in an aging and inefficient capital stock.

Evidence of Technological Inertia

A Review of Previously Published Data

The classic historical study of Soviet technological performance by A.C. Sutton, *Western Technology and Soviet Economic Development,* traced the course of technological innovation in a wide range of civilian industries in the West and in the Soviet Union, asking to what extent Soviet economic development was grounded on an indigenous capacity to innovate or to imitate Western developments and to what extent Soviet growth in technologically advanced industries was built on direct importation of Western plant and equipment. He concluded that, in general, Soviet industry acquired its technology by direct import, in the case of more sophisticated technologies, or by replicating or scaling up original Western models, in the case of less sophisticated equipment.

In 1977, Ronald Amann reviewed the evidence in one of the industries studied by Sutton, the chemical industry. Drawing on more extensive technical sources for the Soviet industry, he found that, in fact, there was no evidence of import of Western equipment for Soviet plastics production before or immediately after World War II. Further, for many of the examples of plastics products in which Sutton ascribed Soviet capability to produce to direct importation of Western plant and equipment, Amann was able to find evidence of Soviet large-scale production of the product at a date earlier than the date of import of the foreign plant and equipment.[5] If the Soviet Union had an indigenous base of technology for plastics production in 1960, why did they choose to spend scarce foreign exchange for an immense import of Western plant and equipment for the chemical industry? Amann speculates that the quality and cost of plastics produced with domestic equipment may have compared unfavorably with the possibilities offered by Western plant. Although he modifies Sutton's interpretation, Amann still concludes:

> In no case has the Soviet Union been the first country to produce a major plastic material on an industrial scale. For most plastics, with the notable exceptions of silicon polymers and PTFE (which are used in the high priority aerospace sector), Soviet production began much later than in the majority of leading Western countries, although in some individual cases Soviet production preceded that of Italy or Japan.[6]

The main conclusion of the Amann, Cooper, and Davies book was that, with the exception of certain priority sections such as high-voltage transmission of electric power, Soviet technology lagged behind Western levels and demonstrated no evidence of catching up.

A more recent (1986) book edited by Amann and Cooper, *Technical Progress and Soviet Economic Development,* suggests that, if anything, technological lags have increased in the preceding decade in such industries as computers, industrial robots, consumer durables, and electronic components.[7] Table 4–2 shows the shares of new technologies in total output of a sample of industries in the Soviet Union and the West estimated by Ronald Amann and Julian Cooper. Without exception, the shares of new technologies are lower in the Soviet Union than in major Western economies.

A study of the Soviet robotics program in *Soviet Automation: Perspectives and Prospects* identifies some of the specific successes and problems encountered in the attempt to introduce industrial robots:

> What has the robotics program accomplished? . . . First, it must be noted that for better or worse, a robotics industry has been established which can now supply the economy with a limited level of services. Some leading enterprises have been able to make effective use of robots to improve production and reduce employment.
> Nevertheless, the industry has been predictably plagued by many of the

Table 4–2
Share of New Technology by Nation, 1982

Technology	USSR	U.S.	Japan	West Germany	U.K.
Oxygen steel, % of total	29.6%	62.1%	73.4%	80.9%	66.1%
Continuously cast steel, % of total	12.1	27.6	78.7	61.9	38.9
Synthetic fibers, % of total	51.2	91.2	83.8	83.1	78.6
Polymerized plastics, % of total	46.4	87.5	80	73	79.3
Numerically controlled machine tools, % of total metal-cutting tools	16.6	34	52.8	20.6	27.7
Nuclear power, % of total (1983)	8.6	9.2	10.7	11.3	11.0

Source: Ronald Amann and Julian Cooper, *Technical Progress and Soviet Economic Development*. New York: Basil Blackwell, 1986.

general problems of introducing new technologies in the USSR. . . . In many cases, designs are not well-coordinated with needs, components such as D.C. motors and numerical control systems are in short supply, poorly tested and prepared equipment is shipped, and the absence of key auxiliary equipment renders the robots useless when they arrive at the enterprise. With limited use of microprocessors, sensing devices, and more advanced drives, the technology remains at a relatively low level.[8]

One telling piece of evidence on Soviet technological problems is the observation that, in both intra-CMEA and hard-currency trade, the Soviet Union relies on raw materials and primary products—notably, oil and gas—for a major share of export earnings while importing substantial amounts of machinery, equipment, and technology-based intermediate goods, a trade pattern common to the less developed countries. Table 4–3 presents estimates by Morris Bornstein of the shares of technology and technology-based products in Soviet exports to the OECD countries. He finds that, in 1982, this category of exports made up only 9.3 percent of Soviet exports to the OECD countries. Of all Soviet exports to the OECD, only 3.8 percent could be considered highly or moderately technology-intensive.[9]

Evidence Concerning Military Technology from
Interviews with Scientists and Design Engineers

This author and economist Susan Linz are carrying out a series of interviews with Soviet emigrés whose work in the Soviet Union involved the development and introduction of new technologies. Our sample is drawn from the Soviet machine-building, metal-working, energy, and heavy industrial sectors of the

Table 4–3
Share of Technology-based Products in OECD Imports from
the USSR, 1970–82

	1970	1975	1980	1981	1982
Technology and technology-based products	22.80%	15.62%	13.53%	10.54%	9.32%
Highly R&D-intensive	0.43	0.43	0.61	0.28	0.19
Moderately R&D-intensive	2.49	3.20	5.17	4.23	3.62
Non–R&D-intensive	19.88	11.99	7.75	6.03	5.51
Other products	77.20	84.38	86.47	89.46	90.68
Total imports	100.00	100.00	100.00	100.00	100.00

Source: Morris Bornstein, *East–West Technology Transfer: The Transfer of Western Technology to the U.S.S.R.* Paris: OECD, p. 120.

economy—sectors that have enjoyed priority access to engineering resources, capital investment, and foreign exchange. As of fall 1987, we had completed only thirty-one interviews, the accounts of which confirm many of the conclusions we draw from the literature on innovation published in the Soviet Union. On the other hand, the evidence from interviews shows a range of variance in circumstances and in levels of performance that is broader than we see in the published literature. Further, the answers of our respondents lead us to place very different emphasis on what appear to be important and minor determinants of the innovative potential of their industries. I shall comment on some of these differences in the pages that follow.

Comparisons based solely on civilian industry may provide a biased estimate of Soviet performance since it is well known that sectors deemed vital to national security have priority access to high-quality domestic and foreign equipment and materials. In spite of its favored access to domestic technologies, however, the Soviet military is handicapped by the low technological levels of many of its supplying sectors and, for this reason, is likely to find itself at an increasing disadvantage as rapid introduction of technologically advanced weapons threatens to shift the East–West balance of nuclear and conventional forces. The Soviets continue to devote massive resources to research and development and to acquisition of foreign technologies, but some of the technologies required to build advanced military systems are in the areas where Soviet performance is weakest—computers, industrial robots, and numerically controlled machine tools. In other key military technologies shown in table 4–4, a U.S. Department of Defense publication estimates that the United States enjoys a positive but narrowing technological lead. These include:

Aerodynamics: The Soviets have sophisticated aerodynamics research facilities, but most of the important aerodynamic principles have been developed in the West.

Table 4–4
U.S. and Soviet Advantages in Military Technology

Basic Technology	U.S. Superior	U.S. and Soviet Union Equal
Aerodynamics and Fluid dynamics		X
Computers, software	X	
Directed energy, laser		X
Electro-optical	X	
Guidance, navigation	X	
Life sciences	X	
Materials	X	
Microelectronic materials, Integrated circuit manufacturing	X	
Nuclear warheads		X
Optics	X	
Power Sources		X
Production manufacturing	X	
Propulsion	X	
Radar sensor	X	
Robotics, machine intelligence	X	
Signal processing	X	
Signature reduction (stealth)	X	
Submarine detection	X	
Telecommunications	X	

Source: Richard DeLauer (under secretary of defense, research and engineering) *The FY 1985 Department of Defense Program for Research, Development and Acquisition.* (n.p., n.d.)

Chemicals: The Soviets give high priority to such areas as chemical explosives and chemical warfare, but Soviet fuels, lubricants, and industrial fluids fall short of Western standards and the Soviet Union turns to the West for sophisticated diagnostic equipment.

Directed energy: The Soviets carry on extensive research on military applications of lasers, radio-frequency energy, and particle beams.

Electronics: The Soviets demonstrate theoretical capabilities comparable to those in the West, but have difficulty translating R&D results into production.

Electro-optics: The West leads in basic R&D, material quality, and fabrication in most advanced electro-optical technologies relevant to reconnaissance, communications, and navigation.

Oceanographics: The Soviet oceanographic research program is the largest in the world.

Manufacturing: The Soviets are international innovators in welding and match world standards in sheet-metal forming.

Materials: Soviet capabilities for producing light metal alloys are strong. They appear to trail the West in leading-edge technologies such as refractory and superalloys, powder metallurgy, ceramics, and composites.

Nuclear power: Soviet theoretical understanding of nuclear weapons physics is probably on a par with the West's. They have rapidly expanding R&D and construction programs for nuclear reactors.

Power sources: The Soviets are the world leaders in the development and application of magnitohydrodynamic power generation.

Propulsion: The Soviets have aggressive R&D programs in ramjet propulsion and liquid-propellant missiles.[10]

Confronting a weak technological base, designers of Soviet weapons choose designs that are simple, rugged, and easy to maintain. A 1986 assessment by a U.S. government agency says:

> The simplicity (relative to Western standards) chosen by Soviet designers has entailed trade-offs. Design simplicity increases reliability and reduces development and production costs. It has allowed the production of capable weapons by a labor-intensive industrial base without substantial investment in new manufacturing methods. The choice of a simple design, however, has frequently resulted in a less sophisticated weapon, often restricted in application to a single military mission.[11]

Since the mid-1960s, the Soviet Union has offset its technological disadvantages in the military sector by producing larger quantities—sometimes overwhelmingly larger quantities—of weapons. This sustained and costly effort has helped to secure Soviet status as a military superpower, but accelerating technological competition is estimated to have increased the burden of Soviet defense spending from 12–14 percent in 1970 to about 15–17 percent in 1982.[12] In another area of competition, the exploration of space, the Soviet Union is carrying on a series of programs that are larger and more ambitious than current U.S. efforts in spite of less sophisticated technology.

Barriers to Innovation

Many Western and Soviet sources address the factors that foster or impede adoption of new technology in the Soviet economy.[13] To evaluate these arguments, we need to remind ourselves of some of the generalizations that have emerged from studies of contemporary innovation in the West. First, private firms devote resources to R&D in the expectations of private benefit, so privately financed R&D is concentrated in areas in which the benefits of discovery can be captured, at least partly, by the innovating firm in the form of increased profits and improved competitive position. Where the benefits of innovation cannot be internalized—for example, in the case of a search for a new variety of food crop that cannot be patented—then research, if it is done at all, is more likely to be carried out by an academic or public organization rather than by a private firm.

Christopher Freeman identifies the following characteristics of successful innovating firms:

1. Strong in-house professional R&D,
2. Performance of basic research or close connections with those conducting such research,
3. The use of patents to gain protection and to bargain with competitors,
4. Sufficient size to finance R&D expenditures over long periods,
5. Shorter lead times than competitors',
6. Readiness to take high risks,
7. Early and imaginative identification of a potential market,
8. Careful attention to the potential market and substantial efforts to involve, educate, and assist users,
9. Strong entrepreneurship to coordinate R&D, production, and marketing, and
10. Good communication with the outside scientific world as well as with customers.[14]

Studies in a 1984 volume edited by Zvi Griliches underscore some of Freeman's points and suggest several other features of the process of innovation:

11. The pace of innovation has accelerated, making short lead time more important than ever.
12. Past innovative success appears to offer advantages in future technological competition.
13. On the other hand, small firms appear to have comparative advantages in some industries, such as mechanical engineering, scientific instruments, and computers. Industries that permit and encourage the formation and growth of new innovative enterprises show better economic performance than industries controlled by an unchanging group of members.
14. Users of new technologies today can rarely acquire it through simple purchase of capital equipment alone. The application of new technology often requires a complicated mixture of capital, specialized materials, labor and management skills, and institutional arrangements. Western firms use a multiplicity of institutional arrangements—licenses, cooperation agreements, joint ventures, and subsidiaries—to govern the long-term employment of specialized resources.

15. Firms introducing new technologies require a higher proportion of scientific and technically skilled labor than firms using the same technology later, once the technology is fully established.[15]

Students of the Soviet economy can identify many ways in which it diverges from this model of the innovative firm. However, the Soviet economy does enjoy at least one clear advantage, which is the sheer magnitude of the resources devoted to science, research, and development. Official research programs, presently drafted by ministries and approved by the State Committee for Science and Technology, direct scientific resources to tasks that have highest priority in central plans. Scientists and engineers may focus on the long-run scientific and technological aspects of problems, Soviet sources claim, without concern for short-run considerations of profitability.

The Soviet Union devotes an impressive quantity of resources to research and development. According to table 4–5, the share of expenditure for science in Soviet national income (Soviet definition) rose from 4 to 5 percent between 1970 and 1985. The National Science Foundation estimates that research and development expenditures in the Soviet Union (excluding capital costs) were 3.7 percent of Soviet GNP in 1982 compared with 2.6 percent for the United States, 2.6 percent for West Germany, and 2.5 percent for Japan.[16] A similar share of total labor force, 3.7 percent of workers, or 4.5 million persons, was employed in Soviet science in 1984. Of these, 1.46 million were "scientific workers" according to table 4–6.[17] In the same year, roughly half as many (744,000) scientists and engineers were employed in research and development in the United States. Although the U.S. employment category differs from the Soviet category, the data suggest the major commitment to R&D made by the Soviets. With the cost of capital investment included, the share of Soviet R&D is still larger.

The Soviet Statistical Abstract publishes synthetic calculations of the "effect" of new technology derived from estimates of the productivity differences of the new and old comparison technologies. These calculations, presented in table 4–7, attribute to new technology an annual productivity increment equal to 2 percent of national income in industry. However, the Western estimates of input productivity presented earlier show small positive, or even negative, changes in total input productivity that leave us somewhat doubtful of Soviet ability to use their impressive scientific establishment to foster industrial innovation.

In spite of the advantages claimed for Soviet science, the barriers to innovation are formidable as well. I will group them under four general categories: (1) bureaucratic, organizational barriers, (2) incentive failures, (3) supply monopoly and excess demand, and (4) diversion of high-quality inputs to military use. These factors fostering and impeding innovation are considered, in turn, next.

Table 4–5
Soviet Expenditures for Science and National Income 1965–86

Year	National Income at Current Prices (billion rubles)	Total Government Expenditure	Expenditure on Science from All Sources	Expenditure on Science from Budget	Expenditure for Professional-Technical Education	Science Share of National Income Percentage
1965	145.0	—	—	—	—	—
1970	289.9	154.6	11.7	6.425	1.313	4.0
1975	363.3	214.5	17.4	7.893	2.092	4.8
1976	—	226.7	—	7.897	2.254	—
1977	—	242.8	—	8.189	2.365	—
1978	—	260.2	—	8.777	2.496	—
1979	440.6	276.4	—	9.280	2.578	—
1980	462.2	294.6	22.3	9.946	2.686	4.8
1981	482.1	309.8	23.4	10.862	2.734	4.9
1982	512.9	343.1	24.9	11.720	2.123	4.9
1983	548.1	354.3	26.4	12.712	2.112	4.8
1984	569.6	371.2	27.8	13.233	2.124	4.9
1985	578.5	386.5	28.6	13.625	2.184	4.9
1986	587.4	417.1	29.5	14.237	3.360	5.0

Source: Budget expenditures for science and professional—Technical Education: Ministerstvo finansov SSSR Biudzhetnoe upravlenie *Gosudarstvennyi biudzhet SSSR i biudzhety soiuznykh respublik 1976–1980 gg* Moscow: Finansy i statistika, 1982; *Gosudarstvennyi biudzhet SSSR 1981–1985,* pp. 18–19; *Narodnoe khoziaistvo SSSR za 70 let* Moscow: Finansy i statistika, 1984, p. 633.

Total expenditures for science, all sources: Tsentral'noae statisticheskoe upravlenie SSSR, *Narodnoe khoziaistvo SSSR,* (various years). Moscow: Finansy i statistika 1979, pp. 555, 556; 1982, pp. 520, 522; 1984, pp. 409, 424, 575, 576.

Gross social product, national income: *Vestnik statistiki,* no 2, 1985, 78; *Narodnoe khoziaistvo 1980,* pp. 49, 379; *Narodnoe khoziaistvo 1985,* pp. 45, 411.

Table 4–6
Soviet Science Employment and Structure of Costs

Year	Total Scientific Workers Including Higher Education (thousands)	Total Workers in Science and Science Service (thousands)	Average Annual Wage in Science (rubles)	Estimated Wage Bill in Science Including Social Security (billion rubles)	Total Expenditure for Science Including Investment (billion rubles)	Estimated current and Capital Costs (billion rubles)
1965	664.6	2625	1401.6	3.937	—	—
1970	927.7	2999	1641.6	5.268	11.7	6.4
1975	1223.4	3790	1890.0	7.665	17.4	9.7
1980	1373.3	4370	2154.0	10.093	22.3	12.2
1981	1411.2	4500	2200.0	10.593	23.4	12.8
1982	1431.7	4470	2200.0	10.522	24.9	14.4
1983	1440.0	4471	2329.2	11.143	26.4	15.3
1984	1463.8	4508	2350.0	11.335	27.8	15.1
1985	1491.3	4554	2428.8	11.835	28.6	14.6
1986	1500.5	4546	2498.4	12.153	29.5	14.2

Source: All science including higher education and average wage in science: V.P. Groshev, *Narodno-khoziaistvennyi nauchnyi kompleks*. Moscow: Mysl', 1985, p. 40 *Narodnoe khoziaistvo SSSR za 70 let* Moscow: Finansy i Statistika, 1984, p. 412.
Science and science service: Tsentral'noe statisticheskoe upravlenie SSSR. *Narodnoe khoziaistvo SSSR* (various years). Moscow: Finansy i statistika, 1985, 1984, pp. 409, 1985, 64.
Note: Wages bill in science estimated from employment times average wage plus estimated social security payment into the budget. Capital and current costs in science estimated as total cost less estimated wage bill.

Table 4–7
Effect of New Technology, 1970–86

Year	National Income in Industry (billions current rubles)	Estimated Effect from New Technology (billions current rubles)	Technology's Effect as a Percentage of National Income from Industry
1970	148.3	2.607	1.76
1971	—	—	—
1972	163.6	2.997	1.83
1973	173.3	3.543	2.04
1974	186.3	3.697	1.98
1975	191.2	3.832	2.00
1976	199.7	3.980	1.99
1977	210.4	4.193	1.99
1978	215.2	4.340	2.01
1979	226.5	4,479	1.98
1980	238.1	4.785	2.01
1981	248.0	4.400	1.77
1982	266.8	4.800	1.80
1983	254.1	5.100	2.01
1984	262.2	5.400	2.06
1985	263.6	6.000	2.28
1986	259.0	6.200	2.40

Source: V.P. Groshev, *Narodno-khoziaistvennyi nauchnyi kompleks*. Moscow: Mysl', 1985, p. 211. *Narodnoe khoziaistvo SSSR za 70 let*, p. 75, 122.

Organizational Barriers to Innovation

A strong theme emerging from the Thornton-Linz interviews is the bureaucratic environment in which scientists and design engineers function. In their descriptions, initiation of a new project is preceded by a prolonged *perepiska* or correspondence between the ministry and subordinate units over the terms of implementation. This accounts for much of the delay in completing Soviet construction projects, they say. Each stage of a design project is supported by a large amount of paperwork and is reviewed at several higher levels of the ministerial hierarchy.

The Soviet industrial ministry is a large, vertically integrated bureaucracy that assumes responsibility for firms producing a particular product. Ministries are designated all-union, union-republic, and republic ministries depending on whether they are administered directly by the center, by a republic alone, or by a combination of republic and central authority. In many respects, the administration of a large all-union or union-republic ministry can be compared to the management of a Western cartel. The ministry has effective monopoly control over its group of products, allocating output targets and often assigning customers to its member enterprises. New enterprises are set up with the approval of the central ministry itself, and any substantial capital investment by member enterprises must be approved by the ministry and included in plan documents as well. While Gorbachev's proposals for reform would give the enterprise considerably more autonomy, the authority of the ministries is undiminished as of mid-1988.

Ministers are appointed by the government through the *nomenklatura* process, and their tenure tends to be stable for many years. The work of a ministry is carried out through divisions known as "administrations" and "chief administrations." There are branch and functional administrations, each headed by a deputy minister. Ministry research and development functions are directed by the Chief Technical Administration of the ministry. The scientific research institutes, information services, and some facilities for engineering and development of the branch usually are attached directly to this administration. However, design bureaus, preliminary engineering facilities, and experimental or prototype construction facilities may be attached to a variety of different organizations. They may be part of a complex scientific research institute, a scientific production organization that is subordinate to the Ministry Technical Directorate, an association, or an enterprise.

Since the late 1960s, ministries have been instructed to integrate research, design, and development facilities into unified complexes. One type of organization bringing together research and development facilities is the Scientific Research Institute (referred to by its Russian initials, NII), which unites basic and applied research, frequently in an academic institution, with engineering design, prototype testing, and experimental construction. The research arm of the organization, which plays the lead role, may be administered by the Academy of Sciences, by a branch ministry, or jointly by the academy and a branch ministry.

A second type of organization intended to link innovators and users is called a Science Production Association (NPO) when it develops new products or a Production Technical Organization (PTO) when it develops new processes. An NPO can link all the stages of innovation from research through prototype construction. Table 4–8 presents a schematic of the organizations and functions that are linked in an NPO. Depending on their size, NPOs may be subordinated to the Technical Administration of a ministry or to an intermediate ministerial organization such as an all-union industrial association. In addition, large enterprises (and, sometimes, not-so-large enterprises) may have their own design or technological bureaus and experimental production facilities; such units are common in Ministry of Defense plants.

In theory, the integration of research and development units into larger organizations is intended to cut lead times and focus work on the needs of clients in production. But in spite of organizational reforms, numerous barriers to innovation remain: (1) research organizations remain isolated from production and are poorly supplied with capacity for constructing models and prototypes, (2) separate development activities are fragmented, and

Table 4–8
Organization of Research and Development in a Science Production Association

	Scientific Research Institute or VUZ	Branch Research Institute or VUZ	Design Bureau (Konstruktorskoe Biuro)	Experimental Production Plant	Enterprise, Association	Scientific Production Association
Fundamental research						
Pure science	X					X
Basic research	X					X
Applied research						
Technical definition	X	X				X
Technical proposal	X	X				X
Preliminary draft (eskiznyi proekt)	X	X				X
Development						
Technical specification			X			X
Design			X			X
Preliminary engineering			X			X
Engineering						
Prototype, pilot facility (opytno-konstruktorskaia rabota)				X		X
Serial production					X	X

Source: N.I. Kotkov et al., "Ekspertno-statisticheskii analiz organizatsionnykh form sviazei v protsesse peredachi i ispol'zovaniia nauchno-tekhnicheskikh resul'tatov," *Kompleksnaia oraganizatziia issledovanii.* Moscow: Nauka, 1981, p. 7.

(3) research units in separate ministries find themselves duplicating the same work several times over.

Isolation of Research and Development. The separation of Academy of Sciences scientists from scientists and engineers in the branches impedes the flow of fundamental innovation into application; the separation of the NPO design bureau from the enterprise clients that will ultimately produce and use its equipment sometimes results in impractical designs that are expensive to construct and inefficient to use in practice. The majority of major research organizations and lead design bureaus are in a few large cities, far from the enterprises that will ultimately use their designs.

The network of design bureaus attached to the Siberian branch of the Academy of Sciences provides an example of some of the problems. This scientific complex includes fifty-five research institutes of the Academy of Sciences, eleven branch design bureaus, and seven economically self-sufficient academy design bureaus (*khozraschetnyi*). According to a series of reports in *Izvestia,* these design bureaus have problems in balancing their basic and applied research, and, further, all research activities are undersupplied with experimental and prototype production facilities.[28]

The research institutes spend a minority of their time on applied problems, but this effort brings in the majority of their income. Their applied work subsidizes their basic work.

The branch design bureaus were set up to provide design of prototypes and experimental production facilities for the applied research of the academy institutes; they are subordinated both to the academy and to their branches for this reason. However, since their budgets come from the branch ministries, their activities are diverted to specific branch needs and away from activities serving the academy's research interests. Experimental production facilities have regular production plans and they are often used to circumvent equipment supply problems. When they can, the branch ministries designate their design bureaus as branch institutes, effectively withdrawing them from basic research support for the academy institutes. The Academy of Sciences institutes sets up their own *khozraschetnyi* design bureaus in response, but, says the *Izvestia* commentary, the design and experimental production base in these is inadequate to support the Siberian research effort. A case in point is the Catalysis Institute, which is developing a valuable method to produce high-grade gasoline directly from natural gas. The institute is building two prototype units in its own machine shops, but, with nine-hundred research associates, it has only twenty workers in its machine shops.

Two surprising findings that emerge from the ongoing Thornton-Linz interview study of Soviet design engineers are the engineer's disinterest in and disregard of costs in the design process and the small share of new technological developments that actually found their way into use in production. Many of the engineers interviewed treat as naive our questions about whether their new prototypes cost less to produce than old models or whether the newly developed equipment will lower the costs of users. A frequent answer was, "Cost estimates were made in a different division," although one engineer did answer, "Oh, yes, I know what you mean; I did my engineering diploma paper on the cost saving afforded by one of our designs."[19]

Rather than costs, the engineers defined their work in terms of technical problems. With some notable exceptions, they spoke of general, and even fairly specific, research goals as coming from higher up in the ministerial hierarchy. An example is an engineer in one of the transportation ministries. His department would receive foreign vehicle parts and components that might be used in the equipment produced by his ministry but that were protected by foreign patents. His department would be assigned the task of designing an alternative component to achieve the same technical result in a different way without infringing on the foreign patent. (Such conscious comparison with the products of competitors is, of course, practiced by firms all over the world.)

The separation of technical from economic considerations may be one factor in explaining the small share of new prototype technologies that actually are put into serial production. An engineer who worked in a design bureau for motor transport for almost twenty years reported that the plan of his division required the production of a new prototype vehicle each year. In answer to the question, "How many of these vehicles found their way into serial production," he responded, "One and one-half."

Another engineer who directed the lead design institute in an energy-producing ministry, whose organization designed several new models of equipment each year and who, individually, had received "dozens" of Inventor's Certificates (patents), reported that only one major piece of equipment developed by his organization was ever put into production. He reported that this equipment was put into production for a couple of years and was then discontinued because it was too expensive to maintain.

The Soviet press confirms the failure to put new designs into general use. *Izvestia* reports: "Unfortunately, . . . the introduction of scientific achievements is, as a rule, local in nature. As many as 80 percent of all new developments are still introduced at only one enterprise, fewer than 20 percent are introduced at three or four enterprises, and only 0.6 percent are introduced at five or more production facilities."[20]

Fragmentation of Research and Development. The fragmentation of the separate stages of development, design, preliminary engineering, and construction of prototypes contributes to the long lead times between development and diffusion. Organizations that have developed a patentable innovation register it with the State Committee for Inventions and Discoveries. The proposed patent is subjected to examination and, if it is certified, is then published in the *Bulletin for Inventions and Trademarks*. Subsequently, enterprises that make use of an Inventor's Certificate in serial production for the first time must file a form listing the dates of use and estimated economic savings. It is these forms, presumably, that serve as the basis of estimates of the "effect" of new technology. A study by J.A. Martens and J.P. Young, based on innovations certified in the late 1970s, showed that two years after receipt of an Inventor's Certificate, 23 percent of Soviet innovations had been introduced into production; the corresponding figures for the United States and West Germany were 66 and 64 percent, respectively. Since the time between application and certification of Inventor's Certificates is, itself, measured in years, the Martens and Young measures are actually a conservative estimate of the true lags.[21]

The Gorbachev reforms propose to deal with the organizational fragmentation by eliminating unproductive research institutes and design departments in many ministries by consolidating others into Super-Scientific Production Complexes on the scale of East Germany's Large-Scale Industrial Research Centers or the Soviet Ye. O. Paton Institute of Electric Welding in Kiev, and by integrating other ministerial NPOs into Inter-Branch Research Organizations. Inter-Branch Research Organizations are a response to the perception that most major technological breakthroughs have potential application in more than one sector. (For example, the development of a low-corrosion heat pump can change the design of nuclear-power stations, car radiators, district heating units, refrigerators, and many other capital goods, each of which is in a separate Soviet ministry.) But such consolidation also lengthens the hierarchical distance between designers and the users of their products.

Duplication of Research. The desire of each industrial ministry and of each individual branch of the equipment ministries to have a separate research and development capacity is merely one facet of the general urge for self-sufficiency of Soviet ministries. It reflects the weakness of incentives and lack of institutional mechanisms fostering transfer of new processes across ministerial boundaries. A 1985 article in *Ekonomika i organizatsiia promyshlennogo proizvodstva* complains that "over 200 scientific research institutes and design bureaus are separately engaged in developing automated control systems for various users."[22] Another article in this journal reports: "The policy of having plants produce their own instruments, which has been adopted in recent years, seems . . . to be economically unjustified. . . . Why . . . must designers develop new items every time when it is possible that someone has already developed them and they are already being produced at other plants? At the present time this information is not available."[23] An article in *Sovetskaia Rossiia* reports that the RSFSR machine-building complex administered 433 scientific research and design organizations.[24] Nationally, the machine-tool ministry alone had 106 scientific research institutes and design bureaus.[25] In the energy sector, each of the separate fuel ministries has its own research effort directed to the transmission of liquids through pipelines. Such anecdotal evidence describing the proliferation of scientific research organizations is voluminous and repetitive. Some of the proliferation of research and development facilities apparently occurs through upgrading of ordinary design and specifications departments. Some design engineers interviewed in the Thornton-Linz project reported that they began working for design bureaus that were subsequently designated "scientific research and production organizations." The change, we were told, increased the status of the organization. But the resulting proliferation reduced the average resource base of each research and design unit.

Attempts to reduce duplication within the ministerial framework are costly in themselves. One design engineer who worked for ENIMS (Experimental-Scientific Research Institute of Metal Cutting Machines) was assigned the task of designing computer-aided metal-cutting machines but was denied the right to design and produce the associated computer controls. Computer controls were the responsibility of the Ministry of Instrument Making, Automation Equipment, and Control Systems, a defense-related ministry that gave low priority to the ENIMS projects. The inevitable result was delay in civilian machinery projects that could neither produce their own nor extract components from other more powerful partners.

One symptom of separation and duplication of R&D is the slow diffusion of new processes into general production discussed earlier. Another symptom is the continued production of new units of equipment embodying obsolete technologies for long periods of time after small quantities of a superior model are already available. One example is the continued supply of new open-hearth capacity to Soviet industry for decades after oxygen steel capacities were already installed in a few plants.[26] Apparently, the costs of structural change are immense in the planned economy.

Access to Information. Although there are sometimes barriers to horizontal flow of information between units in different ministries, many of the scientists and engineers interviewed in the Thornton-Linz project said that their access to some kinds of information in the Soviet Union was superior to their access to information in a U.S. engineering office. Still, U.S. suppliers, they say, provide brochures, detailed manuals, and frequent visits by salespeople to inform designers about products and components that are available. In the Soviet Union, a Soviet designer could get similar data only by making visits to supplying plants.

On the other hand, Soviet design bureaus are obliged to provide valuable technical information, blueprints, and designs to other organizations without compensation when instructed to do so by their ministries, so Soviet design engineers frequently commented that they were dismayed to have to pay for information in the United States that was available without charge in the Soviet Union.

Further, the extensive research-information infrastructure in the Soviet Union gives the Soviet scientist and engineer access to detailed technical information on virtually every field of science and engineering. The All-Union Institute of Scientific and Technical Information in Moscow employs about 6,000 full-time staff and approximately 25,000 part-time reviewers in the publication of more than two dozen monthly journals abstracting important engineering and patent information from all over the world. Most of the respondents in the interview sample had access to technical libraries containing Soviet abstract journals, Western technical journals, and a large body of technical publications and handbooks produced by the ministry. Many reported that a special technical-information office in their organization provided them with translations of scientific material of particular relevance to their work.

Incentives to Innovate

A bureaucratic organizational framework impedes the adoption of new technology because it makes the time and money costs of innovation prohibitively high. Bureaucratic price formation impedes the adoption of new technology because it bestows few benefits on the innovating firm and imposes few costs on the backward firm. These environmental variables affect performance by influencing the incentives and, thus, the choices of decision makers in R&D organizations that provide new technology and in the enterprises that put new equipment and new processes to use.

Consider the incentives facing a Western firm that decides to invest in the development of a cost-reducing production process for its own use or in designing new equipment for sale to others. In the market economy, such a decision must meet the same criteria of potential profitability imposed on other investments. The firm that adopts a cost-effective technology enjoys higher profits, at least until competitors innovate themselves and competitive pressures lower the prices of final products in the industry. With private property rights, the developer of a patentable new technology may derive revenues from licensing, sale, or a variety of other joint arrangements with potential users of the technology.

But in the Soviet Union, aside from payment for the initial work done and aside from some small performance bonuses, the individual innovators and the innovating organization do not have the right to derive continuing income from the technology they have developed by licensing or by any other means. The bonuses that R&D organizations do receive are smaller and are paid less regularly than the production bonuses received by industrial workers. Among the Thornton-Linz sample of scientists and engineers, the average annual bonus (usually for timely completion of projects) averaged less than 10 percent of base wages. In only one of thirty-one cases did an engineer report a substantial incentive payment. This was a payment (estimated to be about 40 percent of base wages) to a design group for completion of a major investment project.

Most of the activities of an R&D organization are specified in work orders drawn up by its superior organization—usually a ministry. These activities are initiated with the signing of a contract called a technical assignment, *tekhnicheskoe zadaniie,* describing a scientific research project, *nauchno-issledovatel'skaia rabota,* or the subsequent experimental design project, *opytno-konstruktorskaia rabota.* These activities may be supplemented by additional projects of a limited size initiated by the members of the research organization itself. The terms of these technical assignments specify the expected results, the time schedule of work, the planned level and structure of staffing, and compensation as well as incremental benefits for early completion or above-plan performance and penalties for late or deficient performance. The larger the size of the project, the more levels in the ministerial hierarchy must review and approve the program. The primary determinant of the cost of R&D is the allocation of staff time to the project. (In the financing of projects for capital investment, a standard 2 percent of project cost may be set aside for project specification work.) Incentive payments appear to play a minor role in most industries.

Currently, the amount of deductions going into the economic incentive funds of R&D organizations is determined by an estimate of the annual economic "effect" of the new technology. This effect is estimated using the "Standard Methodology for Determining the Economic Efficiency of New Technology, Inventions, and Rationalizing Proposals" approved in 1977 or by using one of more than eighty sectoral Standard Methodologies modeled on the national document. The formula for calculating the economic effect of new equipment involves estimating the cost-saving enjoyed by an enterprise producing with the new equipment compared to the cost of the same production using old equipment. Such cost-saving is summed (with or without time discount) over the estimated life of the new equipment. A 1986 article reports that it is common practice to use the obsolescent equipment being retired as the bench mark against which to calculate economic effect even when there are alternative new cost-efficient models of equipment available on the domestic market. This article reports that outside checks made by the Minsk *gorkom* and committees of people's control resulted in annulment of about 7 million rubles of the economic effect from introduction of new technology at Minsk enterprises, scientific institutions, and higher educational institutions.[27] Perhaps in response to the dubious content of such calculations, the reward to R&D organizations for introduction of new technology fell from 2.37 percent of the total estimated effect in 1976–77 to 1.16 percent in 1982–83.[28] Thus, in 1985, if the effect of new technology was 6 billion rubles, the innovating organizations in the whole economy received only 69.6 million rubles of compensation.

Incentives for applied engineering design and prototype production are a particular problem. Facilities for bench-shop testing and production of prototypes are in short supply. Prototype construction facilities are frequently diverted to customized production of deficit items for their ministries. They are assigned regular production plans in which the assembly of complicated mock-ups and prototypes may provide less reward than batch production of standard items. There are incentives to a proliferation of nonstandard items since prototype plants are rewarded for number of designs produced and are not bound by the usual price lists in charging for nonstandard items.

When they lack prototype production capacity, R&D organizations sometimes turn to regular production units for special components. Often they are unsuccessful, for the production of such custom components disrupts regular production schedules. Then, the R&D organization is forced to turn to informal channels of supply. The chief designer of one research institute in the Thornton-Linz sample recounts attempts to acquire a diesel engine for a prototype unit by offering the appropriate official of a supplying firm a trip to the Carpathian Mountains.

The barriers to innovation facing the Soviet enterprise are the subject of Joseph Berliner's *The Innovation Decision in Soviet Industry.* Berliner writes: "When an innovation has traversed successfully the long path from conception to general adoption, one can be sure that all along the way there were people for whom it was a matter of great concern whether it succeeded or not."[28] One of his main findings is that the competent manager who concentrates on current production operations can do about as well as the innovative manager; in most situations, the benefits to innovation are slight. Moreover, the attempt to innovate confronts the enterprise with substantial risks, each of which may entail heavy costs for the firm. In addition, he argues, the protectionist Soviet environment shelters the poor performer from the discipline of "the invisible foot"—the pressure of competition provided by a competitive market economy. He concludes that increased innovation in production is unlikely until the balance between reward and risk is altered.

Frequent complaints in the Soviet press make the case even stronger. They report that the current success indicators facing the Soviet firm may have a perverse impact on the innovating firm. One such case discussed in the television program "Science and Life" in 1987 follows the development of a high-performance, low-cost, tungsten-free steel by a scientist in the Azerbaijanian Academy of Science. In spite of its efficiency, the report claims, the Machine

Tool Ministry, *Minstankoprom,* is unwilling to use it because use of a low-cost raw material lowers the value of output and the value of labor productivity statistics of enterprises.

> This steel is approximately one-third the price. Therefore, the turnover of the enterprise will decrease by two-thirds. Labor productivity will be reduced to a third; stimulation funds will disappear. The plant will go broke. I understand the director of the plant who, at my request and out of respect for science, will produce one or two small smelting batches. But, he cannot allow the plant to go broke. The instrument-makers are faced with the same problem. The instruments will be half the present cost. Where is the cost-reduction mechanism? It does not exist.[30]

Our interview data contain many examples in which modernizing enterprises were expected to retool an existing production line and continue previous levels of production simultaneously—normally inconsistent activities. A number of cases are also detailed in which new products or processes were deficient in important ways. An extreme example is the case reported by a designer in the motor-vehicle industry in which a new model could not be assembled once production was started because various components could not be mass produced with the required tolerances that had been achieved by hand-crafting when the prototype was built. In another case, a newly installed unified assembly line was, indeed, more productive than the several separate machines that it replaced when the assembly line was running, but, each time a part needed replacement or a component needed adjustment, the whole assembly line had to be shut down. Before modernization, production had continued on the remaining machines when any one machine was stopped for repair or adjustment.

Excess Demand and the Helpless Customer

Many of the perverse incentives that leave the producer indifferent to product improvement and efficiency would not operate in the absence of an environment of excess demand. There are solid bureaucratic reasons why allocators who cannot capture the profits from a higher price are benefited by prices that are set below market-clearing levels. Only then are they in the position of bestowing benefits in the form of access to products upon friends and constituents and denying access to others. The excess-demand environment allows ministries to pass costs through onto price without concern for loss of customers. Suppliers face little competitive pressure to improve their products when there are queues for their existing goods.

The State Price Committee provides temporarily higher prices for improved products. In 1986, a markup of 30 percent was provided for products of superior quality and corresponding deductions were to be levied on goods with obsolete or deficient attributes. But such markups are determined by bureaucratic rules rather than market forces. When enterprise incentives are adjusted according to bureaucratic measures of product quality, firms trade off unmeasured attributes of their products to increase the bureaucratically measured attributes, so the resulting mix of characteristics is likely to be far from the design that consumers would have rewarded in a market competition. As Gorbachev's economic reform unfolds, there are frequent press reports of price increases. For example, in an interview with the first deputy chairman of the State Committee on Prices, an article in *Izvestia* reports: "In light industry 25 percent of articles are deemed innovations and the price is increased in each case—sometimes by as much as 100 percent."[31] If measured performance improves from such shifts in assortment, then we would expect the frequency of such real or pseudoinnovation to increase, but if price increases outpace the consumer's perception of quality, then consumer welfare will not have improved.

Many observers comment that demand-side influences are far stronger in the military industries. In the military industries, firms are likely to have their own R&D organizations. The military is able to create some small amount of competition by assigning similar research jobs to competing research units. Military users are believed to engage in careful monitoring of the quality of equipment supplied to them.

In 1986, *Gosstandart* was assigned the task of administering an extensive program for monitoring the quality of products at 1,500 civilian enterprises. State Acceptance is an attempt to provide an administrative substitute for the market discipline provided by competition in the West. There are early reports that State Acceptance has, indeed, improved the characteristics of output, but State Acceptance is an incomplete substitute for the long-run service relationship that successful innovative firms establish with their customers in a market economy.

Military Competition for R&D Resources

The share of military R&D is large in the case of both the Soviet Union and the United States. Western estimates attribute more than half, and possibly as much as three quarters, of Soviet R&D to defense. The nine military-machine–building ministries control about 50 design bureaus that are, in turn, supported by almost 150 subsystem and component design bureaus. The Ministry of Aviation, which designs and builds aircraft and missiles for both defense and civil aviation, has 8 aircraft design bureaus supported by 16 component and accessory design bureaus and 10 design bureaus that develop air-breathing powerplants.[32]

In both the United States and the Soviet Union, there are spillovers from military innovation to new civilian technologies, but in the Soviet Union the spillover effects are concentrated on civilian goods produced by the military industries. Other civilian ministries cannot easily learn of new technological developments in military ministries and acquire them.

The Soviet Environment for Innovation

The two factors favoring innovation in the Soviet environment are extensive R&D resources and good communication between applied work and basic science. On all other counts, the incentives to see the process of innovation through are weak and the bureaucratic barriers to such attempts are substantial.

1. Research units are generally separated from production.
2. In the absence of property rights, innovating organizations do not benefit from diffusion of their designs.
3. The majority of specialized designs are used only once.
4. Diffusion of new technology is slower than in the West.
5. Plants installing new technology may be worse off as a result of innovation.
6. In the absence of competition, there are few rewards for expanding into new markets and few costs to lack of flexibility.
7. With excess demand, there are no competitive pressures to provide users with good services and support of equipment.
8. Entrepreneurial functions are divided between the stages of development and investment. Firms investing in a superior process or supplying a superior piece of equipment do not enjoy economic rents.
9. Designers in the civilian sectors lack the continued feedback from users needed for incremental improvements.
10. Ministries control new entry and, under ministerial normatives, a plant with new technology is not necessarily better off.
11. Because of lack of skilled labor, specialized materials, and closely related equipment, foreign equipment is often less productive in Soviet use.

Finally, the Thornton-Linz interview data provide evidence of serious technological and economic deficiencies in many of the new technologies developed by research and design organizations.

Recent official resolutions of the CPSU Central Committee and USSR Council of Ministers providing an administrative framework for a "radical restructuring" of the Soviet economy may allow the gradual emergence of incentives and institutional arrangements furthering adoption of new technologies, but it will be difficult to eliminate barriers and introduce the required rewards in sectors that remain under administrative management.

Technology Transfer

The Soviet Union has always imported Western technology to stimulate the modernization of domestic industries. Its ability to foster growth through infusion of Western plant and equipment increased in the 1970s when rapid increases in the world prices of oil and natural gas gave the Soviet Union a sudden windfall of hard currency to spend.

Technology transfer occurs in many ways. The import of machinery and equipment—or even of whole turnkey projects or production systems—is the most easily measured source of access to superior foreign technologies. Purchase of licenses, technical know-how, and technical assistance—either jointly with the purchase of equipment or separately—may substitute for a domestic R&D program or speed the time it takes a Soviet industry to undertake serial production. The Soviet Twelfth Five-Year Plan gives particular emphasis to the expansion of industrial cooperation agreements. Such agreements establish a long-term relationship between a Soviet enterprise or ministry and its foreign partner. A study of 218 Soviet industrial cooperation agreements with Western firms found that 54.6 percent of these involved coproduction or specialization in production; 27.1 percent provided for delivery of plant or equipment—usually by the Western partner; 7.3 percent were joint ventures, while another 6.9 percent were other types of joint projects; and 4.1 percent were licensing agreements.[33] Information about foreign technologies is provided by extensive efforts to collect and disseminate scientific and technical information from foreign publications and patent descriptions, through trade shows and other forms of scientific exchange. The Western industrial countries attempt to enforce an embargo of export of certain strategic goods to the Soviet Union under the rules of the Paris-based Coordinating Committee. However, press reports cite frequent violations of such restrictions as well as Soviet efforts to acquire Western technologies through industrial espionage. Consider two sources of technology transfer—commodity imports and industrial cooperation agreements—in turn.

Sources of Technology Transfer

Commodity Imports. The Soviet statistical yearbook reports imports valued at 69.1 billion rubles in 1985, of which machinery, equipment, and transportation equipment accounted for 25.7 billion rubles, or 37 percent of the total. (Machinery constituted 47.5 percent of the imports from socialist countries.)[34] Thus, imported machinery and equipment made up more than a third of total investment in machinery and equipment in the Soviet economy in that year, which was 67.6 billion rubles. If they were well chosen and well used, such large-scale imports of equipment could provide a major infusion of new technology. On the other hand, a large part of this machinery import comes from other members of CMEA (Council of Mutual Economic Assistance), whose equipment is often not state-of-the-art. A ranking of major equipment suppliers to the Soviet Union places five members of CMEA (East Germany, Czechoslovakia, Bulgaria, Poland, and Hungary), as well as Yugoslavia, ahead of the top-ranked Western equipment suppliers (Finland, West Germany, and Japan). The United States currently supplies little equipment to the Soviet Union; it ranks seventeenth in importance, after India.

Gorbachev's ambitious program to modernize his country's capital stock during the Twelfth Five-Year Plan—combined with two years of good harvests in 1986 and 1987, allowing a reduction in imports of grain—will no doubt lead to a rising share of equipment and R&D-intensive products in Soviet imports from the West. Soviet industries that have been major recipients of Western industrial capital goods in the eighties include oil and gas extraction, engineering and metal working, distribution equipment for electricity, and chemicals. The smaller shares of such high technology sectors as computers, electronics, and robotics no doubt reflect the impact of Western embargoes.

Industrial Cooperation Agreements. Industrial cooperation agreements establish a long-term contractual relationship between a Soviet organization and a foreign partner or partners. The agenda of the Gorbachev leadership provides for the expansion of such long-term relationships with both the CMEA and the industrialized West.

At their extraordinary Council session in December 1985, the members of CMEA elaborated a program to create mutually compatible technologies throughout the Soviet bloc and to set up a framework for political negotiation of economic areas of specialization in five areas: electronics, automation, nuclear energy, new materials, and biotechnology. A key feature of the CMEA investment program is the allocation of scarce investment resources in the Eastern European economies to long-run projects that are chiefly of interest to the Soviet Union. Joint specialization is already extensive in computers and in nuclear power. In the case of nuclear power, a joint program of production was established around the Soviet pressurized water reactor, the VVER (Light Water Reactor). (The Soviet Union produces a 1,000-MW unit of this type and Czechoslovakia produces a 400-MW unit.) Two international economic associations were set up in 1972 and 1973. Interatominstrument was established in 1972 to produce testing instruments and apparatuses. Interatomenergo was founded in 1973 to construct nuclear-power plants. It combines Bulgaria's Commissariat for Heavy Machine Building, Hungary's Khinmash firm, the German combine Kraftswerksanlagenbau, the Polish association MEGAT, a Romanian heavy-machine factory, the Czech machinery plants Skoda and Vitkovice, and the Soviet association Soiuzglav-zagranatomenergo. The joint Institute of Atomic Research at Dubna is the center of theoretical and experimental endeavors for the CMEA nuclear-power program. It is fully equipped with cyclotrons, a 10-GEv accelerator, six laboratories, computers, and a staff of six thousand. The Soviet Union trains nuclear-power scientists and engineers for the association as well.

The Gorbachev initiatives propose increased reliance on industrial cooperation by means of joint ventures with foreign partners, although the initial regulations for such organizations did more to reassure domestic party members fearful of excessive foreign influence than to entice Western partners. Provisions published in January 1987 provide that the Soviet side must hold 51 percent of the enterprise ownership and appoint the chairman of the board and director general of the firm. The foreign partner may provide the official responsible for quality control. Enterprise profits bear a 30 percent tax, excluding income reinvested in the firm. Repatriation of profits is limited to the amount of foreign exchange earned through export by the firm, and the enterprise is to be subject to Soviet labor and trade-union regulations. Coincident with the new regulations, twenty-one Soviet ministries and more than seventy large firms received the right to deal directly with foreign firms, and the corresponding departments of the Foreign Trade Ministry were transferred to direct ministry control.

Western Barriers to Technology Transfer

Western countries have attempted to impose restrictions on the transfer of technologies having military relevance ever since the Korean War. The members of NATO (not including Iceland) plus Japan control their multilateral export embargoes through the Paris-based Coordinating Committee, COCOM. There has never been full agreement among the members of COCOM on the list of commodities meriting embargo, so the history of East–West trade is marked by frequent violations of the official COCOM agreements and by a gradual narrowing of the list of embargoed goods.

The U.S. government has generally argued for a more restrictive enforcement of embargo than that supported by its Western partners, for whom the Soviet Union has been a larger trading partner. From 1978 to 1982, U.S. attempts to enforce foreign-policy controls on a wide array of East–West trade led to tensions between the United States and other Western powers and to a long-term reduction in Soviet purchases from U.S. suppliers.

In August 1978, President Carter imposed controls on the export of some oil and gas equipment from the United States in response to the Shcharansky and Ginsberg trials. (In 1977, the United States had supplied about one-fourth of Soviet hard-currency purchases of oil equipment.) Export controls were broadened after the Soviet invasion of Afghanistan and the subsequent imposition of martial law in Poland to restrict the growth of Soviet grain purchases from the United States and to reduce the level of government scientific and educational exchange. U.S. relations with Western Europe fell in disarray when the United States pressed for denial of Western European export credits to the Soviet Union and threatened to extend its embargo of GE 25 MW turbines to firms in other Western countries who were licensees of the GE technology.

Some of the U.S. restrictions on trade were lifted in November 1982, and, in January 1987, the Department of Commerce lifted bans on all nonstrategic oil and gas equipment at a time when U.S. manufacturers were badly hit by a decline in worldwide oil and gas drilling, but levels of U.S.–Soviet trade in technology are unlikely to expand rapidly.

The enforcement of a strategic embargo is still a thorny issue between the United States and its allies. In June 1987, Congress debated a ban on imports from Japan's Toshiba Machine Company after the Department of Defense announced that Toshiba and Norway's Konigsberg Vaapenfabrik had sold the Soviet Union more than $17 million worth of computer-controlled milling machines capable of producing the quiet propellers that could render Soviet submarines safe from detection. As Gorbachev's restructuring of the Soviet economy presents Western firms with new trading opportunities, the pressures of foreign competition are likely to limit the sphere in which an enforceable strategic embargo will be feasible.

The Agenda for Economic Reform

The basic features of Gorbachev's radical restructuring of the economic mechanisms are only now emerging in the documents of the June 1987 party plenum and in the laws and regulations published since: the USSR Law on State Enterprise, the Resolution on Restructuring of Material and Technical Supply, and the Resolution on Restructuring the Financial System.[35] (More changes are expected soon, including a major reform of prices.) These proposed reforms include some fundamental changes in the operation of the centrally planned economy:

> Enterprises and associations will gain greater independence. Their incomes and incentives will depend on their performance so as to reward productivity and penalize inefficiency for the firm as a whole and for its workers individually.

Central management will be streamlined, focusing on long-run growth strategy and ending ministerial intervention into routine management tasks.

The processes of price formation, financing, and materials allocation will be changed.

Organizational structures will be changed to reduce bureaucratic barriers between scientific, research, and development organizations and producing enterprises.

Research and development organizations attached to scientific and production associations will become fully self-financing; they will enter into contracts for scientific research and development and will be paid for their work by clients.

Soviet ministries and large enterprises will be allowed to establish direct links with foreign producers including new organizational forms such as joint ventures.

Some democratic processes and elements of self-determination will be introduced into basic economic and government units.

While organizational changes will be introduced only gradually, immediate changes in resource allocation and industrial structure are intended to give the new management system a strong technological base:

Increased resources are allocated to research, development, and prototype production activities.

Machine-building and metal-working sectors are to grow faster than the rest of the economy, with high technology sectors slated for "forced development."

Secondary and higher education will be reformed.

Many of these proposed changes will affect the ability of the Soviet economy to innovate. An improvement in the technological base of research, development, and, particularly, experimental production will increase the productivity of these sectors. An expansion of the output of key machine-building sectors should allow faster diffusion of new models into production. In the long run, a technologically modern industrial plant will require skilled workers—although the main problem facing Soviet industrial managers today is lack of worker incentives rather than lack of education.

Some of the proposed organizational changes could be promising as well. To the extent that enterprises actually do enjoy greater independence to select outputs and inputs, to set prices, and to keep a share of their net income, they may actually come to benefit from the introduction of cost-efficient processes and high-quality products. It looks now as if some sector of industry—notably high-priority heavy industries—will remain subject to state orders (*goszakazy*), and state allocations, while other sectors—presumably those closer to final consumers—will buy inputs and sell outputs in a wholesale trade network at prices negotiated between buyer and seller (*dogovornie tseny*), within guidelines established by the State Price Committee.

As yet, few of these proposed changes have been instituted. At present, buyers are essentially assigned to suppliers. Giving buyers realistic access to alternative suppliers could be an immense step forward if there were an end to the excess-demand environment as well. But in those markets where excess demand persisted, legal access to alternatives would still bestow little practical benefit.

The introduction of negotiated prices for a wider range of goods could, at first, move markets toward market-clearing levels and then provide real incentives for product improvement. However, a pattern of rising prices is likely to generate administrative intervention short-circuiting market influences.

Genuine enterprise independence will require an end to detailed management by the central ministry—clearly one intention of the new program. In the proposals, the operational responsibilities of *Gosplan* (State Committee on Planning), *Gossnab* (State Committee for Material and Technical Supply), and *Goskomtsen* (State Committee on Prices) will be considerably reduced while their administrative responsibilities will be carried out indirectly through reliance on rules and norms. However, it will be particularly difficult for industrial ministries, which will still be organized as industry cartels, to play a passive role in the face of active technological competition between member firms. Under current arrangements, a firm has the obligation to provide technical information, designs, and documentation without charge to others in the ministry upon request. To my knowledge, no one has addressed the question of how property rights in innovations will be exercised by developers or by producing firms.

It is not clear, either, just who will decide on the promising directions for innovation and investment. As of 1988, it is the responsibility of the State Committee for Science and Technology to oversee the construction of a plan for science and technology in every ministry and to decide on the main directions in which centralized resources will be spent for research and development. However, a resolution passed in October 1987 puts research and development organizations attached to production associations on a self-financing (*khozraschet*) basis as well. So long as there are no ownership arrangements, such as licensing of patents, to give innovators a continuing benefit from diffusion of their new technologies, firms are still likely to pay design bureaus and experimental fabricators for short-run contributions, such as breaking supply bottlenecks, rather than to develop fundamentally new processes. In this respect, Gorbachev's proposals may well make research units more responsive to the concerns of the enterprise at the expense of technological developments with the potential to benefit a wide range of users or to introduce fundamentally new processes.

In my view, the attempt to open the economy to direct foreign ties offers the greatest potential for short-term infusion of new technology. But Soviet purchase of goods on current account is still heavily constrained by difficulties in expanding foreign sales. The large-scale introduction of new processes from abroad would require four developments, all of which have been unattainable in the past: establishment of direct links with Western producers offering them direct access to the domestic Soviet market; a major increase in international borrowing; an opening up of society to allow freer exchange in education, technology, and economics; and, possibly, a lessening of tensions with the West to reduce the restrictions imposed from outside. The Asian countries that have enjoyed rapid economic growth have profited from most, if not all, of these links with the world market. The Soviet leadership is seeking membership in Western economic organizations—GATT, the World Bank, and the IMF—but it still manages its economy in isolation from the world market.

It remains to be seen how rapidly and fully the "radical restructuring" will be implemented. Until there is a major change in the incentives facing producers and designers, technological measures imposed from above will not produce a self-sustaining process of technological advance within the economic system. Innovating firms must enjoy real benefits and stagnant firms must bear costs. Organizations developing new products and processes should have a material interest in seeing their innovations used in the whole economy and not in just one firm or one ministry. It is not clear that Gorbachev's new initiatives will eliminate the barriers to innovation in the near term. On the other hand, in the absence of substantial change in economic arrangements of the sort proposed in the Gorbachev programs, the prospects for modernization of the Soviet economy are dim indeed. In the foreseeable future, technology will still constitute the single most important constraint on Soviet power.

Notes

1. E.g., Joseph Berliner, *The Innovation Decision in Soviet Industry* (Cambridge, Mass.: MIT Press, 1976); Ronald Amann, Julian Cooper, and R.W. Davies, *The Technological Level of Soviet Industry* (New Haven and London: Yale University Press, 1977); Ronald Amann and Julian Cooper, *Industrial Innovation in the Soviet Union* (New Haven: Yale University Press, 1982); and A.C. Sutton, *Western Technol-*

ogy and Soviet Economic Development, 1945 to 1965, 3 vols. (Stanford, Calif.: Hoover Institution, 1968–73).

2. *Pravda,* November 9, 1985, p. 1.

3. Ibid., June 26, 1987, pp. 1–5, and June 27, 1987, pp. 2–3.

4. U.S. Congress, Joint Economic Committee, *Soviet Economy in a Time of Change,* vol. 1 (Washington, D.C.: U.S. Government Printing Office, 1979), p. 378.

5. Ronald Amann, "The Soviet Chemicalisation Drive and the Problem of Innovation," in Amann, Cooper, and Davies, *Technological Level,* p. 276.

6. Ibid., p. 275.

7. Ronald Amann and Julian Cooper, eds., *Technical Progress and Soviet Economic Development* (New York: Basil Blackwell, 1986).

8. Jack Baranson, *Soviet Automation: Perspectives and Prospects* (Mt. Airy, Md.: Lomond, 1987), p. 53.

9. Morris Bornstein, *East–West Technology Transfer: The Transfer of Western Technology to the USSR* (Paris: OECD, 1985), p. 120.

10. U.S. Department of Defense, *Soviet Military Power,* 6th ed. (Washington, D.C.: U.S. Government Printing Office, 1987), pp. 112–16.

11. U.S. Central Intelligence Agency, *The Soviet Weapons Industry: An Overview* (Washington, D.C.: U.S. Government Printing Office, 1986), p. 23.

12. Richard Kaufman, "Industrial Modernization and Defense in the Soviet Union," paper presented to the NATO Colloquium, April 1–3, 1987, p. 11.

13. In addition to the sources cited in note 1, see Bruce Parrott, *Politics and Technology in the Soviet Union* (Cambridge, Mass.: MIT Press, 1985). For Soviet assessments, see A.G. Aganbegian and V.D. Rechin, *Upravlenie nauchno-tekhnickeskim progressom na predpriiatii* (Novossibirsk, USSR: Nauka, Sibirskoe otdelenie, 1986). V.N. Arkhangel'skii, *Organizatsionno-ekonomicheskie problemy upravleniia nauchnymi issledovaniiami* (Moscow: Nauka, 1977); M.V. Romanovskii, *Finansy i upravlenie nauchno-tekhnicheskim progressom* (Moscow: Finansy i statistika, 1986); and P.A. Sedlov, *Formy i metody upravieniia NTP* (Moscow: Nauka, 1987).

14. Christopher Freeman, *The Economics of Industrial Innovation,* 2nd ed. (Cambridge, Mass.: MIT Press, 1982), p. 112.

15. Zvi Griliches, ed., *RPD, Patents, and Productivity* (Chicago and London: University of Chicago Press, 1984).

16. National Science Foundation, *National Patterns of Science and Technology Resources,* cited in *US Statistical Abstract 1986* (Washington, D.C.: U.S. Government Printing Office, 1985), p. 581.

17. An interview with academician G.I. Marchuk, president of the USSR Academy of Sciences, tells us that 50,000 scientific workers are employed in institutes of the Academy of Sciences and "more than 800,000 in scientific research of branches of the economy." His statement raises the question of whether the remaining 600,000 scientific workers are employed directly by the military. See *Izvestia,* March 22, 1987, p. 2.

18. *Izvestia,* January 30, 1985, pp. 2, 31, and February 2, 1985, p. 2.

19. I avoid references to specific industries and products to protect the anonymity of those interviewed.

20. *Izvestia,* January 30, 1985, p. 2.

21. J.A. Martens and J.P. Young, "Soviet Implementation of Domestic Inventions: First Results," in U.S. Congress, Joint Economic Committee, *Soviet Economy in a Time of Change,* vol. 1 (Washington, D.C.: U.S. Government Printing Office, 1979), pp. 472–509.

22. E.A. Melnirov, "Engineering Vacuum," *Ekonomika i organizatsiia promyshlennogo proizvodstva,* no. 10 (1985): 34–60.

23. M.B. Rozenman, "Instrument Fitting Plants Are Needed," *Ekonomika i organizatsiia promyshlennogo proizvodstva,* no. 10 (October 1985): 112–13, tr. in Joint Publications Research Service (JPRS), *USSR Report: National Economy,* UNE-86-009 (December 5, 1986), p. 94.

24. *Sovetskaia Rossiia,* September 15, 1987, p. 1.

25. *Sotsialisticheskaia industriia,* August 8, 1987, p. 1.

26. Judith Thornton and Neil Leary, *Are Socialist Economies Inoculated against Innovation?* (Working paper, November 1986).

27. L. Budnikova, "Scientific Technical Progress: Pace, Incentive, Direction," *Narodnoe Khoziaistvo Belorussii,* no. 11 (November 1986): 40; tr. in JPRS-UEAA-87-002 (June 4, 1987), p. 40.

28. V.I. Kudashov, et al., *Upravlenie issledovaniiami i razrabotkami v akademicheskom nauchno-tekhnicheskom komplekse.* (Minsk: Nauka i tekhnika, 1986), p. 167.

29. Berliner, *Innovation Decision,* p. 518.

30. Moscow Television, March 18, 1987, quoted in FBIS (Foreign Broadcast Information Service), *USSR Daily Report,* 20 (March 1987), p. U-2.

31. *Izvestia,* May 20, 1987, p. 2.

32. *Soviet Military Power,* p. 109.

33. United Nations, Economic Commission for Europe, *Statistical Survey of Recent Trends in Industrial Cooperation* (Geneva: ECE, 1983), p. 9.

34. *Vneshnaia torgovlia SSRV 1985g* (Moscow: Finansy i Statistika, 1986), p. 18.

35. Gorbachev's speech to the plenum appears in *Izvestia,* June 26, 1987, pp. 1–5. The USSR Statute on State Enterprise is published in *Izvestia,* July 1, 1987, pp. 1–4. "Statute on State Inspection of Production in Associations and Enterprises" is published in *Ekonomicheskaia gazeta,* no. 50 (December 1986), p. 7. "Resolution on the Restructuring of Material and Technical Supply and the Activity of the USSR Gossnab in the New Economic Management Conditions" appears on *Sobranie postanovlenie pravitelstva SSSR: Otdel,* no. 35 (July 17, 1987), pp. 723–42. "On Restructuring the Financial Mechanism and Enhancing the Role of the USSR Ministry of Finance in the New Conditions of Management," appears in *Sobranie postanovlenie pravitelstva SSSR: Otdel,* no. 36 (July 17, 1987), pp. 747–62.

Part II
External Constraints

5
Soviet Allies in Europe: The Warsaw Pact

Christopher Jones

W hat restraints are set on Soviet military power because of Eastern European participation in the Warsaw Pact? My answer, elaborated in this chapter, is that Eastern European armed forces make important contributions to all missions assigned by the Soviets to the Warsaw Treaty Organization (hereafter the Warsaw Pact or WTO). NATO analysts, inevitably concerned with preparing for the worst case, have aggregated all these missions into an across-the-board Soviet military threat to Western Europe.[1] This view obscures the specific and distinct missions of the Pact. Further, a worst-case analysis preempts investigation of the underlying political objectives that have set the military-political requirements that in turn generate the specific missions of the Warsaw Pact.

The Political Objectives of the Warsaw Pact

Using evidence from military doctrine and force deployments, this chapter argues that the Soviets have used the Warsaw Pact to pursue four basic Soviet political objectives in Europe.

First, the USSR seeks to preserve pro-Soviet Eastern European regimes—that is, the *nomenklatura* of top party/state/economic/military/cultural officials. This stratum is both dependent on Moscow and devoted to the preservation of the WTO/CMEA (Council for Mutual Economic Assistance) bloc as a whole. Each local regime is bound to Moscow by an unstable combination of ideological loyalty, elite self-interest, lack of domestic legitimacy, and fear of the alternative sociopolitical models offered by Western Europe.

The curious dynamic of these national elites, as argued by Valerie Bunce, may be that the weaker these elites are vis-à-vis their own societies, the greater the elites' bargaining power with the USSR over economic subsidies from the CMEA, reduction of military obligations to the WTO, cultural latitude granted to churches, other sociocultural institutions, and autonomy for small-scale independent farmers, artisans, and service industries.[2] Bunce suggests that such deviations from preferred Soviet norms do not indicate greater national independence from the USSR but show greater regime dependence on Moscow. In my view, the pro-Soviet elites of Eastern Europe have continued to face two recurring threats to their power: (1) anticommunist/anti-Soviet popular movements or outright uprisings that threaten to remove the local elite from power and also to reorient the country's military, economic, diplomatic, and ideological relations with the WTO/CMEA and (2) reformist/nationalist groups within local communist parties who seek to resolve the party's crisis of legitimacy by redefining both internal and external policies. The essence of the program of the reformers/nationalists (most notably Nagy, Gomulka, Gheorgiu-Dej, Ceauşescu, Hoxha, Dubcek, and the "horizontalists" allied with Solidarity) is to shift the basis of power from support by Moscow to local constituencies. Such shifts in political base inevitably require significant departures from bloc norms in domestic or foreign policies or both.

Either challenge to the local elites ultimately threatens Soviet control over the internal and external policies of a given state and, in addition, threatens the entire WTO/CMEA system of interlocking, interdependent bureaucratic elites.

A second WTO objective is to prevent the reunification of the two Germanies. The fear of reunification felt by the regimes in the USSR, East Germany, Poland, and Czechoslovakia was initially concern over territories transferred from the Third Reich to the three northern-tier regimes and the USSR as well. Such fears should have been virtually eliminated by the Soviet-Austrian Treaty of 1955, the Soviet–West German Treaty of 1970, the Quadripartite Treaty of 1971 on Berlin, the FRG's treaties of 1971, 1972, and 1973 with Poland, East Germany, and Czechoslovakia, and the reaffirmation of all these treaties in the Helsinki Final Act of 1975 and subsequent development of the ongoing Conference on Cooperation and Security in Europe (CSCE).

According to the West German interpretation of all the treaties just mentioned, the possibility of unification of the FRG and GDR is still open because these treaties describe the inner-German order is "inviolable." The FRG takes this to mean that the border could be changed by peaceful means. The GDR takes this to mean that the inner-German border is permanent. The USSR takes this to mean that as long as nineteen Soviet divisions remain in East Germany, the border will be both inviolable and permanent.

The present fear of the USSR and allied WTO regimes over German reunification probably reflects a Marxist appreciation of the long-term implications of the extraordinary economic power of the FRG and the economic importance of the GDR to the CMEA. West Germany alone exports a dollar value of goods (calculated by the CIA) almost equal to the dollar value of all Soviet and Eastern European exports combined.[3] Within the CMEA, East

Germany is the bloc's second leading exporter (after the USSR), substantially ahead of every other Eastern European state.[4] With only 6 percent of the Soviet population, the East Germans export about 28 percent of the value of Soviet exports and have by far the highest per capita GNP of the entire bloc.

Such export successes in both Germanies suggest no merely superior economic management but preeminence in technology, science, and cultural infrastructure. Were it not for the military-political barriers maintained by the WTO across all of Eastern Europe, the two separate Germanies and Austria would collectively restore a general German hegemony in the economic, technological, scientific, and cultural affairs of the region. A Germany reunified by peaceful processes within the CSCE framework might not constitute a military superpower, but it would undoubtedly constitute an economic superpower certain to displace Soviet influence in the nonmilitary affairs of the region.

The Soviets and the allied regimes in the northern tier of the WTO require more than military insurance against the possibility of German reunification. They need, in addition, to wield a military threat against the FRG in order to persuade Bonn of the otherwise dubious economic benefits of the transfer of West German credits and technology to the GDR and other CMEA states. West German willingness to extend subsidies to the GDR and its allies depends on continued FRG acceptance of the fact that Soviet military power makes accepting the WTO's definition of détente a prerequisite for broad inner-German contacts. This definition of détente says, in effect, that the basis for continued Soviet–West German political cooperation on inner-German contacts is continued Soviet–West German military confrontation.

The third Soviet political objective in Europe is to deter the projection of Western Europe's political power into Eastern Europe in support of challengers to the existing regimes. The instruments of Western Europe's power projection into the WTO/CMEA bloc are economic, technological-scientific, cultural, and ideological. Although NATO has never attempted to project military power into Eastern Europe, its member states have often made symbolic demonstrations of support to the internal opponents of Soviet-backed regimes. This has been true in the upheavals of 1956 in Poland and Hungary; in the Albanian and Romanian defections from the bloc in the 1960s; in the attempt of the Dubcek reformers to put a human face on Czechoslovak socialism; in the challenge mounted by the Solidarity trade-union movement (even neutral Sweden provided extensive "humanitarian" support to members of Solidarity, whose leader received a Nobel Peace Prize); and in the post-Helsinki pattern of defending the human rights of religious, cultural, and intellectual dissidents in Eastern Europe.

NATO's de facto policy of engaging only in symbolic gestures of support to antiregime movements is probably not due to fundamental agreement with the Soviets over the interpretations of the fine points of the agreements stretching from Yalta to Helsinki. More than likely, this restraint is the result of NATO's reading of the indices of the military balance in Europe.

The fourth political objective of the WTO is to call into question NATO's willingness to honor its obligations to the FRG in the event of a Soviet–West German conflict that develops out of an internal political crisis in the GDR. Under Khrushchev, the primary Soviet means for trying to break the security tie of the FRG to its allies was to mount a fearsome nuclear threat to the major cities of German's European allies. Brezhnev extended this threat to the North American allies as well but also began a policy of luring the FRG away from its NATO partners by dangling the promise of closer ties between the FRG and GDR. However, Brezhnev continued to maintain the nuclear threat to all of Europe and North America. His successors found that Soviet nuclear policy toward NATO, rather than decoupling West Germany from its allies, coupled Soviet–German conflict not only to a WTO–NATO conflict but to every aspect of the Soviet–U.S. rivalry as well. By reducing the Soviet nuclear threat to Western Europe in exchange for a symbolic reduction of the U.S. nuclear guarantee to Germany, Gorbachev is trying to reestablish the credibility of a Soviet conventional threat to Germany.

Soviet Military-Political Requirements for the WTO

These four political objectives have been sewn together into a seamless web because East Germany is a socialist state and a German state as well. The military-political dynamic faced by the WTO is as follows: regime crises in Eastern Europe potentially can threaten the East German regime; an internal GDR crisis threatens military confrontation with West Germany; military conflict with the FRG risks a general war with NATO; the WTO must be capable of blunting the projection of NATO power in either an internal GDR crisis or a neighboring crisis in Poland, Czechoslovakia, or Hungary. This dynamic places four military-political requirements on the WTO. Meeting these requirements is vital not only to the Soviet leadership but to the leadership of the pro-Soviet regimes in the region. The requirements are:

1. Organization of the WTO to ensure: (1) a prompt, massive Soviet capability of internal intervention in Eastern Europe, assisted at least symbolically by other WTO armies; (2) preemption of Eastern European defense systems that could offer organized resistance to a Soviet/WTO intervention. Such a capability for national territorial defense would provide a potential shield for the internal opponents of a domestic regime; (3) preparation of local internal-security forces to take responsibility for as much as possible of the mission of repression. Such a capability depends on highly developed liaison agencies with both the local defense ministry and the central agencies of the WTO.

2. Maintaining a credible WTO capability for a prompt and devastating assault on the FRG. This requires mobilization of an elite portion of the Non-Soviet Warsaw Pact Forces (NSWP) to augment the striking power of the Soviet force groups in the GDR, Poland, Czechoslovakia, and Hungary. It also requires complex command and control systems to circumvent the problem of the political reliability of the NSWP forces.

3. Maintaining a residual WTO capability for a prolonged conflict with NATO. This requirement is one for sheer mass of equipment, reserves, and war-mobilization bureaucracies. This policy has a deterrent effect on NATO impulses to aid anti-Soviet/anticommunist movements in Eastern Europe.

4. The WTO must lend credence to the Soviet nuclear threat against Western Europe by making an elaborate show of preparation for a nuclear conflict, the likely outcome of which is the incineration of Eastern Europe. The goal of this nuclear capability, maintained by the Soviets, is to deter NATO from the use of nuclear weapons to offset WTO advantages in conventional strength.

The Military Missions of the Warsaw Pact

The military-political requirements placed on the Warsaw Pact by the allied regimes of the WTO/CMEA bloc generate five specific missions. Attention to the devices for fulfillment of these missions suggests that the Warsaw Pact is not organized for the strategic objective of conquering Western Europe but for the more modest and more urgent objective of preserving the East–West status quo in Europe. The specific missions of the WTO command are fragmentation of national control over national armed forces; integration of the elite combat forces of the GDR, Poland, Czechoslovakia, and Hungary into a greater socialist army capable of a rapid assault on the FRG; maintenance of a large reserve force excluded from the Combined Armed Forces but still closely linked to the central agencies of the WTO; shifting as much as possible of the burden for backing up internal security forces from Soviet troops to national troops; and the political indoctrination and political monitoring performed by an elaborate interlocking network of Warsaw Pact political administrations charged with the conduct of national, bilateral, and multilateral political activities.

Fragmentation of National Control over
National Armed Forces

Fragmentation of national control over national armed forces is the prerequisite for the pursuit of Soviet objectives on both the internal and external fronts.

On the internal front, this policy results in the denial of national capabilities to defend national territory by national means. Three Eastern European states have such a capability: Yugoslavia, the first communist state to defect from the Soviet bloc; Albania, which signed the Warsaw Treaty of 1955 but ceased active participation in the pact in 1961 and formally withdrew in 1968; and Romania, still nominally a WTO member, but a state that withholds its armed forces from all joint operational activities and pursues an independent security policy in Europe. Western analysts refer to the military postures of these three states as territorial defense strategies. The Yugoslavs call their strategy General People's Defense; the Romanians, War of the Entire People. In practice, these systems will attempt to defend neither the territory nor the people of the states but to provoke as much bloodshed as possible between a Soviet occupation force and the civilian populations. The strategic purposes of the bloodshed are to delegitimize the government that the Soviets are trying to install, to demoralize Soviet soldiers and civilians, and to generate international pressure for a Soviet troop withdrawal. The Soviets are presently facing such a conflict in Afghanistan.

The central administrative agencies of the WTO, which correspond to the agencies of all WTO defense ministries except that of Romania, compete with local defense ministries for effective control over the analogous components of national defense systems. The most important of these agencies are the United Command, which presides over service branches modeled on the service branches of the Soviet Armed Forces; the WTO Staff, which supersedes national staffs in the planning and evaluation of WTO joint exercises; and three agencies concerned with military R&D, production of weapons, and the introduction of weapons systems throughout the WTO. In addition, a centrally coordinated system of officer education trains the bilingual officers necessary for the system to function. Regular joint exercises preempt national capabilities for purely national actions in defense of national territory and also serve as regular practice intervention by Soviet troops. During these joint maneuvers, internal security forces often coordinate their actions and, in addition, the WTO joint political exercises develop liaison with local governmental organizations.

Integration of a Soviet-Bloc Army Capable of Attacking the FRG

Integration of the elite combat forces of the GDR, Poland, Czechoslovakia, and Hungary into a greater socialist army capable of a rapid assault on the FRG is the WTO Command's second mission. The prerequisite for building this force is fragmentation of national command over the analogous components of national armed forces. The Soviets have assembled what the WTO officially calls the Combined Armed Forces (CAF) by linking division-size and smaller Eastern European units to their Soviet counterparts and then combining these bilateral groupings into a coalition that is multinational without being multilateral. This force is built around Soviet troops and is structured to respond quickly to innovations in Soviet doctrine such as operational maneuver groups. This same structure permits rapid regrouping of WTO personnel in the condition of abrupt changes in the conduct of highly mobile battlefield operations.

The Combined Armed Forces of the greater socialist army is held together by Soviet command, control, communication, and intelligence systems. It is led by a greater socialist officer corps whose Eastern European members are trained to take orders in Russian and give commands in their native languages. In the northern tier plus Hungary, there are a total of twenty-nine Soviet divisions (all Category I-full-strength). The total number of NSWP divisions in this area (according to *Soviet Military Power,* 1987) is also twenty-nine (Category I, II, and III). At the present time, probably no more than half this number are integrated into the CAF, although the ultimate objective may be a 1:1 pairing. The nonground forces of the NSWP states— air defense, air forces, and navies—appear thoroughly integrated into the much larger and more sophisticated corresponding Soviet forces in the region.

The pairing of ground forces appears to be the following: In the GDR, six National People's Army (NVA) divisions are garrisoned next to regiments of the Group of Soviet Forces in Germany. After initial training in national units, the two allied armies train together for large-scale maneuvers. This pattern has been extended to Czechoslovakia, Poland, and Hungary, although it not as fully developed there. Very few Polish divisions appear to be paired with Soviet counterparts.

Maintaining a Large Reserve Force

A third mission is the maintenance of a large reserve force excluded from the CAF but still closely linked to the central agencies of the WTO. These forces serve as both reserve and housekeeping units either to resupply the elite forces assigned to the CAF or to provide personnel and equipment to internal security forces. This reserve capability for mass mobilization of Eastern European labor is important in strengthening both the internal and external fronts, particularly in the event of a protracted war with NATO. The Category II and III divisions of NSWP appear to lack the equipment, training, and political preparation necessary for an expedition deep into Western Europe, but their sheer mass is enough to give pause to NATO.

Perhaps the most revealing view of Eastern European military establishments is one that focuses on the military districts of Eastern European states as the basic functional structures, rather than on the national defense ministries. In the USSR, the role of the military district is to train and maintain personnel and material available for wartime transfer to a theater commander. Eastern European military districts play a comparable role for the Soviet commander of the Western Theater of military operations (TVD) but also serve as backups for internal security forces. The peacetime role of the central agencies of the WTO (which supplant national defense ministries) might be best described as maintaining organizational links that connect Soviet force groups to elite Eastern European combat units. These units in turn are connected to training and reserve formations connected in turn to internal security forces.

Shifting the Burden of Internal Security Backup

A fourth mission, emphasized after the WTO reforms of 1969, is shifting as much as possible of the burden for backing up internal security forces from Soviet troops to national troops. Under Soviet and Eastern European military doctrine, national defense ministries are partially responsible for internal security, although they have the additional recourse of calling on WTO allies for further assistance if necessary. In NSWP states, the total number of full-time internal security forces is often 50 percent or more of the full-time ground forces. In the GDR, there are a total of 79,000 Border Guards, State Security Troops, Troops of the Ministry of the Interior, and Transport Police; the total size of the ground forces is 123,000. In Czechoslovakia, the ground forces number 145,000; the Border Troops number 11,000, but the People's Militia, (full-time and part-time) numbers 120,000. In Poland, the Internal Defense Troops, Ministry of Interior Troops, and notorious Zomo antiriot police together number 117,500; the total ground forces are 235,000.[5] In Hungary, the Internal Security Troops and Frontier Guard together number at least 30,000 plus an undetermined number of security police.[6] The Hungarian ground forces number 83,000.[7]

The Eastern European militaries generally maintain what my collaborator, Teresa Rakowska-Harmstone, calls a ratio of distrust of 2:1 or more. That is, for every conscript serving in an Eastern European military, there are at least two cadres (professional officers, technical specialists, non-commissioned officers, internal security personnel, or party members who serve in paramilitary militias)—in other words, individuals who have at least a minor stake in the preservation of the existing regime.[8]

The large quantity of aging equipment in Category II and III divisions in Eastern Europe is more than adequate for combat on the internal front. These training and housekeeping divisions provide basic training and recruitment of the very large paramilitary organizations under the control of local communist parties. These are the People's Militia in Czechoslovakia (120,000), the Workers' Militia in the GDR (500,000), the Citizens' Militia in Poland (200,000), the People's Territorial Militia in Bulgaria (150,000), and the Workers' Militia in Hungary (60,000).[9]

In the past, particularly in 1968 in Czechoslovakia, the overt or threatened use of Soviet troops as the backup for local internal security troops has had the effect of undercutting the legitimacy of the very regimes the Soviets were trying to defend. The inclusions of internal security forces and paramilitary militia organizations in Warsaw Pact exercises after the reforms of 1969 may represent an attempt to interpose the local military forces between local security forces and "internationalist" assistance. As in Poland in 1981–82, the use of a native occupation force is likely to prove much more acceptable to the local population than Soviet/WTO personnel for crushing internal opposition.

This is not to say that the Polish military leadership or at least the middle-echelon officers may not have demurred at actually executing the internal security mission required by WTO doctrine. The point is that there is strong evidence that WTO agencies and the WTO commander himself mobilized Polish ground forces to back up the internal security forces.[10] In the sense, General Jaruzelski not only saved Poland from the consequences of a Soviet intervention; General Jaruzelski also saved the USSR from the consequences of a Soviet intervention.[11]

Political Monitoring and Indoctrination

The last but in many ways most critical mission of the WTO is the political indoctrination and political monitoring performed by an elaborate interlocking network of Warsaw Pact political administrations charged with the conduct of national, bilateral and multilateral political activities. For many Eastern European males, military service is the single most important experience of political socialization into the realities of Soviet–Eastern European relations. Successful socialization of both officers and enlisted personnel is the critical prerequisite for the performance of all the internal and external missions of the WTO. Success in political socialization is what Rakowska-Harmstone calls functional integration into the command hierarchies of the WTO rather than attitudinal integration of personnel who actually are motivated by the official formulas.

She traces this policy to an identical but earlier practice of integrating non-Russians into the Soviet military as functionally reliable personnel for carefully selected assignments. In the Warsaw Pact, coordinated WTO programs of indoctrination make a specific appeal to the national and cultural pride of enlisted personnel and officers. Invoking both the honor of the nation and the threat of enemies (on the western front) serves to stimulate pride in one's unit and acceptance of the discipline required of the unit. Given enough overlapping control mechanisms capable of punishing breaches of discipline, and given appropriate indoctrination about the practical necessity of cooperating with the Soviets within the overall WTO system, Eastern Europeans will reliably perform the specific functions assigned to them, even if they do not endorse the values of the system as a whole. In the WTO, both military training and political indoctrination impress upon following cohorts a lesson not always remembered by their civilian compatriots: the only way to pursue national objectives in Eastern Europe is to function within the system.

The Russian/Soviet Pattern of Allied Military Operations

If the preceding analysis is incorrect, and if the Soviets in the 1980s—or any previous postwar decade—have been trying to develop a capability for the conquest of Western Europe, then all of Russian and Soviet military history suggests that Moscow would not assign any critical roles in such a war to its reluctant allies in Eastern Europe. If the Soviet defense ministry plans to win such a war, it must do so with Soviet forces.

The only allies of Moscow that have been of any military utility in past wars of comparable magnitude have been other great powers fighting the common enemy on distant fronts. The historical evidence suggests that Moscow has unilaterally initiated wars only against grossly inferior adversaries and even then only with the explicit or implicit acquiescence of other great powers. And even in these circumstances, such as the invasions of Finland in 1939 and Afghanistan in 1979, Moscow's military record has been mixed. Should Western Europe ever find itself in a position of gross inferiority to the Warsaw Pact, it will not be because of Eastern European contributions to the WTO.

If the political objectives, military-political requirements, and specific military missions of the WTO are in fact the ones just identified, then Eastern European armies do not constitute limits on Soviet power. The only limits they impose are limits on the worst-case analyses of NATO strategists. Although the Eastern Europeans are the primary source of the Soviet security problem in Europe, the Eastern Europeans are also very much a part of the Soviet solution to the problem.

On Reading Soviet/WTO Military Doctrine and Assessing Soviet Deployments in Europe

By a selective reading of Soviet and WTO military doctrine on European-theater operations and by aggregating the statistical indices of WTO forces, Western analysts have been able to document an alarming analysis of the WTO force posture. This "standard" analysis is that the Soviets have configured the WTO to conquer Europe, by conventional means if possible and by nuclear means if necessary. In this view, no matter who begins the war, the political objective of WTO operations will be a dramatic change in the political status quo in Europe. In contrast, this chapter has been arguing that the offensive posture of the WTO is directed toward preservation of the status quo against two interrelated threats: internal political upheaval in Eastern Europe and the dissatisfaction of Germans on both sides of the Elbe with the continued division of Germany. The offensive capabilities of the WTO are directed against Eastern Europe and against West Germany. For the rest of NATO—on the northern and southern flanks—the Soviet/WTO posture is deterrent/defensive in nature. The following sections will briefly sketch out a case for alternative readings of Soviet deployments in Europe and alternative readings of Soviet/WTO doctrine.

Soviet Garrisons in Eastern Europe

The stationing of Soviet forces in Europe since World War II can be read as deployments of the defense of the status quo. The Group of Soviet Forces in Germany (GSFG), a twenty-division force until its symbolic reduction to nineteen divisions in 1979 in honor of the twentieth anniversary of the GDR, testifies at least to Soviet determination to prevent the reunification of Germany and a corollary determination to intimidate the FRG. The capability of the GSFG to advance beyond the Rhine, however, is entirely dependent on other echelons of Soviet personnel.

The deployments of the late 1980s and the historical evolution of these deployments strongly suggest that the Soviet objective is not to maximize the WTO threat to Germany's allies. In Poland, the key corridor for massive Soviet assault on Western Europe, the Soviets have stationed only two ground forces divisions—the Northern Group of Forces (NGF). These forces have served primarily—or at least in large part—as political-diplomatic symbols of the Soviet right to move troops into Poland without legal protests from inside or outside Poland. By itself, the NGF does not significantly increase the threat posed to Western Europe, although it does enhance the capabilities of the GSFG against West Germany.

Czechoslovakia, which shares a border with the FRG, did not have a Soviet garrison either during the outbreak of the Cold War or during the extremely tense years of the late 1950s and early 1960s (the time of various Berlin crises; the devastating losses suffered by the GDR as the result of mass defections through Berlin; the expansion of the Bundeswehr to the status of NATO's preeminent conventional force; the thorough nuclearization of Soviet and U.S. force postures in Europe; and the initiation of joint WTO exercises designed around the use of nuclear weapons). The five-division Central Group of Forces (CGF) entered Czechoslovakia in 1968 as an occupation army to put down a reform movement led by an independent faction of the

Czechoslovak Communist party. Prior to 1968, there is serious reason to doubt that the Czechoslovak People's Army (CSPA) had the overall capabilities necessary for combat with the U.S. and West German forces based in Bavaria.[12] There is no question that the establishment of the CGF and the integration of units of the CSPA has significantly enhanced Soviet power-projection capabilities against the FRG and perhaps even against Western Europe. But from a historical standpoint, this increase in offensive capabilities against West Germany was a consequence of defensive actions on the internal front. Severe demoralization of Czechoslovak society during the early and mid-1970s, coupled with popular disturbances in Poland in 1970 and 1975 and the development of a dissident movement in East Germany during the same period, also suggests a defensive mission for the CGF. Although it is possible to read the Soviet–West Germany Treaty of 1970, the normalization of FRG relations with the GDR, Poland, and Czechoslovakia during the early 1970s, the Berlin Agreement of 1971, the initiation of Mutually Balanced Force Reduction (MBFR) talks in 1973, and the signing of the Helsinki Treaty of 1975 as Soviet deceptions designed to mask a military buildup in the WTO, it is equally plausible to read these developments as efforts to secure Western acceptance of the status quo in Eastern European and inner-German relations.

The same problems of analysis arise in evaluation of the Southern Group of Forces (SGF) in Hungary. This four-division force had as its first mission the pacification of Hungary after 1945. This mission was reemphasized in 1956 and in the first ten years of the Kadar regime. It was only in the mid-1960s that the Hungarian People's Army (HPA) began to participate in multilateral WTO exercises. Since 1969, joint exercises of the SGF, HPA, CFG, and CSPA suggest that the Soviets are capable of increasing the threat to the FRG by marching across Austria to attack the southern frontier of Bavaria, probably assisted by units of the HPA.

Although the ten Soviet divisions in the NGF, CGF, and SGF undoubtedly enhance the Soviet threat to the FRG, in each case there are good historical reasons for seeing the deployment of these troops as Soviet efforts to enhance the capabilities of the USSR against Eastern Europe rather than against non-German NATO members.

According to *Soviet Military Power, 1987,* an additional thirty-three divisions assigned to the central front are garrisoned in the western military districts of the USSR. Although arguments can be made that there are economic, logistical, and intra-WTO reasons for basing these divisions in the USSR rather than Eastern Europe, the geographical fact remains that before invading all Western Europe, these forces must first invade Eastern Europe and then the FRG. By the time they arrive at the banks of the Rhine, they will have offered NATO clear invitations to attack them with nuclear weapons or at least demolish the transportation networks of Eastern Europe and the western USSR.

In his study of conventional deterrence, John Mearsheimer has argued that the attempt to funnel 62 to 64 Soviet divisions through the most likely West German axes of attack will prove a plan for the attrition of the best Soviet units available for combat in the Western theater.[13] Mearsheimer sees such attrition as the most likely result of what he views as the most likely scenario of a NATO–WTO war: a Warsaw Pact mobilization followed by a NATO mobilization.[14] He sees two other possible scenarios. One is a WTO mobilization to which NATO fails to respond out of fear of provoking a Soviet attack; Mearsheimer predicts a Soviet victory in this case. His third scenario is a "standing-start" attack launched by the ready forces in the northern tier. In this case, according to Mearsheimer, the Soviets "would have to settle for capturing a portion of West German territory."[15] In Mearsheimer's opinion, "such a limited victory is hardly an attractive option."[16] This judgment depends on the Soviet political objective, which Mearsheimer evidently assumes to be the conquest of Western Europe. No matter what the Soviet objective, such a limited Soviet victory would prove even less attractive to Bonn.

Mearsheimer's optimistic conclusion about the outcome of the most likely conventional war scenario should also evoke something less than enthusiasm in the FRG. The murderous attrition Mearsheimer expects to be wreaked upon the Soviet army would also be visited on both Germanies, a prospect that long ago converted every major political party in the FRG to advocacy of détente with the WTO.

Jeffrey Simon has argued that in a standing-start surprise attack, the NSWP forces would constitute the majority of available WTO forces. (He counts thirty-seven NSWP divisions to thirty Soviet divisions.)[17] He also offers evidence to argue that "even if the Soviet Union were to mobilize and deploy only its own reserves and not rely on the active participation of non-Soviet forces, it would still need NSWP support."[18] He argues that this support would take the form of logistical aid and protection of Soviet flanks. In any of his cases, the Eastern Europeans would play a vital role in a Soviet attempt to defeat NATO as a whole.

This chapter has already argued that probably no more than fifteen of the twenty-nine NSWP divisions counted by *Soviet Military Power, 1987* on the western front are in fact assigned to the external front by the 1:1 pairing mechanisms discussed earlier. Even if I have erred seriously in calculating the number of Eastern European units assigned to the Combined Armed Forces, the evidence on the distribution of state-of-the-art weaponry suggests that only a limited portion of the Eastern European forces are capable of taking on the front-line forces of the Bundeswehr, the U.S. Army, and the other

NATO forces in the FRG. In an analysis of the different generations of weapons fielded by the NSWP armies, Colonel Richard Martin of the U.S. Army concluded in 1986:

> The prognosis, then, is that the national armies will remain at least one and probably two generations behind the rapidly-modernizing Soviet forces in both equipment and force structure. . . . This will result in major differences in combat capability between the national armies and the Soviet forces. East Germany is a possible exception as is, to a very limited extent, Czechoslovakia. . . . The non-Soviet Warsaw Pact ground formations should not be equated with Soviet forces stationed in Eastern Europe.[19]

The Military Doctrine of the WTO

There remains another contentious issue: how to read the published military doctrine of the WTO on European-theater operations. Portions of this doctrine are changing constantly in step with technological and tactical innovations on both sides. Even within any given fixed time period, portions of Soviet/WTO doctrine on the European theater appear blatantly contradictory in regard to declaratory objectives of deterring war, discussions of how to inflict a quick conventional defeat, and other talk on the necessity of avoiding a general nuclear war with an opponent doctrinally committed to the use of nuclear weapons as a response to conventional defeat. If there is any internal coherence to Soviet/WTO doctrine, one may assume that it arises out of the coherence and compatibility of Soviet political objectives rather than from the coherence of Soviet war plans for achieving a conventional victory in Europe without precipitating a nuclear holocaust. Published military doctrine of the WTO also should be read as a Soviet attempt to communicate to Eastern Europe, Western Europe, and North America how the Soviets would like the states of these regions to evaluate the deployments and capabilities of the WTO forces in the European theater.

Despite the distinct differences among American analysts over the proper interpretation of Soviet military doctrine,[20] there is general agreement on the following Soviet-defined schemata of socialist military doctrine. Military doctrine has two components: the military-political and the military-technical. The Soviets argue that although the two components mutually influence each other, the military-political component is the more decisive in determining the overall nature of military doctrine. The military-technical component consists of four constantly evolving "theories," each of which is concerned with some aspect of the technical capabilities necessary to meet political requirements. The four theories are:

1. *The theory of military art.* This consists of strategy, operational art, and tactics. Strategy is concerned with the use of all possible means—military and political—to achieve a given political objective. Operational art is concerned with the mobilization and support of the military forces necessary to achieve the political objective; in practice, operational art is concerned with assembling and coordinating the military forces necessary for victory in a given theater of military operation (TVD). Tactics covers the particular combat techniques appropriate to specific actions by particular types of troops and specialized forces in a given theater of action.

2. *The theory of military training and education.* This is the systematic preparation of officers and troops at every level to execute the functions demanded by military art. This theory includes the political education of personnel at every level.

3. *The theory of military economics.* This concerns the research, development, and production of the weaponry needed to meet the requirements of military art. It is also concerned with the problems of supplying and sustaining an enormous military machine.

4. *The theory of military organization and development.* This is concerned with creating the bureaucratic structures necessary to coordinate the mobilization of human and material resources necessary to meet the requirements of the three theories previously discussed. This theory also covers the organization of internal security forces and the liaison bureaucracies necessary to link these forces with a national defense ministry.

American analysts have produced divergent readings of the continuing stream of Soviet writings on military art in the European theater. For all practical purposes, most American analysts regard the evolving theory of military art for the WTO as synonymous with Soviet military doctrine. The U.S. debate has been over the continuing changes in Soviet discussions over the optimal techniques for using conventional and nuclear forces in the European theater and the complexities that arise from fighting at different points along the conventional–nuclear spectrum.[21]

Despite their different readings of the role of nuclear and conventional weapons in Soviet/WTO doctrine, Western analysts can agree that the following premises underlie the Soviet/WTO theory of military art: No matter who begins the war, the WTO plans to carry the war to enemy territory with the objective of destroying the conventional and nuclear capabilities of the enemy (though not necessarily by the use of Soviet nuclear weapons). The Soviets hope to minimize damage to the Soviet bloc through a quick and decisive victory. If possible, they would also like to minimize collateral damage to the urban/industrial centers where they are fighting. Many analysts note the persistent lag of Soviet/WTO capabilities behind such doctrinal requirements. But other analysts detect a consistent pattern of Soviet capabilities eventually catching up to the requirements of the doctrine.

Despite the careful readings of the military-technical component of Soviet/WTO doctrine and evaluation of the WTO capabilities required by this doctrine, American analysts have uniformly dismissed the specific military-political axioms that constitute the military-political component of Soviet theater doctrine. Joseph Douglass declares that the political component of Soviet doctrine is the imperative of the victory of communism.[22] Lee and Staar argue that Marxism-Leninism postulates perpetual conflict between socialism and capitalism and anticipates a high probability that the capitalist states will sooner or later launch a war. This requires that socialism be prepared to win the war when it comes.[23] Michael MccGwire, who sees the Soviets primarily concerned with preservation of the status quo in Europe, pays no attention to the intra-alliance role of the military-political axioms of the WTO.

The Functions of the Military-Political Axioms of the Warsaw Pact

The military-political axioms of the Warsaw Pact have a direct influence on the four theories of the military-technical component of WTO doctrine. These military-political axioms form an interlocking and overlapping set:

Joint defense of the gains of socialism against internal and external reaction,

Joint defense of the gains of World War II,

The Marxist-Leninist teaching on war and the military,

The Marxist-Leninist concept of armed defense of the revolution,

The Marxist-Leninist concept of the defense of the socialist fatherland,

The Marxist-Leninist concept of the organic unity of socialist patriotism and socialist internationalism,

The defense of socialism and peace,

Defense against the intrigues of imperialism and reaction to break the unity of the socialist camp and restore capitalism in separate socialist countries,

Defense against revanchism in general and German revanchism in particular,

The unbreakable combat alliance of the armed forces of the socialist states, and

The collective defense of socialism by the fraternal combat alliance of the socialist armies.

These concepts are in one sense slogans, suitable for banners in WTO parades or as the titles of books, chapters, articles, and so on appearing under the name of the WTO commander-in-chief, his WTO subordinates, and high-ranking Soviet officers and also under the joint commissions that write the national histories of each loyal WTO member.[24] Discourses on these slogans fill whole volumes, take up hours of political indoctrination for WTO personnel, and provide subject matter for conferences of WTO staff officers, high-ranking pact political officers, and military historians. The force of these overlapping concepts comes neither from their internal logic nor from ceaseless repetition, but from the fact that these phrases are written into a series of legal and political documents enforced by the armed forces of the WTO. These documents include the Warsaw Treaty of 1955, the renewal of the treaty in 1985, and the bilateral treaties of the Soviet Union with every WTO member except Romania; the 1977 Soviet constitution and the Eastern European constitutions revised after 1977; the party programs of all WTO states except Romania; political declarations of the political Consultative Committee of the WTO and lower ranking agencies; and the statements of party, state, and military officials of the WTO countries delivered at major WTO ceremonies, national anniversaries, and party congresses.

The circular logic of these phrases is both historical and ideological. The argument runs as follows: The victory of socialism in every WTO state, including the USSR, was the result of joint efforts of workers and soldiers from many socialist countries. The responsibility for the defense of the socialist revolution and the gains of socialism in each fraternal country is the common internationalist duty of allied socialist countries and specifically of their fraternal military alliance, the Warsaw Pact. The WTO armies have the responsibility of joint defense of the socialist fatherland against internal and external reaction, revanchism, and its imperialist allies. To fulfill the obligation of socialist patriotism, the armed forces of these states must forge a combat alliance for the joint struggle against reaction, imperialism, and revanchism. The combat alliance of the fraternal armies requires an identity of views on military art, on military training, on weapons production, and on the organization of national defense systems.[25] In other words, if an Eastern European state accepts the military-political axioms of the WTO, it must structure its national armed forces to meet the requirements of the common military-technical component of WTO doctrine.[26]

Alternative Military-Political Axioms and
Alternative Defense Postures in Eastern Europe

The significance of WTO doctrine cannot be understood solely from the perspective of the WTO posture against NATO. Its significance also derives from the Soviet military posture against the three independent communist regimes of Eastern Europe: Yugoslavia, Albania, and Romania. Each of these three states adheres to the military-political axiom of national control over national armed forces for the sole mission of defense of territory by national means. The military-technical component of these heretical doctrines is a territorial defense posture designed to offer prolonged political resistance to a Soviet military occupation of these states. The strategic objective of these defense ministries is the same as that of the late 1980s Afghan resistance: to prevent the consolidation of power by a pro-Soviet native government installed by the superior military forces of the USSR.

Even without elaborating on the details, obligingly provided at length by the defense ministries of these states,[27] it is obvious that the military-technical components of the doctrine of the three Eastern European military heretics are dramatically different than the military-technical components of the common doctrine of the loyal WTO states. Military art (strategy, operational art, and tactics) emphasizes defensive/harassment actions with small arms by a large paramilitary force led by a small, highly mobile regular army commanded by an officer corps schooled in guerrilla war and closely linked to local party organizations. For these officers, the criterion of success is not military defeat of their opponent, but political stalemate between the occupation regime and the political resistance led by the local communist party (or even a successor nationalist regime).

Military training and education, conducted independently of the WTO, addresses an entirely different kind of war than that planned by the WTO against its high tech/nuclear opponents in the West. Likewise, the types of military weapons required and supporting economic infrastructure and logistics systems are very different from the WTO counterparts. The organization of the national defense ministry and national defense systems is focused on functioning while under foreign military occupation, unlike the WTO focus on the mobilization of personnel for combat beyond national territory.

In Yugoslavia, Albania, and Romania, national control over national armed forces has not only denied the USSR an assured capability for unopposed intervention, but has also denied the Warsaw Pact offensive use of these forces on the external front. In these three states, independent defense ministries have also been the basis for independent security policies in Europe—policies that are almost indistinguishable from the neutral and nonaligned states in the CSCE system.[28]

This historical record in Eastern Europe strongly suggests that national control over national armed forces does not generate the problem of political reliability that has drawn the attention of NATO analysts. National control over national armed forces has generated what the Soviets recognize as a far worse problem: political unavailability, i.e. nonacquiescence of Eastern European militaries to USSR security policies and intervention within the WTO. In practice, every independent Eastern European defense ministry has stood down from the WTO order of battle, has raised troublesome political barriers to a Soviet military intervention, and has pursued independent security policies.

In short, these three states have invited other Eastern European states to oppose all of the principal Soviet military-political objectives in Europe: (1) assuring a Soviet capability of unopposed military intervention, (2) mounting a credible military threat to the FRG as insurance against the possibility of German reunification, and (3) deterring NATO from active support of anti-Soviet developments in Eastern Europe by threatening NATO with a war of attrition.

The activization of the Warsaw Pact in the early 1960s can be traced in part to a Soviet attempt to preempt the efforts of Polish officers to adopt a national doctrine that would have resulted in national control over Polish armed forces for missions determined by Warsaw.[29] For the same reasons, much of the reorganization of the WTO in 1969 can be traced to efforts of Czechoslovak officers in 1968 to develop an independent military doctrine that would have transferred control of the Czechoslovak military to Prague.[30]

On the basis of the examples set by Yugoslavia, Albania, and Romania, General Samoilenko was fully justified in concluding in 1981 that "The slightest departure of any state from the principle of collective defense of socialism weakens the whole system of socialism and produces a threat to the sovereignty of the fraternal countries."[31] Another Soviet specialist on the WTO had in 1975 called for "a sharp class struggle with the forces that propagandize various theories of 'neutralism,' 'nonalignment,' 'an interbloc position' and 'reliance on one's own forces.' "[32] In that very year, the volume edited under the auspices of the former WTO commander, I.I. Iakubovskii, made the same point:

> The experience of the political cooperation of the socialist countries shows that their unity is a natural phenomenon and that the course of building socialism in isolation from the world confederation of socialist countries, one basis of which is the theory of 'reliance on one's own forces' propagated by the Mao Zedong group, is reactionary and harmful to the world socialist system. The course of building socialism in isolation is advantageous to the reactionary imperialist forces, which are striving, by the means of stirring up nationalist, anti-Soviet moods, to wreck the unity of the social countries,

to isolate them from the most powerful socialist country, the USSR, and to deal with the socialist countries one by one.[33]

The Applications of WTO Military Doctrine

Within the WTO system, common doctrine plays a critical role both as a proscriptive policy wielded against further defections from the bloc and as a prescriptive policy providing for the intermeshing of Soviet and Eastern European military bureaucracies. The theory of military organization and development requires corresponding national military systems with defense ministries organized on the Soviet model. The existence of comparable structures makes it possible for WTO agencies to preside over analogous agencies and to facilitate the transfer of real administrative authority to the Soviet agencies. The interlocking command structure in turn makes it possible to attach Eastern European components to their Soviet counterparts. The practical application of the WTO theory of economics assures national dependence on bloc-wide sources (mainly Soviet) and the functional readiness of loyal WTO forces to use standard-issue Soviet equipment, even if somewhat dated. If the Eastern European forces linked to Soviet forces lag in technical capability, the Soviet commanders should nonetheless have a clear idea of what can be accomplished with earlier generations of Soviet weapons.

A common WTO theory for military education and training makes it possible for the alliance to standardize officer education and troop training. Cooperation in these areas also assures the preeminent position of Soviet military academies as the gateways to the top commands of Eastern Europe because the Soviet midcareer academies are both the oracles of doctrine and the designated institutions for preparing Warsaw Pact officers for the requirements of allied execution of WTO military art. The shared theory of military art is the basis for common exercises.

In addition to binding the alliance together through the interlocking system of bilateral treaties, party programs, and other political documents, the common military-political axioms provide the texts for the common indoctrination and education programs necessary to prepare personnel for the enforcement of the WTO military-political axioms. The military-political axioms also require WTO liaison with national security troops and paramilitary forces assigned to the internal front. The title of Marshal Kulikov's 1981 book on the WTO neatly sums up the unity of internal and external missions: *The Collective Defense of Socialism*. As V.I. Fomin explained in the concluding chapter to a 1984 volume, *Organization and Development of the Armies of the European Countries of the Socialist Confederation:*

The collective defense of the socialist gains of the workers, as experience shows, permits the party and state leaderships of the fraternal countries not only to unite their military forces, but also more rationally in the course of military organization and development to approach the determination of the size and structure of their armed forces and of the development of one or another branch of their armed services or types of troops and services.[34]

Conclusion

The military-political axioms of the WTO can be read as a critically important element in the WTO system for structuring postures on the internal and external fronts and for linking these two fronts into one continuous theater of military action. From a purely cynical point of view, the military-political axioms of the WTO are mere justifications. But even cynical justifications identify at least some de facto missions: (1) preemption of Eastern European capabilities of self-defense; (2) assurance of Soviet capabilities to intervene in Eastern Europe in support of local security forces; (3) preempting a response of "West German revanchism" to "threats to the gains of socialism" in the GDR by preparing a devastating assault against the Federal Republic; and (4) deterring any attempt by NATO members to support a change in the status quo in Eastern Europe, including East Germany.

The military-political axioms of the WTO explain, with no apology, the aggressive military posture of Soviet/WTO forces toward West Germany and Eastern Europe. This military posture is, as its commanders proclaim, the optimal defense of the pro-Soviet regimes of Eastern Europe. Soviet/WTO forces in the European theater jointly threaten adversaries and allies alike, holding the populations of both alliances common hostages to a status quo that lacks legitimacy in either half of Europe.

With the steady refinement during the 1970s and 1980s of the mechanisms of the integration of Soviet and Eastern European military personnel on both the internal and external fronts, the Soviets have been able to shift the WTO's emphasis from sheer mass to qualitative factors. The superior mechanisms of the 1980s permit reliance on smaller quantities of qualitatively better forces.[35]

On the external front, this has permitted the Soviets in the MBFR negotiations that began in 1973 to focus on maintaining a 1:1 ratio between the Bundeswehr and the Soviet-force groups in the northern tier. The Soviets retain very large forces outside this region. Moscow appears to be moving toward acceptance of a 1:1 ratio between the Eastern Europeans and the non-German forces in the western sector covered by the MBFR negotiations.[36] If any troop reductions do result from either the MBFR talks or the forthcoming

CSCE negotiations covering the region from the Atlantic to the Urals, such troop reductions will at a minimum preserve if not actually enhance Soviet capabilities on the internal front. These capabilities do not depend on raw numbers as much as on preemption of independent defense capabilities. Reduction of Eastern European forces may further limit Eastern European residual capabilities for self-defense while preserving an overwhelming Soviet/WTO advantage against each loyal member of the pact. Reduction of the absolute size of the Bundeswehr and other NATO forces will more than compensate for equivalent or even larger reductions of WTO personnel. NATO reductions will diminish the capabilities of the Bundeswehr while making the FRG more dependent on less capable allies.

In addition, the Soviets have obtained FRG and NATO recognition of the political and territorial status quo in Eastern Europe through the various treaties signed by West Germany in the early 1970s and by NATO in the 1975 Helsinki Final Act.

In the U.S.–Soviet treaty on the elimination of intermediate-range nuclear weapons in the 500–1,000- and 1,000–5,000-km range, the Soviets are obtaining a symbolic reduction of the U.S. commitment to respond to a conventional assault on Germany with a U.S. nuclear reprisal against the USSR. To obtain this symbolic reduction of the U.S. nuclear guarantee to Germany, the USSR has been willing to make a symbolic reduction of its nuclear threat to the FRG and its allies. These symbolic reductions on both sides shift the terms of the military confrontation back to the WTO capability for a conventional assault on West Germany.

The analysis of the doctrine, deployments, agencies, and programs of the WTO presented in this chapter suggest that the question to ask about the Eastern European role in the WTO is neither that of the political reliability of Eastern European personnel nor the degree to which Eastern Europeans place limits on the use of the WTO against NATO. If the analysis in this chapter is correct, then the doctrine and force posture of the WTO reveal the limits deliberately set by Soviet leaders on the projection of Soviet military power into Europe. The question to ask about the Eastern Europeans is how the WTO uses them to assure the projection of Soviet power against fellow alliance members and against the FRG. An additional question for NATO is whether it is willing to accept in principle what it accepts in practice: the permanence of the Soviet military threat to Eastern Europe and to the Federal Republic of Germany. Conscious acceptance of this principle is the only possible basis for arms control agreements with the USSR in the European theater and in the U.S.–USSR nuclear balance.

Notes

1. For instance, see U.S. Department of Defense, *Soviet Military Power, 1987* (Washington, D.C.: U.S. Government Printing Office, 1987), pp. 63–68.

2. Valerie Bunce, "The Empire Strikes Back: The Evolution of the Eastern Bloc from a Soviet Liability," *International Organization* (Winter 1985).

3. The CIA figures for 1985, the most recent available, list West German exports at $183.9 billion. The Soviet figure for the same year is $87.0 billion; the total for the Eastern European members of the CMEAS is $98.4 billion; the combined Soviet–Eastern European figure is $185.4 billion. Central Intelligence Agency, *Handbook of Economic Statistics, 1986* (Washington, D.C.: U.S. Government Printing Office, 1987), pp. 24–25.

4. Ibid.

5. All statistics from International Institute of Strategic Studies, *The Military Balance 1986–87,* (London: IISS, 1987) pp. 49–53.

6. William J. Lewis, *The Warsaw Pact: Arms, Doctrine and Strategy* (New York: McGraw-Hill, 1982), pp. 193–94.

7. *Military Balance, 1986–87,* p. 52.

8. Teresa Rakowska-Harmstone, "The Price of Cohesion and Performance Expectations," p. 325, in Harmstone, Christopher Jones, and Ivan Sylvain, *The Warsaw Pact: The Question of Cohesion, Phase II,* vol. I (Ottawa: Department of National Defense, 1984).

9. *The Military Balance, 1986–87,* pp. 49–53.

10. See the interview with Col. Ryszard Jerzy Kuklinski in *Kultura* (Paris), no. 4 (1987), esp. pp. 39ff, (translated for author by Teresa Rakowska-Harmstone).

11. Teresa Rakowska-Harmstone, "Poland," in Harmstone et al., *The Warsaw Pact,* vol. II.

12. See Condoleeza Rice, *The Soviet Union and the Czechoslovak Army 1948–1983* (Princeton, N.J.: Princeton University Press, 1984), ch. 4.

13. See "The Prospects for Conventional Deterrence in Central Europe" in John Mearsheimer, *Conventional Deterrence* (Ithaca, N.Y.: Cornell University Press, 1983).

14. Ibid., p. 166.

15. Ibid.

16. Ibid.

17. Jeffrey Simon, *Warsaw Pact Forces: Problems of Command and Control* (Boulder, Colo.: Westview Press, 1985), p. 1.

18. Ibid.

19. Richard C. Martin, "Warsaw Pact Force Modernization: A Second Look," in Jeffrey Simon and Trond Gilberg, eds., *Security Implications of Nationalism in Eastern Europe* (Boulder, Colo.: Westview Press, 1986), pp. 213–14.

20. For example, see Douglass Hart, "The Hermeneutics of Soviet Military Doctrine," *The Washington Quarterly* (Spring 1984).

21. For a chronological account of the evolution of these positions, see Harriet F. Scott and William Scott, *The Armed Forces of the USSR,* 3rd ed. (Boulder, Colo.: Westview, 1984), pp. 38–73. For an interpretation stressing the role of nuclear forces in Soviet theater war-fighting plans, see Joseph Douglass, *Military Strategy in Europe* (New York: Pergamon, 1974). For an ongoing analysis of the role of conventional weapons in Soviet theater doctrine, see the following articles by Phillip A. Petersen and John G. Hines: "The Conventional Offensive in Soviet Theater Strategy," *Orbis* (fall 1983); "Strategic Frontiers," *Washington Quarterly* (fall 1986); and "Changing the Soviet System of Control," *International Defense Review* (November 1986). For an argument that the Soviets seek nuclear and conventional superiority for the purpose

of neutralizing North America and China in order to conquer Europe, see William T. Lee and Richard F. Staar, *Soviet Military Policy since World War II* (Stanford, Calif.: Hoover Institution Press, 1986); for an analysis at odds with Lee and Staar, see Michael MccGwire, *Military Objectives in Soviet Foreign Policy* (Washington, D.C.: Brookings Institution, 1987). For a view of the shift to nonnuclear strategies, see Mary C. Fitzgerald, "Marshal Ogarkov on the Modern Theater Operation," *Naval War College Review* (fall 1986). For a sweeping but brief overview, see William E. Odom, "Soviet Force Posture: Dilemmas and Directions," *Problems of Communism* (August 1985).

22. Douglass, *Soviet Military Strategy in Europe*, p. 163.

23. Lee and Starr, *Soviet Military Policy since World War II*, pp. 24–29.

24. For example, the current (as of 1988) WTO Commander-in-Chief (C-in-C), V.G. Kulikov, *Kollektivnaia zashchita sotsializma* (*Collective Defense of Socialism*) (Moscow: Voenizdat, 1982); the current chief of the WTO Staff, A.I. Gribkov, *Nadezhnyi shchit mira i sotsialisma* (*The Reliable Shield of Peace and Socialism*) (Moscow: Voenizdat, 1985); the former WTO C-in-C, I.I. Iakubovskii, *Boevoe sodruzhestvo bratskikh narodov i armiii* (*The Combat Confederation of the Fraternal Peoples and Armed Forces*) (Moscow: Voenizdat, 1975); a former deputy chief of the Soviet Main Political Administration, P.I. Efimov, ed., *Boevoe soiuz bratskikh armiii* (*The Combat Union of the Fraternal Armed Forces*) (Moscow: Voenizdat, 1974); a prominent political officer associated with WTO affairs, V.F. Samoilenko, *Osnova boevogo soiuzai: internatsionalism kak faktor oboronoi moshchi sotsialisticheskogo sodruzhestva* (*The Basis of the Combat Alliance: Internationalism as a Factor of the Defensive Power of the Socialist Confederation*) (Moscow: Voenizdat, 1981); V.T. Login, ed., *Opyt voin v zashchitu sotsialisticheskogo otechestva* (*Experience of Wars in Defense of the Socialist Fatherland*) (Moscow: Nauka, 1985); I.I. Mintz, ed., *Zashchita zavoevanii sotsialisticheskikh revoliutsii* (*Defense of the Gains of Socialist Revolutions*) (Moscow: Nauka, 1986). For an example of the joint Soviet-Eastern European military histories, see Ia. Berets et al., eds., *V bratskom soiuze (Iz istorii sovetsko-vengerskikh otnoshenii)* (*In Fraternal Alliance [From the History of Soviet–Hungarian Relations]*) (Moscow: Voenizdat, 1979).

25. See the itemization and discussion of most of these principles in the works cited in the previous footnote and also in D.A. Volkogonov et al., eds., *Armii stran Varshavskogo dogovora* (*Armies of the Countries of the Warsaw Pact*) (Moscow: Voenizdat, 1985), pp. 10–20.

26. On p. 18 of the Volkogonov text cited in the previous note, the discussion of the military-political axioms is immediately followed by this passage:

> The military-strategic basis of the combat alliance of the fraternal socialist countries and their armed forces is conditioned by the unity of their goals and tasks in securing the reliable defense of their socialist achievements through united, collective efforts. A primary role is played by the commonality of military-strategic views, identical understanding of the laws, regularities of war, of the principles of military art and of military organization and development (*stroitel'stvo*). . . . Proceeding from this, the military science of the countries of socialism, which in its bases is identical, define the common principles of military organization and development (*stroitel'stvo*), the direction of development and the character of the strategic use of armed forces, the forms and methods of the preparation of the country, the army and navy of a possible war, the material-technical provisioning of military actions and also the methods of leadership of armed forces and the administration of troops.

The text notes that the basis of the military unity of the allied states "is the defense of the gains of socialism from the imperialist aggressors by the united efforts of the countries of the socialist confederation."

27. See Alexander Vukotic et al., eds., *The Yugoslav Concept of General People's Defense* (Belgrade: Medunarodna Politika, 1970). See also A. Ross Johnson, "Yugoslav Total National Defense," *Survival* (March/April 1973); Iulian Cernat et al., eds. *National Defense: The Romanian View* (Bucharest: Military Publishing House, 1976); Mehmet Shehu, *A propos de l'experience de al guerre de liberation nationale et du development de notre armee nationale* (Paris: Editions GIT/LeCoeur, 1969).

28. See Bengt Sundelius, *Foreign Policies of the Neutral and Non-Aligned States* (forthcoming).

29. See Teresa Rakowska-Harmstone, "Poland," pp. 65–90, in Harmstone et al., *The Warsaw Pact,* vol. II.

30. Christopher Jones, *Soviet Influence in Eastern Europe: Political Autonomy and the Warsaw Pact* (New York: Praeger, 1981), pp. 95–105.

31. V.F. Samoilenko, *Osnova boevogo soiuza,* p. 268.

32. M.S. Kirichenko, *Nadezhnyi strazh mira (Reliable Guard of Peace)* (Minsk: Belarus, 1975), p. 75.

33. I.I. Iakubovskii, *Boevoe sodruzhestvo,* pp. 119–29.

34. V.I. Fomin, "Zakliuchenie" (Conclusion) in P.A. Zhilin, ed., *Stroitel'stvo armii europeiskikh stran sotsialisticheskogo sodruzhestva, 1949–80 (The Organization and Development of the Armed Armies Forces of the European Countries of the Socialist Confederation, 1949–80)* (Moscow: Nauka, 1984), p. 299.

35. See Simon, *Warsaw Pact Forces.*

36. For background on MBFR, see John G. Keliher, *The Negotiations on Mutual and Balanced Force Reductions* (New York: Pergamon, 1980).

6
The Limits to Long-Distance Intervention: Soviet Capabilities for Power Projection in the Third World

Michael T. Klare

I n assessing the military capabilities of the Soviet Union, Reagan administration officials consistently emphasized the threat posed by Soviet "power-projection" forces—that is, forces configured for show-of-force and military intervention in distant, predominantly Third World areas.[1] "We must recognize," former secretary of defense Caspar Weinberger told the Senate Budget Committee in 1982, "that in recent years the Soviet Union has been greatly increasing its ability . . . to project military power into [non-European] areas, such as the Persian Gulf and the Caribbean."[2] The intent of this buildup, in the administration's view, is to provide Moscow with a significant military presence in strategic Third World areas and thence to diminish Western power and influence. "The Soviet Union has pushed its traditional policy of global expansionism to a new dimension in recent years and has emerged as a mature global power," Weinberger declared in 1982. "It now has the power and reach to challenge our interests almost anywhere in the world."[3]

Similar assertions have been made in each successive edition of *Soviet Military Power,* the U.S. Department of Defense's unclassified assessment of Soviet capabilities. Thus, in the first (1981) edition of this survey, it was stated that "The USSR's enhanced confidence in its capabilities to project power through a variety of military means has widened Soviet options and has been a key factor underlying its increased activities in Africa, the Middle East, Asia and Latin America."[4] Similarly, in the 1983 edition, it was reported that "Soviet development of increasingly capable armed forces has enhanced Moscow's ability to challenge Western interests in nearly every corner of the globe."[5] Comparable language has appeared in successive editions of this survey, each of which has contained a section on "Soviet power projection" or "Soviet global ambitions."

The impression given by these and other Pentagon pronouncements on Soviet military moves in the Third World is that Moscow has sought, and largely obtained, a substantial power-projection capability of the sort long possessed by the United States. Such a capability, on the U.S. side, is assumed to consist of all those military assets needed to transport fully equipped U.S. forces many thousands of miles to distant battlefields in sufficient strength to overcome any local resistance to U.S. penetration. Typically, such assets include airborne and airmobile infantry; sea-based infantry ("marines") with organic amphibious assault vessels; aircraft carrier battle groups; long-range cargo planes and vessels; and "special" forces equipped for guerrilla and counterinsurgency operations. The United States possesses a large inventory of such assets, and, under the Reagan administration buildup, added significantly to its power-projection capability.[6]

In the 1983 edition of *Soviet Military Power,* the Department of Defense asserts that the USSR has sought, and largely acquired, similar capabilities:

> Over the past decade, the growing capability of Soviet armed forces to pro-
> ject power to great distances has helped the USSR to sustain and consolidate
> many new military outposts. . . . The Soviets have traditionally maintained
> their naval infantry and airborne forces at high levels of readiness. Since
> 1972, naval infantry and airborne unit training, equipment, and
> deployments have also been matched by comparable enhancements to Soviet
> airlift, sealift, and mobility infrastructure.[7]

With slightly different wording, the same theme has recurred in later editions of this survey and in other Department of Defense assessments.

Administration analysts also assert that these Soviet "enhancements" were stimulated by and carried out in conformance with an explicit policy of using military force to expand Soviet power and influence in the Third World. "A major manifestation of the Soviet Union's global ambitions since the 1960s has been its steadily expanding presence and reach beyond Soviet borders to the most distant oceans and throughout the Third World," notes the 1985 edition of *Soviet Military Power.* "This military presence abroad has supported a continuing, aggressive Soviet foreign policy aimed at expansion of Soviet influence around the world."[8]

Some analysts have gone further, charging that Soviet military moves in the Third World are intended to provide Moscow with a capacity to impede Western access to vital overseas supplies of oil and strategic raw materials. "Soviet statements clearly reflect the USSR's understanding of the extent to which the United States and Western Europe currently depend on imports of vital strategic raw materials from the developing regions," notes the first edition of *Soviet Military Power.* With this in mind, "the Soviets are . . . seeking to develop a viable oil and strategic minerals denial strategy."[9] A similar view was advanced by Noel C. Koch, then principal deputy assistant secretary of defense for international security affairs, in 1985. "While the defense strategists of the democracies focus on the nuclear threat and then on conventional conflict of the World War II variety," he told a group of arms exporters, "the Soviet Union is quietly going after key global resources and global choke-points."[10]

It is on this basis that the Reagan administration called for a significant expansion of U.S. power-projection capabilities. "The increasing inter-dependence of the world over the past decade has made our access to foreign markets and vital natural resources more critical than ever," Weinberger told the Council on Foreign Relations in 1982. "Because Soviet military power has acquired a global reach, we need mobile and flexible forces, particularly to prevent Soviet conquest of the oil fields and major targets in the Mideast."[11] Similar comments appeared in Weinberger's annual budget reports to the U.S. Congress.

This perspective on the Soviet threat, and on the proper U.S. military response to it, has been generally accepted by the U.S. Congress and the public at large. While Congress voiced some doubt about certain aspects of Mr. Reagan's military program, it largely approved his requests for a signifi-cant buildup in U.S. power-projection capabilities. Nonetheless, a number of Western analysts have questioned the validity of administration assertions on the power-projection issue. These analysts contend that Soviet power-projection capabilities are not as formidable as suggested by the Department of Defense and that their configuration does not provide evidence of a Soviet drive to expand its capacity for military intervention in the Third World. "Despite [recent] improvements," Dennis M. Gormley observed in *Survival,* "current Soviet force projection capabilities represent, at best, only a rudimen-tary potential to project into and to sustain power in distant crisis areas."[12]

All this has led to a vigorous debate on the magnitude of Soviet capabilities and the doctrine governing their use. While overshadowed by the more prominent debate over the magnitude and configuration of the USSR's nuclear arsenal and its conventional armies arrayed against NATO, the debate on power-projection forces has important policy implications. So long as a pessimistic assessment of Soviet capabilities and intentions remains domi-nant, we are likely to see a continuing expansion of U.S. military capabilities along with a generally antagonistic stance regarding Soviet behavior in the Third World; if a less alarmist assessment were to prevail, we might see a slowdown in U.S. force improvements and a more tolerant response to Soviet activities. Moreover, since several successive U.S. administrations have held that U.S. readiness to negotiate new limits on strategic arms is contingent on Soviet restraint in the Third World, the power-projection debate could affect the outcome of future U.S.–Soviet arms control talks.

Given these stakes, it is important that we clarify the threat posed by Soviet power-projection forces. By looking at them closely and by evaluating their strength and potential utility, we can achieve a more precise net assessment of Soviet capabilities. Such an evaluation can also tell us if the Soviets have been systematically enlarging their interventionary capabilities, whether they have achieved some semblance of parity with the United States in this field, and whether their more effective forces are a means to deny the West essential raw materials.

A Note on Sources

Lacking access to classified data, I naturally had to rely on public sources. Fortunately, there are many valuable unclassified sources on this topic. I have drawn in particular on three: *The Military Balance,* published annually by the International Institute for Strategic Studies; *Soviet Military Power,* published annually by the U.S. Department of Defense; and John M. Collins' *U.S.–Soviet Military Balance 1980–1985,* published in 1985 by Pergamon-Brassey's.

For data on specific vessels and aircraft, I have relied on *Jane's Fighting Ships* and *Jane's All the World's Aircraft,* both published yearly. Other useful information can be found in professional journals, notably *Air Force, Army, Military Review, National Defense, Naval War College Review, Survival, The Defense Monitor,* and *U.S. Naval Institute Proceedings.*[13]

Soviet Power-Projection Capabilities

The first thing that must be understood about Soviet capabilities is that, in contrast to the United States, the Soviet Union deploys very few forces that have long-range power projection as their *primary* mission. Whereas many sizable U.S. units—for example, the Army's 82nd Airborne Division and 101st Airmobile Division—are primarily intended for combat in Third World areas, most Soviet forces with a power-projection capacity are intended primarily as augmentation for Soviet forces in Europe or along the Sino–Soviet border and only secondarily for combat in remote Third World areas.[14]

With this in mind, it should be noted that most of the forces described shortly are included in this assessment because they are the Soviet forces that most clearly resemble U.S. power-projection capabilities, not because they have any formal power-projection function as such. While Moscow may on occasion employ them in a power-projection capacity, they usually have other missions that are normally given greater attention in the Soviet military writings.

All this having been noted, we can turn to our survey of Soviet capabilities. While power projection entails the employment of a wide spectrum of forces, weapons, and systems, we will concentrate here on the three basic components of such a capacity: (1) mobile ground forces, (2) tactical air-power, and (3) air and naval mobility assets. Other important components, including access to overseas bases, will be discussed later, though in somewhat less detail.

Mobile Ground Forces

The mobile-infantry component of the Soviet Union's power-projection capability is comprised of four basic combat formations: the Soviet Naval Infantry, Soviet airborne divisions, Soviet air-assault brigades, and Soviet Special Designation Forces (*Spetsnaz*). These are the formations that are light and mobile enough to be moved quickly to distant battlefields and thus are the forces that Moscow would probably rely upon in conducting interventionary operations abroad.

The Soviet Naval Infantry (SNI), or *Morskaya pekhota,* consists of some 16,000 soldiers, organized into three 3,000-man brigades (one each assigned to the Northern, Baltic, and Black Sea fleets) and one 7,000-man division (assigned to the Pacific Fleet). The original Naval Infantry was formed prior to World War I, but was disbanded after World War II. Reactivated in 1963, the current SNI has evolved slowly from a force of only 4–5,000 troops organized into several small regiments to its present size and configuration. Organic SNI assets include some 110 PT-76 light amphibious tanks and 200 T-54 and T-55 medium tanks, plus 1,045 BTR-60 armored personnel carriers (APCs) and a variety of light artillery pieces.[15]

Although often compared to the U.S. Marine Corps, the SNI is much smaller (with only 16,000 troops, it is approximately one-twelfth the size of the Marine Corps) and intended for rather different purposes. Whereas the Marine Corps is configured as a self-sufficient fighting force with its own air arm and logistical support system, the Naval Infantry is largely designed to serve as a flanking force for neighboring land armies and thus lacks an integral air arm and logistics service.

When employed in exercises—the SNI has not seen active combat since 1945—these units have been used to seize ports and beachheads on the coastal flanks of enemy concentrations (usually in parallel with a land offensive by friendly ground troops) and to dislodge enemy forces from key islands and straits astride the "choke points" that must be traversed by Soviet warships on their way to and from the high seas.[16] Lacking an organic air arm, the attacking SNI forces are dependent for air cover on any ground-based air support within the theater of operations. Possessing only four to five days' worth of supplies, the SNI also requires rapid reinforcement by follow-on ground troops. "[SNI] units would act as spearheads of an operational landing in conjunction with ground forces," James Hansen of the Defense Intelligence

Agency (DIA) wrote in *National Defense*. "This concept is markedly different from that of U.S. Marine Corps units, designed to fight on their own with organic air support."[17]

Although primarily oriented toward Europe and the China/Japan/Korea theater, some small SNI detachments have served afloat in show-the-flag operations in the Middle East and Africa. This has led some analysts to suggest that the Soviets intend to employ the Naval Infantry as an amphibious intervention force akin to the U.S. Marines.[18] Although Moscow could certainly use these forces for short-term, limited missions against lightly armed opponents, the SNI is wholly unequipped for sustained combat against a determined opponent. Most crippling, of course, is the lack of organic, sea-based airpower; without an integral air arm, SNI forces would be at a severe disadvantage in any overseas encounter with an adversary possessing even limited air support. "Lack of staying power, limited lift capacity, and the need for land-based aircraft support suggest that the Soviet Naval Infantry's primary wartime mission is to seize and control such critical areas as the Dardanelles," wrote Keith A. Dunn of the National Defense University, "rather than the force projection mission usually attributed to the U.S. Marines."[19]

While it is likely that the Naval Infantry will continue to grow at the same unhurried pace we have witnessed since the 1960s, there is no evidence of a determined and rapid Soviet drive to convert the SNI into a global intervention force oriented toward the Third World. As noted by naval expert Michael MccGwire: "The gradual buildup and present size [of SNI forces] do not support the theory that the reactivation of the Naval Infantry in 1963 signaled a Soviet intention to develop a Western-style overseas intervention capability."[20]

Soviet Airborne Forces, or the *Vozdushno desantnye voyska* (VDV), consist in 1988 of seven active divisions of about 7,500 paratroopers each, with an eighth division employed for training purposes. Each division consists of three regiments plus assorted artillery, signals, and supply units. Mobility and fire support for these units is provided by the air-droppable BMD-1 infantry fighting vehicle, which comes equipped with a 73-mm. smoothbore gun and an AT-3 "Sagger" antitank guided missile (ATGM) system. Some 330 BMDs are supplied to each airborne division.[21]

With a total troop strength of 52,500 (compared to 33,000 in the two U.S. airborne/airmobile divisions), the seven divisions of the VDV provide Moscow with a significant airborne assault capability. For this reason, these units are often described in the West as a long-range power-projection force much like the U.S. Marine Corps. "Because of their mobility," the 1981 edition of *Soviet Military Power* observed, "the Soviet Union's seven airborne divisions are particularly well-suited for the rapid introduction of combat forces into a foreign country."[22] To support this assessment, U.S. analysts stress that VDV units spearheaded the Soviet occupation of Prague in 1968 and Kabul in 1979. However, while these incidents certainly suggest that the VDV could be used in a projection role, it is important to note that "power projection" connotes operations in distant, noncontiguous areas and that both Czechoslovakia and Afghanistan are contiguous to Soviet territory and within range of regular Soviet forces. Also, we need to consider what *other* roles the VDV are intended to perform, in order to fully assess their capacity for long-range power projection.

As in the case of the SNI, Soviet doctrine and exercises suggest that the primary mission of the VDV is to spearhead a major ground advance by seizing key objectives—bridges, river crossings, airstrips, military bases, and the like—behind or on the flanks of enemy lines. During the 1981 "Zapad" maneuvers, for instance, airborne units were used to spearhead the advance of an "operational maneuver group" (OMG)—a multidivision combined-arms force designed to penetrate deep into NATO territory.[23] Soviet doctrine also stresses the use of airborne forces (in concert with the OMGs) to seize or destroy NATO nuclear-weapons sites and command-control-communications (C³) centers at the very onset of an East–West conflict. According to V.D. Sokolovsky's authoritative text on Soviet military doctrine, the VDV is charged with "such missions as capture and retention or destruction of nuclear missiles, air force and naval bases, and other important objectives deep within the theaters of military operations."[24]

True, these forces are available for other purposes in the absence of East–West conflict. Indeed, events in Afghanistan suggest that Moscow is prepared to use them in a classical power-projection role, when and if deemed necessary. However, the VDV would experience severe operational disabilities in any sustained overseas deployment against well-equipped adversaries. If forced to fight on their own, such units would have little protection against enemy armor and aircraft, and they would quickly run out of fuel and ammunition. Casualties would also prove a significant burden and probably would be denied anything beyond rudimentary treatment. For these reasons, Soviet writings on airborne operations stress the need for a rapid linkup with ground forces.[25] Even with recent improvements in firepower and mobility of the VDV, Gormley observed in 1982, "the Soviet Union still requires close coordination between the airborne forces and the main body of advancing ground force units, especially for missile, air and artillery fire support."[26] This is, indeed, the scenario that was followed in the two major instances of VDV deployment—in both Czechoslovakia (1968) and Afghanistan (1979), early-arriving airborne units were reinforced almost immediately by regular ground troops carried by truck from staging areas in the Soviet Union.[27]

In a Third World encounter, however, a linkup with regular Soviet ground forces would be almost impossible (except, of course, in Afghanistan and other contiguous nations). Soviet transport aircraft are not, as we shall see, capable of moving heavy ground units over long distances, and a lack of significant sea-based air support would leave Soviet transport planes vulnerable to enemy air strikes. "In conflicts far from the USSR," the Joint Chiefs of Staff (JCS) noted in 1981, VDV effectiveness "would be hampered by the limitations of Soviet long-range airlift and the lack of immediately available tactical air forces."[28]

It is, therefore, apparent that the VDV, as now constituted, possesses only a modest power-projection capability when deployed any distance from the Soviet periphery. In recognition of this fact, the 1981 edition of *Soviet Military Power* suggested that while the VDV might be able to defeat "the indigenous forces of a number of less developed countries," it was "not suitable for operations against a well-armed [Third World] adversary."[29] Moreover, the seven Soviet airborne divisions comprise *the* strategic reserve of the Soviet General Staff. Thus it is unlikely that Moscow would commit them far from home when there is any likelihood of a crisis arising in a more critical area, such as Eastern Europe, the Far East, or non-Russian areas of the USSR itself.

Soviet Air Assault Brigades, of which about ten have been established, are a relatively recent addition to the Soviet military lineup. These units, which number about two-thousand soldiers each, are thought to be under the operational command of Soviet frontal commanders (in contrast to the VDV, which is under the direct command of the Soviet General Staff). Each brigade comprises two parachute battalions and two BMD-equipped assault battalions; firepower is provided by sixty-four BMDs and some thirty artillery pieces.[30]

Some Western analysts have viewed these air assault brigades as an adjunct to the VDV and suggested that they possess a significant power-projection responsibility. Giving credence to this view is the fact that one of the brigades has been deployed in Afghanistan.[31] However, while it is certainly possible that these units will be used in future interventionary operations abroad, the evidence suggests that they are largely intended for use in Europe and on the Soviet periphery.

In contrast to the VDV, which is under General Staff control and is capable of long-range deployment on short notice, the air assault brigades are assigned to Military District commands (in time of war, *front* headquarters) and are largely dependent on intratheater lift capabilities (helicopters and medium transport planes). Soviet doctrine and exercises indicate, moreover, that the principal role of the brigades is to spearhead a breakthrough in enemy lines or to seize key objectives just behind those lines. Their mission, according to Captain Edwin W. Besch of the Army Intelligence and Threat Analysis Center, "would include seizure of important lines of communication, bridges, mountain passes, and the like, probably within the tactical depth (50–100 kilometers) of the enemy's rear in direct support of front (or army) operations."[32] These brigades are also thought to figure in Soviet plans for the use of OMGs to seize nuclear-weapons sites and other critical NATO installations at the outbreak of an East–West conflict.[33]

Clearly, the new Soviet air assault brigades represent a significant threat to defending forces on NATO's front lines. It does not appear likely, however, that they would be employed in interventionary operations any distance from the Soviet periphery.

Soviet "Spetsnaz" forces are the rough equivalent of U.S. Special Operations Forces (SOF). At the present time, there are approximately sixteen Spetsnaz brigades serving with Soviet ground forces and four brigades of naval Spetsnaz (one for each fleet) assigned to the Soviet navy.[34] Each brigade is composed of several parachute battalions and is believed to number some 1,000–1,200 men. This adds up to rough total of about 20,000–24,000 Spetsnaz troops, compared to about 16,000 active-duty soldiers and 15,000 reservists in the U.S. SOF lineup. Like their American counterparts, Spetsnaz troops are trained in reconnaissance and sabotage tactics, and they are expected to operate for long periods of time behind enemy lines.[35]

In the event of a major East–West conflict, the Spetsnaz would be given the same sort of behind-the-lines missions as would the U.S. Army's Special Forces: to collect intelligence on enemy capabilities; to blow up bridges, rail lines, communications facilities, and the like; and, where possible, to stir up civilian resistance to military authorities. Some Spetsnaz personnel have also been deployed in Afghanistan, where they reportedly spearheaded the December 1979 assault on the palace of then president Hafizullah Amin.[36] It is doubtful, however, that the Spetsnaz are designed or equipped to participate in long-range interventionary operations far from the Soviet periphery.

From all that we know, these units are primarily oriented toward the European theater. Most Spetsnaz personnel are trained to speak Western European languages and, according to the U.S. Department of Defense, are trained at installations designed to look like NATO military bases, complete with mock-ups of US Lance, Pershing, and other missiles systems.[37] Furthermore, while U.S. doctrine stresses the employment of SOF cadres in insurgency and counterinsurgency operations in the Third World, Spetsnaz forces do not appear to have an equivalent mission.[38] As in the case of Soviet airborne brigades, therefore, it appears that these forces have a limited power-projection function.

Airlift and Sealift Forces

To move any of its forces to distant Third World battle zones, the Soviet Union would rely on its strategic mobility assets: long-range cargo planes and amphibious assault ships.

Soviet airlift capabilities are largely assigned to the Military Transport

Aviation (*Voenno transportnaya aviatsiya* or VTA) branch of the Soviet Air Force. In 1986, primary VTA assets included 260 Antonov An-12 "Cub" medium transports, 310 Ilyushin IL-76 "Candid" jet transports, 50 Antonov An-22 "Cub" heavy transports, and a handful of the new Antonov An-124 "Condor" heavy transports. (Soviet aircraft names given in quotation marks are NATO designations; all proper, or indigenous, ship and aircraft names are given in italics.) Another 265 An-12s are deployed with other air force commands, giving the Soviet Union a grand total of 885 military transport planes (excluding the few An-124s). In a crisis, the Kremlin could also make use of the 1,600 passenger aircraft in the Aeroflot fleet.[39]

Once a relatively neglected branch of the air force, the VTA has received more attention since the 1970s, as reflected in the replacement of older, obsolete aircraft with more modern and capable variants. Thus, the propeller-driven An-12—first introduced in 1959 and long the mainstay of the VTA fleet—is now being replaced by the jet-powered IL-76. Similarly, the twenty-year-old An-22s are now being joined by the vastly more capable An-124s. These improvements will significantly enhance the operating capabilities of the VTA—particularly as relates to the delivery of heavy and out-sized equipment—but will not result in a larger fleet of aircraft, since older planes are being replaced by fewer numbers of modern craft.[40]

In total numbers, the VTA fleet compares favorably with the U.S. airlift fleet, now consisting of 216 C-130 *Hercules* turboprop transports (another 300 or so are in the Air Force Reserve), 269 C-141B *Starlifters,* 36 KC-10 tanker-transports, and 70 C-5A *Galaxy* heavy transports.[41] However, these U.S. assets enjoy significant advantages over their Soviet counterparts—particularly with respect to speed, range, and payload. More significantly, these U.S. transports can be refueled in the air (giving them virtually unlimited reach), while none of the Soviet transports possess this important ability.[42]

Despite these limitations, the Soviets have employed VTA forces in a power-projection capacity on several notable occasions. In 1973, during the October War in the Middle East, Moscow flew some 930 cargo sorties to Egypt in order to replace critical stocks of arms and ammunition. Four years later, in 1977–78, the Soviet Union airlifted hundreds of tanks, APCs, and artillery pieces to Ethiopia during its war with Somalia. Soviet aircraft also flew some 25,000 Cuban troops to Angola during the civil war that followed independence in 1975 and carried the initial contingent of Soviet forces in Afghanistan in 1979.[43]

It is safe to predict that the VTA will again perform such functions when and if the need arises in some future Third World crisis. It must be noted, however, that VTA forces are not fully suited to this mission: they cannot travel far from the Soviet periphery unless refueling facilities are available along the line of flight; they cannot be escorted by Soviet combat planes (since no Soviet fighters possess the range or air-refueling capacity enabling them to accompany the transports on long-distance flights); and they cannot carry large numbers of tanks and other heavy weapons. Thus, as noted by Gormley, "The Soviet Union must substantially improve her airlift capability, if she seriously contemplates a *direct* and sustainable military role" in Third World operations (emphasis in the original).[44]

In the event of a major war, moreover, VTA aircraft would be fully engaged in the transport of Soviet forces from garrisons in the interior to staging area in Eastern Europe or the Far East. (It is important to remember that critical Far Eastern bases such as Vladivostok are served by only one, highly vulnerable rail line and that the strategic naval base at Petropavlovsk has no overland connections to the Soviet mainland and is highly dependent on air transport.) And while VTA capabilities are being steadily improved, Gormley finds that "the current *and prospective* VTA inventory appears insufficient to meet the needs of both strategically vital contingencies on the Soviet periphery as well as operations in regions elsewhere" (emphasis added).[45] All this being true, we can expect the Kremlin to exercise extreme caution in committing large numbers of VTA aircraft to sustained supply operations in remote Third World areas.

Soviet amphibious lift consists of some 35 special-purpose vessels designed to carry Naval Infantry troops and equipment across the high seas to distant battle zones. Current Soviet holdings in this category include 2 *Ivan Rogov*–class amphibious assault transport docks (LPDs), 19 *Ropucha*-class vehicle-landing ships (LSTs), and 14 *Alligator*-class LSTs. Altogether, these ships displace an estimated 152,600 tons when fully loaded. The Soviet navy also possesses 42 smaller amphibious vessels and other short-range amphibious ships such as the *SMB* and *Vydra* classes (*Polnocny*-class landing ships) that are intended for coastal assault operations in the Baltic or in other protected bodies of water. By comparison, the U.S. amphibious fleet consists of 60 ocean-going vessels, displacing some 970,000 tons when fully loaded— giving the United States a sixfold lead in tonnage over the USSR.[46] This Soviet disadvantage is somewhat mitigated by the large Soviet merchant fleet, which can be pressed into military service as required.

The Soviet amphibious fleet was normally confined to home waters, where it was generally used (in the course of exercises) to support Naval Infantry landings on the flanks of Soviet ground forces. In the 1980s, however, small amphibious squadrons with embarked SNI detachments have accompanied Soviet warships on patrols in the Indian Ocean, the Eastern Mediterranean, and in the waters off of West Africa. Deployed in this manner, amphibious forces have provided Moscow with an important symbol of political power. In a crisis, such forces could also be used to rescue Soviet advisors from war-torn areas, to facilitate the delivery of arms and equipment to allies, and to seize critical port facilities. However, the small size of these forces (a typical SNI deployment in these waters numbers five hundred to one thousand men) and the lack of carrier-based air support significantly limit the combat potential of such units when faced with any sort of organized resistance. As suggested by the JCS in 1981, "the lack of sea-based tactical air support greatly limits Soviet ability to carry out amphibious landings against heavy opposition."[47]

Because ocean-going amphibious forces are specifically designed for long-range assault operations, their growth and development provide a good indication of a nation's intentions in the power-projection area. Thus, in seeking to corroborate its claims of a Soviet drive in this area, the Department of Defense has highlighted recent Soviet improvements in amphibious lift—notably the introduction, in 1978, of the *Ivan Rogov* assault ship. Such improvements, observed the 1981 edition of *Soviet Military Power*, are among the principal features of a determined Soviet effort "to provide a formidable projection into distant waters."[48] The fact is, however, that Soviet enhancements in amphibious lift have been relatively meager, not to mention slow in coming. The *Ivan Rogov* has been joined by only one other vessel of this class (a third is reported to be under construction), and even these new ships, impressive as they are, displace only one-third the tonnage of the largest U.S. amphibious ships, the *Tarawa*-class LHA (landing ship helicopters).[49] No other signs of a Soviet drive in this area have since been detected, and so we must conclude that long-range amphibious assault remains a relatively *low* Soviet priority.

Tactical Air Support

If lightly equipped expeditionary forces are to prevail in any encounter with well-equipped Third World adversaries, and particularly those possessing an air combat capability, they must have some tactical air support. For the United States, this requirement has long been satisfied through the deployment of large aircraft carriers with their complement of modern combat planes. This formidable capability, now comprised of fourteen active carriers (one more is being refitted, and one is under construction), can be augmented through the deployment of Tactical Air Command (TAC) warplanes, all of which can be refueled in the air in order to permit long-distance flights. For the Soviet Union, however, this requirement poses considerable problems: Soviet carrier-borne aircraft are few in number, and Soviet ground-based aircraft cannot be transported easily to distant battle zones.

As of 1988, Soviet carrier-based airpower consists of the 40 or so Yakovlev Yak-38 "Forger" V/STOL (vertical- and short-takeoff-and-landing) fighters deployed in groups of twelve to thirteen on the three *Kiev*-class VTOL carriers. (A fourth carrier of this class was undergoing sea trials in 1987.) The Yak-38 can carry up to 2,000 pounds of bombs and rockets, and it has a combat radius of about 200 miles. The U.S. carrier-based force, by comparison, consists of about 900 fixed-wing combat aircraft (A-6s, A-7s, F-14s, and F/A-18s), all of which can carry in excess of 10,000 pounds of ordinance over ranges of up to 550–750 miles.[50] The aircraft of the Soviet Yak-38 fleet are so few and possess such limited range that they provide but a meager capability for power projection ashore.

In recognition of this limitation, the Soviets are beginning to assemble a fleet of large-deck carriers similar to those long possessed by the United States. A 65,000-ton vessel (twice the displacement of the *Kiev* VTOL carrier but only about two-thirds the size of U.S. *Nimitz*-class carriers) is now under construction at Nikolayev on the Black Sea. While it is expected that the ship will have aircraft catapults and arresting gear like U.S. attack carriers, it is still too early to determine the nature of its ultimate configuration. Because the development, installation, and testing of such a system—the like of which has never been produced in the Soviet Union—will take many years, it may not be until the early 1990s before we can determine the deployable air strength of this class of warships.[51] In the meantime, Soviet sea-based air support will be limited to the forty (to become fifty-two when the fourth *Kiev*-class carrier becomes operational) not-very-potent Yak-38s.

Soviet ground-based tactical air units, assigned to the Frontal Aviation (FA) branch of the air force, are the only other possible source of air support for deployed ground forces abroad. Current FA holdings include some 5,150 combat aircraft, most of which are based in or near Eastern Europe or along the southern and eastern borders of the USSR.[52] These aircraft are primarily designed to support Soviet ground troops in any clash with NATO or Chinese forces and to strike enemy installations behind the line of combat.

Theoretically, some of these planes could be diverted for military operations overseas, but Moscow would face a significant problem in attempting to do so. Most Soviet fighters have a limited (under-600–mile) combat radius, and none are equipped for aerial refueling. As noted by Keith Dunn: "This reduced range, coupled with the lack of in-flight refuel capabilities, makes it difficult for the USSR to redeploy its FA assets rapidly over long distances."[53] To get around this problem, Moscow would have to ship its fighters by sea and then find a friendly air base in the zone of conflict from which to conduct operations—a slow and risky process and not one that is likely to instill Soviet leaders with considerable confidence when it comes to planning long-range power-projection operations.

Net Assessment

It is clear, from all of the preceding, that the Soviet Union possesses a wide variety of forces that could, if needed, be pressed into service for military intervention in distant Third World areas. For the most part, however, these forces are not designed to fight on their own but require support from Soviet ground armies and land-based aircraft, thus limiting their effective operating range to countries bordering on or close to the USSR itself. In addition, many of these forces are intended primarily for other military functions—some of a strategic nature—and thus are not likely to be committed to a distant Third World contingency except under extraordinary circumstances. Very few Soviet military units can be said to have power projection as their principal mission, and those units—e.g., the *Ivan Rogov*-class transport ships with their embarked Naval Infantry detachments—represent a paltry capability when compared to equivalent U.S. forces. In sum, the Soviet Union possesses a rather limited capacity for military intervention against well-equipped Third World adversaries located any distance from the Soviet periphery.

This overall assessment of Soviet interventionary capabilities is generally shared by other analysts who have studied the available data.[54] "At present," Dennis Gormley wrote in *Survival*, "the Soviet Union possesses only minimal capabilities to project and sustain military power far from her borders." Given their operational limitations, Soviet Naval Infantry units "provide Moscow with only limited potential for power projection ashore, accept under benign conditions." Similarly, with their lack of integral air support, the seven Soviet airborne divisions "would face serious difficulties if confronted by strong defenses" in remote-area operations. "Most importantly," he concluded, "the Soviet Union is seriously short of requisite air transport capability to undertake simultaneous operations in strategically vital contiguous theaters, as well as in non-contiguous third-world conflicts."[55]

A similar assessment was offered by Keith Dunn of the National Defense University. In areas close to the Soviet Union, he wrote, Moscow could draw on its heavy concentrations of air, sea, and ground forces to overcome a Third World opponent. "However, as one moves further from the USSR, Soviet combat and force projection capabilities become less significant and in some cases insignificant."[56] Dunn cautioned against using Afghanistan as a yardstick of Soviet interventionary capabilities, since the invasion occurred in an area where superior Soviet-based forces could be brought in almost overnight—a situation "that may not exist as one moves further from Soviet borders."[57]

The limited Soviet capacity for long-range power projection stands in sharp contrast to comparable U.S. capabilities, which provide Washington with a significant capacity for military intervention against determined and well-equipped adversaries located many thousands of miles from the American heartland. As noted by the International Institute for Strategic Studies in 1981: "Soviet capabilities to project power over long distances, while growing, remained distinctly inferior to those of the United States."[58]

Some analysts have suggested that the Soviets have sought to overcome this disadvantage in power-projection capabilities by gaining access to basing facilities in the Third World and through the use of "proxy" troops supplied by Cuba and other Soviet allies. Thus, in the 1983 edition of *Soviet Military Power,* it is noted that "The basing facilities now available to Soviet maritime forces in Cuba, Vietnam, South Yemen, Angola, Ethiopia, and elsewhere greatly extend the reach and staying power of Soviet air and naval forces."[59] Similarly, in the 1984 edition, it is suggested that "Moscow has been able to enlist the assistance of its Allies [*sic*] as surrogates in situations where it normally would not have easy access or where its participation might be counterproductive to its objectives."[60]

True, the Soviets have succeeded in gaining regular access to air and naval facilities in a number of Third World countries. Soviet ships regularly stop for supplies (and, in some cases, for minor repairs) at Cam Ranh Bay in Vietnam, Dahlak Island in Ethiopia, and the Angolan port of Luanda. Moreover, Soviet reconnaissance and cargo aircraft make regular use of the airstrips at Aden in South Yemen and San Antonio de los Banos in Cuba, as well as those at Cam Ranh Bay and Luanda.[61] These basing arrangements enable Soviet ships and aircraft to remain "on station" in remote areas for longer periods and to undertake routine repair and maintenance work without returning to their home bases in the Soviet Union.

But while such basing arrangements certainly contribute to the operational effectiveness of certain Soviet capabilities, they do not necessarily constitute permanent Soviet *bases* in the sense that is normally signified by U.S. military doctrine. As defined by the Joint Chiefs of Staff, a naval base is a port complex or support facility "for which the Navy has operating responsibilities, together with interior lines of communication and the minimum surrounding area necessary for local security."[62] Such facilities—and their army and air force equivalents—are usually defended (at least in part) by U.S. forces, and their continued occupation by U.S. military personnel is assured by treaty or binding agreement. As of 1988, the United States has 111 such "bases" in the Third World,[63] while the Soviet Union has no facilities that fully fit this description (although Cam Ranh Bay comes reasonably close). For the most part, Soviet "basing arrangements" consist of access agreements that have been granted for certain specified and limited purposes and that can be revoked at any time by the nation involved. Indeed, on several notable occasions—in Egypt in 1972, Somalia in 1977, and Guinea in 1977—the Soviets were denied access to facilities that they had previously been using on a regular basis.[64]

It is unlikely, then, that Moscow can undertake major interventionary operations abroad with the assurance that it will be able to employ these overseas basing facilities to the extent desired. If the host government supports the Soviets' interventionary purposes and there is no risk of incurring significant retaliation, it will presumably allow the Soviets to continue using the port or airstrip in question. If, however, the host government opposes the Soviet action (as many Moslem states opposed the Soviet intervention in

Afghanistan), it may close its ports and airfields to Soviet forces. Under these circumstances, Soviet "basing facilities" in the Third World cannot be considered a major addition to Moscow's net power-projection capability.

A similar assessment pertains to the Soviets' use of "proxy" forces. While the deployment of Cuban forces in Angola and Ethiopia has certainly enabled these two Soviet allies to hold their enemies at bay, they have not provided lasting security and thus constitute a continuing drain on Soviet resources. The much smaller Cuban deployment in Grenada did not significantly alter the outcome of events in that country, and the Cuban military presence in Nicaragua proved to be something of a diplomatic liability when the Sandinistas decided to pursue the Contadora route to regional stability. At this point, moreover, it appears unlikely that Havana can provide additional forces in any strength for new Soviet adventures elsewhere, while Moscow's other major Third World allies—Vietnam, Syria, South Yemen, and Libya—are either bogged down in local conflicts (Vietnam in Cambodia, Syria in Lebanon, and Libya in Chad) or too small and weak to be of much use in a major military undertaking outside of their own territory.[65] The United States, on the other hand, has several allies with significant power-projection capabilities of their own. Britain and France, for instance, each have "rapid-response" forces of various types along with aircraft carriers and other long-range interventionary assets, and the United States can seek assistance from a large number of Third World countries.

Thus, even after factoring in basing arrangements and proxy forces, it is apparent that the Soviet Union suffers from a significant "power-projection gap" vis-à-vis the United States.[66] Moreover, there is no evidence that Moscow is trying to close this gap in a hurry. Hence, only two vessels of the *Ivan Rogov* class were introduced between 1978 and 1986, a time in which the United States was significantly expanding its own amphibious assault capabilities. Similarly, despite some improvements in Soviet air-transport capabilities, the VTA aircraft inventory is actually declining in numbers, while the U.S. inventory is growing in both numbers and total capacity. And while the Soviets will soon deploy their first catapult-equipped aircraft carrier, they are proceeding very slowly and cautiously in the development of carrier technology and thus can be expected to lag behind the United States in this area for many decades to come. In no field can we detect a Soviet effort to rapidly expand its power-projection capability or to significantly diminish its relative disadvantage vis-à-vis the United States.

We must, therefore, conclude that there is no evidence for Secretary Weinberger's assertions that the Soviets have vastly enhanced their power-projection capabilities in recent years or have made the expansion of such capabilities a major military priority. Indeed, the very opposite appears to be the case. While the Soviets have undertaken vigorous efforts to enhance their strategic nuclear capabilities and to modernize their conventional forces in

Europe, they have devoted relatively scant resources to the development of long-distance interventionary capabilities.

This allocation of resources is fully consistent with Soviet military doctrine, which stresses the absolute primacy for preparedness for an all-out conflict with the West—which, it is assumed, will entail intensive combat on the Soviet periphery. As suggested by Commander Steve F. Kime of the National War College: "Soviet military doctrine, reflecting the realities of Soviet politics and history, is concerned with the big war—it is oriented around major conflict and the security of the homeland."[67]

This "continental" approach to security has, in Kime's view, provided Moscow with a vast reservoir of conventional military capabilities that it can draw upon when forces are needed for power-projection elsewhere. The forces so employed are not, however, seen by Moscow as power-projection forces per se; instead, "These capacities are 'spinoffs' of Soviet continental power and are inherent in the massive forces maintained in the USSR and at her periphery."[68] But while the Soviets may choose to employ some of these forces in a power-projection mode, they will never do so at the risk of diminishing their capacity for continental defense. Soviet leaders may "entertain military options at long distances," Kime observed in *Air Force*, "but they judge such options more in terms of *opportunities* than in terms of *necessities* in the service of Soviet national interests." Such "necessities," he added, "exist only in Eurasia and in the intercontinental nuclear equation" (emphasis added).[69]

As Soviet main-force units have gained in strength and mobility, the "spinoff" capacity of Soviet continental power has naturally grown in proportion—thus enabling the Soviets to exercise greater boldness in their pursuit of "opportunities" in the Third World. As Rajan Menon has shown in *Soviet Power and the Third World*, the Soviets were rarely willing to risk the employment of their forces outside of Eurasia in the 1950s and 1960s—a period during which Moscow perceived a significant disadvantage vis-à-vis the West in nuclear arms and modern conventional forces—but were much more likely to consider such moves in the 1970s, when Soviet forces had begun to reap the fruits of the massive military buildup undertaken by Khrushchev's successors in the mid-1960s.[70] But while the Soviets have certainly been more forthcoming in their assistance to distant Third World allies (particularly with respect to arms transfer, military training, and logistical support), such endeavors remain in the realm of *opportunities,* not *necessities,* and thus Moscow has been very careful to avoid making any statement that would imply a commitment to employ regular Soviet forces in the defense of these countries.[71] Moreover, in their post-Brezhnev reassessment of the Third World, Soviet leaders have become much more mindful of the risks associated with such opportunities and, accordingly, have reasserted the primacy of Soviet forces' continental defense responsibilities.[72]

Clearly, this approach precludes an explicit Soviet policy of systematically seeking Third World beachheads from which to impede Western access to strategic raw materials. The Soviets may, in line with their opportunistic approach to Third World upheavals, take advantage of local conditions in order to gain influence in areas of geostrategic interest to the West—but such gains are the product of circumstances, not of a conscious policy of resources denial. Indeed, this ad hoc approach can, and has, led to important Soviet *reversals* in areas of such interest. Thus, when Moscow was invited by Ethiopia to help resist Somalia's 1977 invasion of the Ogaden, the Soviets responded with massive arms aid and the airlift of Cuban troops—even though this ultimately meant the loss of Soviet access to the strategic Somalian base at Berbera on the Gulf of Aden.[73] "If the USSR is primarily interested in putting itself . . . in positions to sever Middle East oil lines," Dunn observed in 1980, "one would have expected that Moscow would have refrained from taking actions that threatened access to Berbera. In fact, by supporting the Ethiopian cause, it did exactly the opposite."[74] The Soviets have behaved in a similar fashion on other occasions, thus removing any credibility from Reagan-administration claims that the Soviets have been guided by a strategy of resources denial.[75]

Conclusion

In line with Moscow's "continental" view of the strategic equation, the Soviets have devoted only a small fraction of their overall military capability to power projection as such, while relying on the occasional use of other forces to resolve those crises or opportunities that may arise in the Third World. This means that Moscow can draw upon a large reservoir of Soviet-based forces when circumstances require their deployment elsewhere—but these forces are not intended for long-range power projection, and they are not likely to be squandered in an unpredictable Third World contingency far from Soviet territory. As suggested by Dennis Gormley: "It is doubtful that Moscow would be willing to tie up—and possibly sacrifice—critical theater resources earmarked for the Eurasian land mass on such potentially risky ventures."[76]

Given this bias, Soviet main-force units have not, for the most part, been designed principally for power projection. Soviet ground forces, which are heavily equipped with tanks and armored vehicles, may prevail in "a certain type of Eurasian land battle," Dunn observed in 1980, but they are "inherently . . . less 'projectable' " to distant Third World areas.[77] And while naval ships and aircraft designed for antisubmarine warfare on the high seas may possess some residual capacity for support of infantry operations ashore, they obviously cannot provide much protection against enemy aircraft designed for close support of tactical forces.

By building up large and well-equipped forces to conduct an all-out war with NATO, Moscow has not necessarily acquired a corresponding capacity to fight effectively in distant Third World contingencies. Given the distinctive characteristics of long-range interventionary operations, the United States—with its historic commitment to the power-projection mission—has consistently maintained a large inventory of forces configured for this specific function. Lacking such specialized forces and not being heavily dependent on distant markets, sources of raw materials, and allies, the Soviet Union obviously has a much less significant capacity to conduct interventionary operations at any distance from its borders.

Notes

1. The Joint Chiefs of Staff have described power-projection capabilities in the following fashion:

> Broadly speaking, the projection of military power involves a nation's ability to use its military forces for influencing events beyond its borders, particularly in areas where it has little or no permanent military presence. Power projection may entail the direct defense of national interests in forward areas, peacetime demonstration of military reach and striking power, or material and advisory support to friendly indigenous forces. (Organization of the Joint Chiefs of Staff, *United States Military Posture for FY 1982.* Washington, D.C., 1981, p. 43. Hereinafter cited as JCS, *Military Posture FY82*.)

2. Caspar Weinberger, Statement before the Senate Committee on Budget, Washington, D.C., March 3, 1982 (U.S. Department of Defense transcript).

3. Caspar Weinberger, Remarks before the Council on Foreign Relations, New York, N.Y., April 20, 1982 (U.S. Department of Defense transcript). (Hereinafter cited as Weinberger, Remarks 4-20-82.)

4. U.S. Department of Defense, *Soviet Military Power* (Washington, D.C.: 1981), p. 83. (Hereinafter cited as DoD, *SMP 1981*.)

5. *U.S. Department of Defense, Soviet Military Power 1983* (Washington, D.C., 1983), p. 83. (Hereinafter cited as DoD, *SMP 1983*.)

6. For a description of U.S. power-projection assets and an outline of the Reagan administration's expansion program, see Caspar Weinberger, *Annual Report to the Congress, Fiscal Year 1986* (Washington, D.C., 1985), pp. 193–204.

7. DoD, *SMP 1983*, p. 11.

8. U.S. Department of Defense, *Soviet Military Power 1985* (Washington, D.C., 1985), p. 113. (Hereinafter cited as DoD, *SMP 1985*.)

9. DoD, *SMP 1981*, p. 87.

10. Noel C. Koch, "The Third World: Cockpit of Conflict," *Defense/86* (March/April 1986): 38.

11. Weinberger, Remarks 4-20-82.

12. Dennis M. Gormley, "The Direction and Pace of Soviet Force Projection Capabilities," *Survival*, 24, no. 6 (November 1982): 266. For somewhat similar

assessments, see Michael T. Klare, "The Power Projection Gap," *The Nation* (June 9, 1979): 671–76; and Barry R. Posen and Stephen W. Van Evera, "Overarming and Underwhelming," *Foreign Policy* (fall 1980): 102–7.

13. For further information on these and other sources in the field, see William Arkin, *Research Guide to Current Military and Strategic Affairs* (Washington, D.C.: Institute for Policy Studies, 1981).

14. For discussion of this point, see Cmdr. Steve F. Kime, "Power Projection, Soviet Style," *Air Force* (December 1980): 50–54.

15. International Institute for Strategic Studies, *The Military Balance 1986–1987* (London, IISS: 1986), p. 41. (Hereinafter cited as IISS, *Military Balance 86–87*.) See also James Hansen, "Soviet Vanguard Forces: Naval Infantry," *National Defense* (May–June 1986): 51–60; and Lt. Col. Roger M. Jaroch, "Amphibious Forces: Theirs and Ours," *U.S. Naval Institute Proceedings* (November 1982): 41–48.

16. See Graham H. Turbiville, "Warsaw Pact Amphib Ops in Northern Europe," *Marine Corps Gazette* (October 1976): 20–27.

17. Hansen, "Naval Infantry," p. 52.

18. Jaroch, "Amphibious Forces," p. 44.

19. Keith A. Dunn, "Power Projection or Influence: Soviet Capabilities for the 1980s," *Naval War College Review* (September-October 1980): p. 40.

20. Michael MccGwire, "Parallel Naval Developments," in Michael MccGwire, ed., *Soviet Naval Developments* (New York: Praeger, 1973), p. 165.

21. IISS, *Military Balance 86–87*, p. 37. See also Lt. Col. William P. Baxter, "The Soviet Threat from the Sky," *Army* (April 1981): 41–43; Capt. Edwin W. Besch, "Soviet Airborne and Air Assault Forces—Part I," *U.S. Naval Institute Proceedings* (July 1986): 94–98; James Hansen, "Soviet Vanguard Forces—Airborne," *National Defense* (April 1986): 25–32, 44; and Graham Turbiville, "Soviet Airborne Forces," *Army* (April 1976): 18–27.

22. DoD, *SMP 1981*, p. 91.

23. Besch, "Soviet Airborne and Air Assault Forces—Part I," p. 95.

24. V.D. Sokolovsky, *Soviet Military Strategy* (New York: Crane, Russak, 1975), p. 250. See also Gormley, "The Direction and Pace," pp. 269–71. On the Soviet emphasis on the early seizure and destruction of NATO C^3 and nuclear weapons sites, see Michael MccGwire, *Military Objectives in Soviet Foreign Policy* (Washington, D.C.: Brookings Institution, 1987).

25. See Hansen, "Soviet Vanguard Forces—Airborne," pp. 30–32; and Baxter, "Soviet Threat from the Sky," p. 43.

26. Gormley, "The Direction and Pace," p. 270.

27. Jiri Valenta, "From Prague to Kabul: The Soviet Style of Invasion," *International Security*, 5, no. 2 (fall 1980): 134–35.

28. JCS, *Military Posture FY82*, pp. 47–48. See also Gormley, "The Direction and Pace," pp. 272–74.

29. DoD, *SMP 1981*, p. 91.

30. IISS, *Military Balance 86–87*, p. 37. See also Besch, "Soviet Airborne and Air Assault Forces—Part I," pp. 94–98; Maj. Roger E. Bort, "Air Assault Brigades," *Military Review* (October 1983): 21–38; and Hansen, "Soviet Vanguard Forces—Airborne," pp. 27–28.

31. Capt. Edwin W. Besch, "Soviet Airborne and Air Assault Forces—Part II," *U.S. Naval Institute Proceedings* (August 1986): 99.

32. Ibid. See also Hansen, "Soviet Vanguard Forces—Airborne," p. 27.

33. See Bort, "Air Assault Brigades," pp. 27–32.

34. IISS, *Military Balance 86–87*, pp. 37, 41.

35. See Robert S. Boyd, "Spetsnaz: Soviet Innovation in Special Forces," *Air University Review* (November-December 1986): 63–69; Joseph Hansen, "Soviet Vanguard Forces—Spetsnaz," *National Defense* (March 1986): 29–37; David R. Kohler, "Spetsnaz," *U.S. Naval Institute Proceedings* (August 1987): 47–55; Viktor Suvorov, "Spetsnaz: The Soviet Union's Special Forces," *International Defense Review* (September 1983): 1209–16; and "US and Soviet Special Operations," *Armed Forces Journal* (February 1987): 48–52.

36. See Hansen, "Soviet Vanguard Forces—Spetsnaz," p. 36; Valenta, "Prague to Kabul," pp. 135–36.

37. An artist's impression of a Spetsnaz training facility appears in DoD, *SMP 1984*, p. 69. See also Boyd, "Spetsnaz," pp. 65–67; and Suvorov, "Spetsnaz," pp. 1212–15.

38. According to Suvorov, a Soviet army defector writing under a pseudonym, "Spetsnaz units are not tasked . . . to engage in guerrilla warfare." Suvorov, "Spetsnaz," p. 1210.

39. IISS, *Military Balance 86–87*, p. 39. See also John M. Collins, *U.S.–Soviet Military Balance 1980–1985* (Washington, D.C.: Pergamon-Brassey's, 1985), pp. 115, 253; Besch, "Soviet Airborne and Assault Forces—Part II," pp. 99–101; and William Schneider, "Soviet Military Airlift," *Air Force* (March 1980): 80–86.

40. Collins, *U.S.–Soviet Balance*, p. 253.

41. IISS, *Military Balance 86–87*, p. 27.

42. Collins, *U.S.–Soviet Balance*, p. 255.

43. Dunn, "Power Projection or Influence," p. 35.

44. Gormley, "The Direction and Pace," p. 274.

45. Ibid. See also Dunn, "Power Projection or Influence," p. 35.

46. IISS, *Military Balance 86–87*, pp. 23, 40. See also Collins, *U.S.–Soviet Balance*, pp. 214–15.

47. JCS, *Military Posture FY82*, p. 47. See also Gormley, "The Direction and Pace," pp. 268–69.

48. Dod, *SMP 1981*, pp. 50–51.

49. For comparison of U.S. and Soviet vessels, see *Jane's Fighting Ships 1986–87* (London: Jane's, 1986), pp. 593–94.

50. Ibid., p. 556. See also *Jane's All the World's Aircraft 1986–87* (London: Jane's, 1986), pp. 273–74; and Collins, *U.S.–Soviet Balance*, pp. 226–27.

51. See Dod, *SMP 1985*, pp. 99–101. See also *Jane's Fighting Ships 1986–87*, p. 556.

52. IISS, *Military Balance 86–87*, pp. 39, 41–45.

53. Dunn, "Power Projection or Influence," p. 33. For characteristics of U.S. and Soviet tactical aircraft, see Collins, *U.S.–Soviet Balance*, pp. 218–22.

54. In addition to authors cited in notes 55–57, see Posen and Van Evera, "Overarming and Underwhelming," pp. 102–7; and Rajan Menon, *Soviet Power and the Third World* (New Haven: Yale University Press, 1986), pp. 90–128.

55. Gormley, "The Direction and Pace," p. 274.

56. Dunn, "Power Projection or Influence," pp. 44–45.

57. Ibid., p. 45.

58. International Institute for Strategic Studies, *Strategic Survey 1980–1981* (London, IISS: 1981), p. 17.

59. Dod, *SMP 1983*, p. 11.

60. Dod, *SMP 1984*, p. 123. See also Richard Shultz, "Soviet Use of Surrogates to Project Power into the Third World," *Parameters*, 16, no. 3 (1986): 32–42.

61. Dod, *SMP 1984*, pp. 124–26.

62. Joint Chiefs of Staff, *Dictionary of Military and Associated Terms* (Washington, D.C., 1984), p. 246. For discussion, see Dunn, "Power Projection or Influence," p. 40.

63. "Military Installations and Properties," *Defense/85*, p. 51.

64. See Dunn, "Power Projection or Influence," pp. 40–43; and Menon, *Soviet Power*, pp. 231–34.

65. For discussion, see "Soviet Geopolitical Momentum: Myth or Menace?" *Defense Monitor*, 25, no. 5 (1986): 1–32; and Menon, *Soviet Power*, pp. 125–27.

66. The author first uses the term *power-projection gap* in Klare, "Power Projection Gap," p. 676.

67. Kime, "Power Projection," p. 53. See also Steve F. Kime, "The Soviet View of War," *Comparative Strategy*, 2, no. 3 (1980): 205–21.

68. Kime, "Power Projection," p. 51.

69. Ibid., p. 53.

70. Menon, *Soviet Power*, pp. 1–18.

71. Ibid., pp. 74–88.

72. See Francis Fukuyama, *Moscow's Post-Brezhnev Reassessment of the Third World* (Santa Monica, Calif.: Rand, 1986).

73. Menon, *Soviet Power*, pp. 230–31.

74. Dunn, "Power Projection of Influence," p. 42.

75. Menon, *Soviet Power*, pp. 231–33.

76. Gormley, "Direction and Pace," p. 274.

77. Dunn, "Power Projection or Influence," p. 54.

7

Third World Clients and Third World Dilemmas for Soviet Foreign Policy

Melvin Goodman

I n 1945, the Soviet Union was a continental power whose military focus was the defense of the homeland and whose military reach was limited to regions contiguous with its own borders. Today it is a global power with worldwide naval deployments and the ability to monitor Western naval forces; it has gained access to naval and air facilities in strategically located client states and is a factor to be considered in any regional crisis or conflict. This expanded scope of activities, moreover, is backed by economic and political capabilities for projecting influence in Africa, Asia, and Latin America that would have been impossible in the first years after World War II.

Moscow's success in achieving many of its Third World objectives—securing a military position in every major region of the globe, challenging the West and China, and influencing the governments of key regional states—has been accomplished almost entirely through the use of military instruments of policy. Through military assistance and the use of surrogate forces, the Soviets have served the national security needs of key Third World countries and have reaped the benefits. More than a dozen friendship and cooperation treaties have been signed with various Third World states that form a framework of Soviet global interests.

The evolution of the USSR's Third World policy since the mid-1950s has reflected its perceived national interests and its ability to capitalize on international developments. Although ideology has shaped Moscow's world view, it has not been a major factor in determining Soviet interests or behavior. And though its policy in the Third World has been keyed to its ambitions vis-à-vis the United States, Moscow has not allowed concern for bilateral relations with the United States to deter it from pursuing its global interests.

The scope of Soviet military activities in the Third World expanded significantly in the 1960s and 1970s, when the USSR began a steady increase in the size, capability, and range of operations of its forces in support of Soviet political goals. The rapid and impressive expansion of the Soviet navy since the 1960s has led to a continuous naval presence in the Mediterranean, the Indian Ocean, the South Atlantic off the coast of West Africa, and the South China Sea. Soviet naval forces now use facilities for a variety of purposes in about a dozen Third World countries that provide the USSR with intelligence and surveillance capabilities, various training opportunities, and support for Soviet interests abroad. Soviet naval forces abroad underscore Moscow's commitment to specific policies or local regimes and must be taken into account at times of regional crises.[1]

Despite the long list of Soviet successes in the Third World, which must include Angola, Cuba, Ethiopia, Syria, and Vietnam, the USSR has confronted serious setbacks in such key nations as Egypt, Guinea, and Somalia and has encountered problems that promise to become more intractable in the near term. Soviet operational planning has not helped Arab client regimes against the Israelis over the years, nor has it led to any sustained success for Ethiopian forces against the Eritreans. Soviet inability to train and discipline the Afghan army is a major reason for Moscow's inability to limit the insurgency in Afghanistan, which has become more pervasive since the Soviet invasion in December 1979. The Soviets have had even less success in translating their limited military influence in key Third World states into political and diplomatic influence. Huge amounts of military assistance to Arab clients have not led to a Soviet role at various Arab–Israeli negotiations since 1973 or in talks in southern Africa since the late 1970s that dealt with Angola, Mozambique, Namibia, and Rhodesia.

The Soviets themselves have acknolwedged more recently that the appeal of Soviet-style orthodox formulas for the Third World has declined significantly. Soviet party officials and academicians have recorded that the completion of the "first stage" of the national liberation movement has been completed. The "second stage," which will involve economic advancement and independence, is understood by the USSR to offer fewer opportunities to aid national liberation struggles and increasing demands for economic assistance. At the same time, the deterioration of East–West relations from 1975 to 1985 meant that the increased requests for economic aid competed for limited resources with a Soviet military establishment trying to match the Western military buildup and with the non-Soviet Warsaw Pact states demanding greater amounts of Soviet assistance.

In addition to a series of economic problems that will place limits on Moscow's ability to increase assistance to Third World clients, there are a series of political factors that will complicate the expansion of Soviet influence. In such key states as Afghanistan, Angola, Ethiopia, Mozambique, and Nicaragua, the Soviets are backing either "weak" regimes without legitimate authority or clients that are facing strong insurgency movements. The USSR, in fact, is no longer primarily a supporter of national liberation movements but has become a counterinsurgency power. This places the USSR in the awkward position of supervising a military process that generally weakens the economic development of these states because of the costs of fighting insurgencies.

The introduction of Soviet force also creates a series of regional problems for the Soviets. For example, one can identify diplomatic and political problems in the Middle East and Southwest Asia following the invasion of Afghanistan or in Southeast Asia following the Soviet buildup in Vietnam, particularly in Cam Ranh Bay and Da Nang, which provides Moscow with its only operating military base between Vladivostok and the east coast of Africa. The USSR's growing presence in Vietnam includes naval units, a composite air unit, and a growing infrastructure for communications, intelligence collection, and logistics support.[2]

The Soviets, in some areas, have become victims of their own success. Since the late 1960s, they have dramatically increased their military agreements and deliveries in the Third World, doubled the number of Soviet military personnel outside the Warsaw Pact countries and Afghanistan, and sharply increased naval deployments over an expanded area through access to naval facilities and ports of call. The expansion of Soviet capabilities has had geostrategic benefits for the USSR, enabling it to break out of its traditional realm in the Baltic Sea and the Black Sea. Soviet air and naval power can now be projected virtually anywhere in the world; Moscow enjoys intelligence-gathering facilities in strategic regional locations, and Soviet military air transport can deliver tanks, troops, and self-propelled artillery into key outlying locations.[3] Moscow's expanded presence, however, has led to serious contradictions and complications in Soviet policy as choices have to be made between Iran and Iraq as well as Syria and Iraq in the Middle East, Algeria and Morocco as well as Algeria and Libya in North Africa, and Somalia and Ethiopia on the Horn of Africa. Specific Soviet involvements in Afghanistan, Cuba, Syria, and Vietnam, moreover, have led to regional problems in Southwest Asia, Latin America, the Middle East, and Southeast Asia, respectively.

Afghanistan as Success and Failure

The invasion of Afghanistan in 1979 stands out as an example of the introduction of military power in one state that has created a series of problems for the Soviets elsewhere in the region. On the one hand, there are military benefits associated with a protracted Soviet presence in Afghanistan. Soviet forces are in a combat environment for the first time since the second World War, and Afghanistan has become a huge testing ground for fighter aircraft, armored helicopters, and various rocket launchers. Soviet writings refer to various new concepts dealing with command and control, and Soviet forces have essentially switched from tank-heavy mechanized units to small-unit tactics and helicopter operations.[4] Afghanistan's difficult terrain and poor transportation network made progress against the insurgency slow and costly, and ultimately the Soviets seem to have realized that the strategic advantages of any "victory" were to be had, if at all, only after a long, expensive effort.

On the other hand, counterinsurgency problems in Afghanistan as well as in Angola, Ethiopia, Kampuchea, and Nicaragua in general exacerbate the risks of getting deeply involved in a client state, the problems of sinking excessive investments into unsteady political systems, and—consequently—the economic problems within the world socialist system. The Afghan invasion has further damaged already poor relations with Pakistan and Iran and has created strains with such clients as India and Iraq. These states, like others in the Third World, see the USSR engaging in heavy-handed direct military intervention, clumsily trying to prop up an ineffective puppet regime. The invasion undermines the USSR's claim to be the "natural ally" of Third World nonaligned countries as well as similar claims made on Moscow's behalf by such countries as Cuba and India.

Regional Implications of the Soviet Invasion of Afghanistan

Maintaining the current Afghan regime in power and rebuilding the Afghan military has required a long-term Soviet military presence in the country involving some 100,000 Soviet troops. A decision to move decisively against the insurgents would have required a massive increase in the Soviet presence—a move Moscow clearly was not prepared to make. Indeed, General Secretary Gorbachev announced on February 8, 1988, that the USSR was prepared to begin the complete withdrawal of Soviet forces from Afghanistan in May 1988 and that a large number of troops would be removed in the early stages of withdrawal regardless of whether the Afghans manage to agree on an interim government.[5] The Soviet leadership thus has stated an interest in troop withdrawal despite its failure to deal with the pervasive nature of the Afghan insurgency or to leave behind an Afghan army that can deal with the insurgent problem. Ultimately, under the April 1988 Geneva Accords, the Soviet withdrawal from Afghanistan actually began.

Moscow's preoccupation with its problems and basic objectives within Afghanistan has presumably left little time or incentive to consider the impact of its position there on its interests in the Middle East and Southwest Asia. The Soviets undoubtedly want to expand their influence in this broader region, and their decision to invade Afghanistan may have reflected, in part, their long-term regional objectives. The invasion, however, undermined the USSR's position in the immediate region and may have left a permanent scar on Soviet relations with the area. This could limit Moscow's ability both to capitalize on its projection of force and to arrange a favorable and enduring shift in the regional balance of power, particularly in view of the long period that it will take to consolidate control over such a defiant country and tenacious resistance.

Most Third World states, while physically and psychologically far removed from Afghanistan, were offended by the brutality of the Soviet takeover—particularly the execution of Amin. A prolonged and ruthless Soviet effort to destroy the Islamic insurgency in Afghanistan will have continuing repercussions on the perceptions of these states, particularly those that are Muslim. Soviet clients, especially the ones that have accommodated a Soviet military presence and concluded a friendship treaty with the USSR, must not have doubts about the desirability and risks of their involvement with Moscow. And the states bordering the USSR or Afghanistan, specifically Iran and Pakistan, clearly are suspicious of future Soviet objectives in the region.

Pakistan

Moscow's policy in Afghanistan undermined its relations with Pakistan, which moved closer to both the United States and China. Pakistan provided refuge to over two million Afghan refugees, served as the main staging area for insurgent operations, and joined the forefront of those Islamic nations demanding the withdrawal of Soviet forces. The Soviet invasion has increased Islamabad's fear of the USSR and the Soviets have tried to play on this fear, as well as on Pakistan's internal difficulties, to pull that country into accommodation with the Afghan regime.

The Soviets have combined blandishment and pressure to encourage Pakistan to limit assistance to the Afghan insurgents. They have tried to persuade Islamabad that it is "not too late" to cease all aid to the rebels. They have begun to increase their economic assistance to Pakistan despite Islamabad's continued refusal to consider a settlement to the Afghan problem without an early withdrawal of Soviet troops.

The Soviets simultaneously have put pressure on Pakistan, taking advantage of the weak central authority in Pakistan. Soviet commentary implies that Pakistan's security position will be difficult if it does not stop supporting the insurgents. The USSR has threatened to exercise "hot pursuit" against the Afghan rebels, and there have been violations of Pakistani airspace and bombing of refugee camps by Afghan and Soviet aircraft.[6] Soviet rhetoric supports antiregime elements within Pakistan, particularly the Movement for Restoration of Democracy.

Moscow could also try to intimidate Islamabad by encouraging the Afghans to heat up the campaign for an independent Pushtunistan or by encouraging the ambitions of such anti-Pakistani tribal groups as the Buluchis. Pakistani Baluchistan has been in periodic rebellion against the central government for decades, and some Baluchis are probably willing to probe for signs of Soviet willingness to support their efforts to secure an independent Baluchistan. A long-term Soviet military presence in Afghanistan will mean greater tensions between Afghanistan and Pakistan, which will in turn increase the Soviet temptation to use the Baluchi and Pushtun issues against the Islamabad government. Henry Bradsher has argued, for example, that Soviet motives for protecting a new client state in Afghanistan could "coincide nicely with a Soviet desire" to acquire a port on the Indian Ocean at some Baluchi harbor such as Gwadar, but any additional thrust of Soviet power in the region will encounter political resistance from such traditional antagonists in the region as Iran and such traditional allies as India.[7]

Iran

The Soviet presence in Afghanistan has been a source of major friction in Soviet–Iranian relations, hampering dialogue and feeding mutual suspicions. The shah opposed the communist takeover in Kabul in April 1978, and the Khomeini regime has consistently condemned both the Soviets' intervention of December 1979 and their continuing presence. Iran has taken in over a million Afghan refugees and has called for an Islamic solution in Afghanistan and a Soviet withdrawal. Tehran has voiced strong support for the insurgents, permits insurgent groups to operate from Iranian territory, and—according to Soviet media commentary—trains and equips some of these groups.

Soviet media frequently criticize Iran's attitude and argue that the insurgency is a creature of the United States, which is also alleged to be supporting counterrevolution in Iran. In late May 1983, for the first time, *Izvestia* charged that Iran was allowing insurgents to use its territory as a base of operation.[8] An *Izvestia* article in late July contained a more detailed indictment of Iranian support for the insurgents and claimed these activities had been steadily increasing.[9] More recently, *Izvestia* charged that the Iranian air force and ground forces had "carried out over 60 acts of aggression" against Afghanistan and that Iran has "aligned itself with the United States and its allies" in participation in subversive activity against the Kabul government.[10]

Moscow has responded to its perceptions of Iran's activity by stepping up its own military operations on the Afghan-Iranian border. A major incursion of Soviet forces into Iranian territory occurred in April 1982, the same month that Moscow signed an arms agreement with Iraq and a month after an article in *Pravda* revealed Soviet frustration with Iran.[11] While the incursion itself may have been inadvertent, the Soviet willingness to operate in close proximity to the border and risk antagonizing Tehran revealed an increasing sensitivity to the actions of Iranian-supported insurgents and a decreasing concern about potential damage to bilateral relations. The *Pravda* article provided the first outpouring of Soviet grievances against the Iranian regime. It listed a long series of complaints, including closure of a Soviet consulate, reductions in embassy staff, and denial of visas to Soviet journalists. This and subsequent articles have warned that right-wing elements close to Khomeini are succeeding in whipping up anti-Soviet sentiment. Although avoiding criticism of Khomeini himself, these official commentaries indicate that the Soviets do not believe significant improvement in bilateral relations will occur while he remains in power.

Since the naming of Eduard Shevardnadze as minister of foreign affairs in July 1985, however, the Soviets have signaled that they do not intend to let differences with Iran over Afghanistan interfere with broader interests in Iran. In September 1985, for example, a group of Soviet experts visited Iran and agreed that expanding hydrotechnical facilities on border rivers was the most obvious direction for future cooperation. Soviet and Iranian officials met in January 1986 to plan for the tenth session of the Permanent Committee for Economic Cooperation between the USSR and Iran, which was held in December of that year. (The ninth season had been scheduled for 1980 but postponed repeatedly.) In addition to discussing a joint shipping company on the Caspian Sea and sending Iranian gas exports to Europe through the USSR, the Permanent Committee discussed a possible joint project to build dams over the Aras and Atrak rivers along the border. The Iranians also want the Soviets to send back several hundred technicians who were pulled out of Iran in 1985 because of Iraqi air raids on major industrial projects, including a steel plant in the central Iranian city of Isfahan and several power stations.

On the political front in 1986, Soviet first deputy foreign minister Korniyenko visited Iran in February, which marked the highest-level Soviet official to visit Iran since the revolution. No tangible improvement resulted from the visit, but Korniyenko met with the Iranian oil minister regarding the resumption of natural gas shipments to the USSR, the level of hostile rhetoric subsided, and the promise of improved relations was restored. In June, the head of the Soviet diplomatic mission in Tehran delivered a message from General Secretary Gorbachev to Iranian president Khameini and, the following day, the director general of the Soviet State Committee on Economic and International Cooperation for Asia and the Middle East met with the Iranian deputy minister for international and economic affairs and announced the USSR's readiness to improve bilateral relations.[12]

Although there does appear to have been a shift in Soviet policy toward Iran under Gorbachev, relations between the two countries probably will be strained as long as Soviet troops remain in Afghanistan. Prior to the invasion of Afghanistan, the Soviets had used the crisis in U.S.–Iranian relations to strengthen their ties to the Khomeini regime and to improve their image as a defender of "antiimperialist" revolutionary causes. Although bilateral ties never became close, the invasion and occupation aroused latent anti-Sovietism in Iran's new leadership and triggered a protracted deterioration in relations. Iran's attitude had been reflected in numerous actions, including harsh anti-Soviet rhetoric, the postponed replacement of the Iranian ambassador to Moscow for a year,[13] and an assault on the Soviet embassy in Tehran in December 1982. The following year, the Iranians arrested a number of Tudeh Communist Party leaders, banned the party, and expelled eighteen Soviet officials for illegal intelligence activities. Public trials of Tudeh officials began in December 1983 and continued in 1984, culminating in prison sentences and some executions.

Continued, albeit sporadic, signs of anti-Soviet activity from Tehran indicates that those members of the Khomeini regime urging an active anti-Soviet posture have prevailed and that the Iranian leadership for the most part remains well aware of the history of Soviet intervention in its country in this century. In 1920, Soviet forces occupied Gilan—the northernmost province of Persia—in an attempt to rid the area of British forces. The following year, however, when Soviet policy shifted from active promotion of revolution to collaboration with national governments, the Soviets withdrew their forces. During the second World War, the Soviets occupied all of northern Iran and, along with British forces, secured Iran and the Persian Gulf corridor as an important supply line to the USSR. The Azerbaijan Democratic Republic was formed in 1945 with Soviet support, but heavy pressure from both the United States and the United Kingdom compelled Soviet forces to withdraw the following year. The Azerbaijan Democratic Republic collapsed when Iranian troops reentered the area on the pretext of supervising national elections.

Just as the Soviets used a friendship treaty with Afghanistan to justify their invasion of that country in 1979, the Soviets invoked the 1921 Russian–Persian Treaty to justify their occupation of Iran during the second World War. Article six of that agreement gives the USSR the right to introduce troops into Iran if a third party should try to carry out a policy of usurpation through armed intervention in Persia or should seek to use Persian territory as a base of operations against the Soviet Union. The article provides, however, that the Soviets would withdraw such troops when the danger to the USSR was removed.[14] Article five of the treaty commits both sides to prevent the presence on their territory of forces or organizations that might be regarded as a menace to the other side.[15] Immediately after the seizure of the U.S. embassy in Tehran in November 1979, the Iranian government announced the unilateral abrogation of articles five and six of the treaty. The Soviets have not formally responded to the Iranian action, and Moscow's continuing public affirmation of articles five and six provides the USSR a plausible rationale should it choose to intervene militarily in Iran.

India

India has long been one of the most important targets of Soviet attention in the Third World, both as a partner in containing China and as a cornerstone of Soviet influence with the nonaligned movement. The return of Indira Gandhi to power was reassuring to the Soviets who were confident of her continued interest in close ties with the Soviet Union and opposition to U.S. policies. The quick rescheduling of the late defense minister Dimitri Ustinov's trip to India in March 1984, which was postponed during then general secretary Andropov's final illness, testified to Moscow's interest in protecting its New Delhi connection. The assassination of Indira Gandhi and the accession to power of her son, Rajiv Gandhi, created a problem for the Soviets because he was not well known to the Soviet leadership and was rumored to have political and cultural ties to the West.

Despite Moscow's initial apprehension, India's dependence on the Soviets for economic and military aid remains considerable, and Indo-Soviet relations continue to be cordial. Although not comfortable with the Soviet position in Afghanistan, India has muted its criticism of the Soviet occupation. India was far more sensitive to any signs of change in U.S.–Pakistani relations as a result of the Soviet invasion of Afghanistan than to the Soviet occupation itself. India opposes greater superpower involvement in the region and is particularly concerned that significant U.S. arms sales to Pakistan will increase prospects for regional instability and conflicts. Indian media have expressed consistent opposition to U.S. arms deliveries to Islamabad and their potential use against India.[16] Moscow has played to this concern by highlighting U.S. sales of "sophisticated" arms to Islamabad and by charging Pakistan with a buildup of forces on the Indian border and the exacerbation of tension along that border.

Over the long run, however, the removal of Afghanistan as a buffer between the USSR and South Asia could well have prompted some segments of the Indian political elite to explore alternatives to dependence on the Soviet Union. The Soviet presence at the Khyber Pass would ultimately have been worrisome to India as well as Pakistan. Some Indians may have reexamined the Soviet–Indian friendship treaty in view of Moscow's use of a friendship and cooperation treaty with Afghanistan to justify the 1979 invasion. Although increased concern with the Soviets would not have driven New Delhi into the arms of the United States, Rajiv Gandhi's government signaled a willingness to improve relations with the United States, and agreements on military and computer sales were negotiated. The Indian government might also have recognized the importance of reducing tensions with both Pakistan and Bangladesh as a result of a protracted Soviet presence in Afghanistan and increased superpower involvement in the Indian Ocean.

The Islamic Community

The Islamic community was almost unanimous in its continuing opposition to the Soviet presence in Afghanistan. Most Arab states either signed the initial request for an urgent Security Council meeting to condemn the Soviet presence or have expressed indignation in some other form. Each year, the Islamic Conference Organization condemned the Soviet presence in Afghanistan and demanded the unconditional withdrawal of Soviet forces. At the meeting in Casablanca in 1984, for example, only Libya, South Yemen, and Syria refused to support the resolution, and only the latter two deigned to recognize the government in Kabul. At the February 1988 meeting in Kuwait, the organization passed another hardline resolution by consensus and allowed an Afghan insurgent delegation to lobby on behalf of the resolution.

Moscow's oppression of Islam forces in Afghanistan has reinforced fears of communism in the region and did considerable damage to the image of the USSR. The invasion and occupation also drew international attention to the drama in Southwest Asia, thereby distracting some attention from the Arab–Israeli conflict. The Soviets probably counted on Arab opposition to the U.S.–Israeli alliance to limit opposition to the invasion. Regional tensions and the acquisition of Soviet arms, Moscow may have reasoned, would turn out to be more important to many Islamic nations than events in Southwest Asia. To some degree this proved to be a valid view. Moscow's Arab clients have been reluctant to risk alienating the Soviets when other issues preoccupy them. For example:

Syria's isolation, involvement in Lebanon, and dependence on Soviet military support tempered its reaction to Afghanistan.

While the Soviet invasion of Afghanistan reinforced Iraq's mistrust of Moscow and further strained an already cool relationship, the war between Iraq and Iran forced Baghdad to moderate its opposition.

Libya's preoccupation with the United States offset what might have been a natural empathy for the Islamic insurgents in Afghanistan.

South Yemen's dependence on Soviet military assistance as well as the violent internal conflict in January 1986 assured support from Aden on the issue of Afghanistan.

Despite the pull of more pressing problems, however, the suspicions of these nations regarding Soviet intentions in Southwest Asia as well as Soviet support for the extremists in the civil strife in South Yemen have been fortified and could work to limit Moscow's ability to expand its influence with them.

Whatever Moscow's ultimate intentions toward the Persian Gulf in the wake of the Afghan invasion, for example, Saudi Arabia appears to believe that the USSR's objective is to encircle the conservative oil-producing nations and to gain access to oil. For the Saudis, this is the essential explanation for Soviet activities in Ethiopia, South Yemen, and North Yemen; for Moscow's readiness to take advantage of discord in Iran; and for the Soviet invasion of Afghanistan. The war on the Horn of Africa, the Camp David Accords, the ouster of the shah, and the seizure of the Grand Mosque added the Riyadh's anxiety.

The USSR and Saudi Arabia have not had diplomatic ties since the late 1930s. The Soviets have long been eager to reestablish their diplomatic presence in Riyadh, but all past efforts have been rebuffed. Since the Arab–Israeli war in October 1973, the Soviets frequently have signaled a willingness to resume a diplomatic dialogue. They have been doing so under Gorbachev as well. Soviet press commentaries occasionally contain long and sympathetic accounts of Saudi policies and often play upon Saudi disenchantment with the Camp David Accords. Both *Pravda* and *Izvestia* have emphasized that the Soviet Union and Saudi Arabia have never had any "irreconcilable" conflicts.[17]

The Afghan invasion certainly set back whatever hopes the Kremlin may have had about establishing diplomatic and commercial relations with Saudi Arabia. Moscow presumably was not surprised at Saudi Arabia's vehemently hostile response to the invasion, including Riyadh's willingness to strengthen its security relationship with the United States. The Soviet probably did not anticipate, however, Saudi ingenuity in organizing the Islamic Conferences, which have condemned the USSR, called for assistance to the insurgents, and stamped the current regime in Kabul as unacceptable. As a result, Riyadh now appears to the USSR as a more competent opponent of Soviet interests. The Soviets may have to cope with a Saudi Arabia that is even more willing to counter the spread of Soviet-supported radical regimes in the Arabian peninsula and more anxious to cement a "special relationship" with the United States. Soviet concern is reflected in its frequently expressed view that the United States is seeking to create a new alliance including Pakistan and the conservative Gulf states.

Despite Saudi differences with the Soviets over Afghanistan, there is no indication that Riyadh made any attempt to block the USSR's establishment of relations with two of the smaller Gulf states—Oman and the United Arab Emirates (UAE)—in the fall of 1985. The action by these states reflected their shifting perceptions of regional dynamics and ultimately could presage warmer relations between the Soviets and Saudi Arabia. Both were trying to demonstrate their international independence and desire not to be seen as puppets of the United States. Both had agreed to increase cooperation with the United States during the early 1980s, when they felt themselves threatened. At that time, Libya, Ethiopia, and South Yemen had signed a Tripartite Pact, which appeared to be aimed at increasing subversion against the conservative states of the region. The Soviet invasion of Afghanistan marked an additional threat to the region but, by 1985, the Soviet threat and the tripartite arrangement appeared far less substantial. At that point, Oman and the UAE probably felt that the time was right to establish some balance in their relations with the major powers in the region.

The Soviets have yet to gain from the establishment of diplomatic relations with the two conservative Gulf states. Oman has announced its support for the Soviet participation in an international conference on the Middle East, but had yet to allow the Soviets to establish a permanent diplomatic mission. The USSR has had diplomatic contacts with representatives of Qatar and Bahrain, but their is no sign of progress toward the establishment of diplomatic relations. Over the long term, the Saudis may become more receptive to Soviet overtures, particularly if they believe that the United States has abandoned its role as honest broker in Arab–Israeli negotiations and if they continue to have difficulty purchasing arms from the United States, but there is no indication of an exchange of diplomatic relations.

Syria as Independent Actor and Dependent Client

Hafez al-Assad's rule as president of Syria since 1970 has surpassed all expectations. Before Assad's accession to power, Syria had experienced more than a dozen coups and attempted coups following the departure of French forces in the wake of the second World War. In addition to bringing stability to Damascus, Assad has managed to emerge from wars with Israel and series of regional crises over the past decades as a major actor in the Middle East. The Syrian president is the key arbiter of Lebanese politics and has managed to limit Palestine Liberation Organization chairman Yasir Arafat's role in Lebanon. Assad has made it difficult for Arafat and Jordan's King Hussein to coordinate a strategy for the region that does not take into account Syrian policies and interests. He also continues to be the major Arab supporter of Iran in the Iran–Iraq war although, as a result, Assad has found himself isolated from the Arab mainstream on this issue. The Soviets have not supported Assad on all of these issues over the years, but it has been Soviet military and economic support that has enabled Assad to pursue his independent foreign policies.

Soviet setbacks in the Sudan and Egypt in the early 1970s, not long after Assad's emergence, led Moscow to broaden the base of Soviet ties in the Middle East and the Horn of Africa, as well as to concentrate on Syria as the new linchpin of the Soviet position in the region. The Soviets quickly made contacts with Algeria and Morocco on the Maghreb as well as South Yemen in the Arabian peninsula, but the key efforts were made with Iraq, Libya, and Syria in order to buttress the Soviet position in the region and to isolate Egyptian president Sadat. The Arab–Israeli October War of 1973 provided the Soviets with a major opportunity to mount an airlift and sealift of supplies to Egypt and Syria. In the first days of the war, however, the bulk of the supplies went to Damascus and the Soviets primarily seemed concerned about the deterioration of the Syrian position. Sadat wrote in his memoirs that the Soviets made an effort to arrange a cease-fire in the first day of fighting because of Moscow's concern for the Syrian–Israeli front.

Although the 1973 war dealt a major blow to Soviet–U.S. détente, the Soviets did manage to improve their regional position as a result of the hostilities. Iran and Iraq reestablished diplomatic relations after the war, and there was also a reconciliation between the Ba'athist regimes of Syria and Iraq, thus improving Assad's position in the region. The Soviets also profited from the solidarity of the oil-producing Arab states, which resulted in a total embargo on oil exports to the United States and led Soviet commentator Georgi Mirsky to write that the embargo dispelled the myth of the "alleged fragility and illusoriness of Arab solidarity."[18] The Soviets also benefited from the crisis within NATO due to Western European opposition to the supplying of Israel from U.S. bases in Europe. Differences over policy toward the oil embargo exacerbated tensions within the alliance still further, and the Common Market was strained by the failure of key Western European states to come to the aid of the Netherlands, which was hit by a total oil embargo.

As Robert Freedman has concluded, however, the central Soviet concern during the postwar period was Moscow's relations with Syria. Soviet leaders went out of their way to emphasize their support for President Assad during his trip to Moscow in 1974 and the final communiqué for the visit emphasized the need to "further strengthen" Syria defense capability. The Syrians "reemphasized the importance" of Soviet participation in all stages of the peace process in the Middle East, and the Soviets supported Syria's "lawful inalienable right" to use "all effective means" to free its occupied lands.[19] Soviet weapons deliveries in the wake of the war, which were largely paid for by wealthier Arab states and provided the Soviet Union with valuable hard-currency reserves, included more than 850 replacement tanks (primarily T-61s) and scores of MiG-21 fighter aircraft, and eventually made Syria the second largest importer of Soviet arms in the world with deliveries valued at over $5 billion during the five-year period 1976–80. (Two other important Middle Eastern states, Libya, Iraq, were first and third in purchases from the USSR during this period, according to annual studies by the U.S. Arms Control and Disarmament Agency.) Soviet-bloc arms supplies accounted for about 90 percent of Syrian weapons stockpiles during this period, and Soviet-bloc economic assistance concentrated on specific projects in Syria including railroad lines linking the port of Latakia with the industrial areas of the interior as well as oil refineries, phosphate plants, and land reclamation.

Although Syrian domestic unrest and regional isolation led the Assad government to improve its relations with the Soviets, Damascus continued to pursue its own policy interests in ways that challenged and even compromised Soviet goals in the region. Indeed, large-scale Soviet military deliveries—included a massive, continuous resupply in 1973 during the actual course of hostilities—not only failed to achieve military success for Syria in its various wars with Israel, such deliveries also did not lead to significant Soviet political influence in Damascus or diplomatic influence in the region. The Soviets, for example, played no role in the Syrian–Israeli disengagement agreement of 1974, which returned to Damascus territory lost in the 1973 war as well as the city of Kuneitra lost in 1967, and Soviet commentators even warned the Arabs that it was not in their interest to exclude the USSR from peace negotiations in the area.[20] More importantly, in 1976 President Assad sent 4,000 Syrian troops and 250 tanks into Lebanon in support of President Suleiman Franjieh against defiant units of his Lebanese army and the Palestine Liberation Organization. The Syrian presence eventually grew to more than 15,000 troops despite Arab opposition and significant Soviet criticism of Assad's efforts to plunge a "knife into the back" of the Palestinian movement.[21] In July, Soviet general secretary Brezhnev personally called for Assad to "take all possible measures to end its military operations against" the Palestinians.[22] Soviet pressure tactics eventually included delays in the deliveries of military equipment and spare parts and in signing a new arms agreement with Syria.

Despite the differences over Arab–Israeli negotiations in the Middle East, Lebanon, and the Iran–Iraq war, the Soviet–Syrian relationship remains close.[23] In terms of credits, military cooperation, and economic assistance, Syria is the favored Soviet client in the Middle East and trails only Cuba and Vietnam as the favored Soviet client in the Third World. President Assad traveled to Moscow in April 1987 and signed a communiqué that reaffirmed Moscow's willingness to upgrade Syria's military capacity. Western diplomats in the Middle East believe, moreover, that the Syrians will soon receive more sophisticated fighter aircraft, surface-to-surface and surface-to-air missiles, and additional military technicians. The Soviets have also rescheduled Syria's military debt from accumulated purchases, which is believed to have reached $15 billion. (In March 1987, the Soviets agreed to reschedule Egypt's military debt as well.)[24]

Nevertheless, Moscow's significant presence in Syria coupled with Syrian dependence on Soviet military equipment has not led to genuine Soviet influence over policy making in Damascus. As Alvin Z. Rubinstein has written: "What seems to be influence turns out instead to be the joint interests of the two parties."[25] The importance of Soviet military assistance and the presence of Soviet military and economic advisors were not sufficient to dissuade Syria from intervening in Lebanon against the Palestinians in 1976, to prevent Syrian attacks against the Palestinians in the 1980s, or to prevent Syrian–Iranian cooperation against Iraq since the beginning of the Iranian–Iraqi war in 1980. On several occasions, for example, the Soviets have been unable to convince the Syrians to reopen the pipeline that pumps Iraqi oil to the Mediterranean. Until 1987 the Soviets were unable to prevent Syrian authorities from confiscating Soviet weaponry sent to the PLO through Syria. The Soviets have also been opposed to Syrian support of the largest Shi'ite militia, the Amal, during its attack on Palestinian refuge camps in 1985 in addition to recent Syrian support for anti-Arafat rebels in the internecine battles of the fragmented PLO. Finally, Syrian troops remain in Lebanon at significant political, financial, and personal cost despite criticism from the Soviets.

Indeed, Soviet influence in the region has not progressed since Moscow's ouster from Egypt in 1972. The Soviets have been mere observers in the Arab–Israeli peace process since the October War in 1973 and they have been unable to exploit the Iranian–Iraqi war since 1980 in order to gain ground in the Persian Gulf. The Syrians have been unhelpful in Moscow's efforts to get a resumption of the Geneva conference or another international conference for a Middle East settlement, and the Soviets face the risk that Jordan's King Hussein's efforts to support an international conference could lead to a joint negotiating strategy with the PLO that could move Arafat closer to the West. The Soviets, moreover, were passive for the most part during the Israeli invasion of Lebanon and, except for a few statements critical of the invasion, did very little until full-scale war between Israel and Syria appeared to become a possibility. The Soviets pressured the Syrians to accept a cease-fire agreement at that point and, more importantly, delayed resumption of military supplies to the Syrians after Israel had attacked Syrian missile batteries in the Beka'a. The Soviets presumably realize that Syrian efforts to play a larger regional role in the Middle East merely complicate Moscow's goal of diminishing Western influence in the region.

Cuba as Independent Actor and Dependent Client

Just as Assad's rule as president of Syria since 1970 has lasted longer than most experts had expected, Fidel Castro's rule of almost three decades in Cuba, the longest tenure of any Cuban government since the island gained formal independence from Spain in 1902, was not anticipated. During this period, Castro has wiped out the 30 percent illiteracy rate that existed prior to the revolution, eradicated the system of sinecures that characterized the Batista regime as well as the widespread administrative corruption of the past, provided a new role for Cuban women, engaged in a series of militant activities throughout the Caribbean, Central America, and South America, and transformed Cuba's private-enterprise system into a centralized, state-controlled economy that resulted in growing inflation, disorganization, bureaucratic chaos, and inefficiency.[26] Meanwhile, Castro has emerged as a leader of the nonaligned movement and has committed his Soviet-equipped and trained armed forces to military roles in Africa. Castro has, indeed, established a large military presence in Africa and the Middle East totally out of proportion to Cuba's size and resources, and at the expense of the Cuban people. Castro sees his support for revolution as an integral and critical part of Cuba's foreign policy, and the revolutionary success in Nicaragua is perceived as a vindication of the Cuban emphasis on armed struggle.[27]

Cuba's relationship with the Soviet Union began in 1960 after a small guerrilla force had toppled a U.S.-backed dictatorship with only marginal involvement from the Moscow-oriented Communist party. These Soviet ties were probably the critical element that enabled the Castro regime to consolidate its revolution and to withstand U.S. efforts to weaken and isolate it within the hemisphere.[28] Since 1960, Moscow has provided Havana with about $9 billion in military equipment at nominal cost to Cuba, thus emphasizing Havana's importance to Soviet planners.[29] After very large deliveries from 1981 to 1985, Cuba in 1986 received modest quantities of new equipment, including MiG-23 aircraft, MI-8 helicopters, T-62 tanks, and BM-21 rocket launchers. The Soviets continue to support Cuba's military with 2,800 military advisors. Soviet military assistance, moreover, has transformed the Cuban Ministry of the Revolutionary Armed Forces (MINFAR) into a modern military establishment staffed with professionally trained individuals who attended military academies in Cuba or the Soviet Union. Under the leadership of Raul Castro, Fidel's brother, the MINFAR has emerged as Cuba's strongest institutional force and the major repository of specialists trained for Cuba's new organizational life along the lines of a Soviet bureaucratic system.[30]

During the 1980s, the Soviets also have furnished Cuba with over $4 billion in economic assistance and subsidies per year. Although Soviet subsidies declined somewhat in 1986 due to the lower market price of oil, and Soviet financial help was not sufficient to solve Cuba's hard-currency shortages, the USSR continues to provide most of Cuba's oil supplies and has agreed to provide Havana with 2.5 billion rubles in new credits between 1986 and 1990, an increase of 50 percent over the five-year period ending in 1985. One project that Soviet credits will fund is completion of the first phase (two of four reactors) of the Cienfuegos nuclear-power station.[31] Soviet–Cuban economic collaboration is coordinated through the Intergovernmental Soviet–Cuban Commission for Economic, Scientific, and Technological Cooperation, which was established in 1970 and held its first meeting in Havana in 1971. Cuba was admitted into COMECON the following year, which entitled it to "preferential" conditions in economic cooperation and meant an even closer coordination of the Cuban economy with commodity, trade, and planning agreements of the other Soviet-directed COMECON states.

Although Castro's ties to the Soviets have been essential to the survival of his regime and to his role as a regional and even global actor, there have been serious sources of disharmony in the Soviet–Cuban relationship and Cuba has not always been a compliant client state. In the late 1960s, for example, there were major Soviet–Cuban differences over the role of armed struggle, the capacity of communist parties in leading revolution in Third World countries, the appropriate economic-development model for Cuba, and the required level of Soviet military commitments to Cuba.[32] Throughout this period, the Cubans viewed armed struggle as the correct path to revolution, downgraded the leadership of Third World communist parties, and were not inclined to support bourgeois reformist governments in Latin America. Meanwhile, the new leadership in the Soviet Union took a more pragmatic and cautious approach to the Third World and was more interested in expanding state-to-state relations through normal trade and diplomatic ties, particularly in South America and Africa. The invasion of the Dominican Republic by the United States in 1965 was a sharp reminder of Cuba's national–security vulnerability in the region; the invasion of Grenada in 1983 was a similar reminder to the Soviets and led to Soviet–Cuban strains over the role of "armed struggle" in the region.

The chilly relationship that dominated Soviet–Cuban ties in the 1960s due to the Soviet emphasis on the "peaceful road to socialism" and the Cuban commitment to armed struggle as a revolutionary strategy was followed by a cycle of cooperation in the 1970s marked by the Soviet and Cuban ventures in Angola and Ethiopia. The Cuban interventions in Angola and Ethiopia not only demonstrated Cuba's usefulness to the Soviets in the Third World but also provided the Castro government with additional leverage in negotiating favorable economic- and military-aid agreements with the USSR throughout this period. By the end of the 1970s, most of Cuba's trade was conducted with COMECON countries (with the USSR alone accounting for 65 percent of Cuba's trade) and Soviet trade subsidies on Cuba's sugar exports and petroleum imports deepened the island's economic dependence on the USSR.[33] Cuba's Five-Year Plans during this period were coordinated closely with the USSR, and Cuba's General Directorate of Intelligence (DGI) began to work closely with the KGB. The Revolutionary Armed Forces also established closer ties with the Soviet military, and Soviet military deliveries (including the first MiG-23 fighter aircraft and several submarines) allowed Cuba to become a regional military force. Soviet military assistance thus allowed Cuba to maintain more diplomatic missions, intelligence operatives, and military troops abroad than any other developing country. As Robert

Pastor has concluded, the Soviets are willing to fill Cuba's "gap between its internal resources and its external capabilities . . . not because of altruism, but because the Soviets are assured that what the Cubans do abroad will serve their purposes."[34] Both Moscow and Havana gained new international status in the Third World as a result of their efforts in Angola and Ethiopia.

Cuban–Soviet cooperation in the Third World and Cuban dependence on Soviet economic and military assistance does not mean that their relations are without irritants. These include:

> A coup attempt in Angola in 1977 against Agostinho Neto (who was favored by Cuba) by Nito Alves, leader of a pro-Soviet extremist faction, suggested continuing differences in orientation between Moscow and Havana. The Soviets reportedly backed the coup attempt and the Cubans helped to defeat it.

> The Eritrean independence movement continues to plague the Mengistu government in Ethiopia, but Cuba has never permitted its forces to challenge Eritrean self-determination. The Soviets in the meantime have wavered between support for use of force against the Eritreans and support for a negotiated settlement.

> Revolutionary successes in Central America are extremely important to Fidel Castro but of less strategic concern to the Soviet Union. Cuba has publicly opposed the low level of attention that the Soviets have given to Nicaragua's economic and military needs, and even complained about conciliatory Soviet statements in the face of increasingly hostile U.S. pronouncements about the Sandinistas.

> The Soviets appeared to distance themselves from Maurice Bishop's leadership struggle with Bernard Coard in Grenada and kept an extremely low profile in the wake of the U.S. invasion in 1983. Cuba actively sought to prevent the U.S. invasion and Castro ordered his soldiers in Grenada to fight.[35]

These differences on regional matters were recorded at the 27th Congress of the Communist Party of the Soviet Union in 186, when General Secretary Gorbachev stressed the importance of East–West security matters and the importance of controlling the arms race and Fidel Castro reminded his Soviet audience that Third World issues also demanded attention and that national liberation struggles were not fought without great costs. As if to urge Gorbachev to meet Soviet obligations abroad despite his preoccupation with economic reform at home, Castro noted that Third World countries expect that they "will receive maximum solidarity from the socialist community in their struggle for just economic gains."[36]

Cuban and Soviet views differ on regional issues but their disagreements are not as significant or as contentious as the differences in the 1960s over revolutionary struggle and the role of armed force. Nevertheless, the presence of diverse interpretations about the Third World serves to identify and highlight sources of conflict between the USSR and Cuba that could contribute to the renewal of friction in the near term. The possible sources of tension between the two states include lukewarm Cuban support for Soviet efforts at détente and arms control with the United States, any overextension of Cuban support for the Sandinistas, and Cuban activism for revolutionary movements in Central and South America in general in opposition to Soviet efforts to maintain cordial relations with as many of the countries in the region as possible.

Conclusions and Outlook

Clearly the Soviets have expanded and extended their role and influence in the Third World since the 1950s. U.S. acceptance of Soviet strategic parity as well as prolonged U.S. difficulties in Vietnam made the USSR more attractive as an alternative to U.S. support in many Third World countries. Increased military and economic assistance as well as a more expansive military presence characterized greater Soviet involvement in the Third World. Soviet and Cuban military forces allowed Agostinho Neto to remain in power in Angola and enabled Mengistu Haile Mariam in Ethiopia to deal with an invasion from Somalia and two separate secessionist threats. The Soviet invasion of Afghanistan in 1979 raised serious questions about the outlook for Soviet power-projection capabilities and intentions in the Third World as well as the possibility that the "Vietnam syndrome" (the fear of becoming entangled in unpopular military conflicts in the Third World) had compromised the ability of the United States to challenge Soviet expansion in the developing world. Soviet access to naval and air facilities in Ethiopia and Afghanistan raised even more serious questions about the security of Western sea lines of communication through the Suez Canal and the Strait of Hormuz. Answers to these questions often ignored the dilemmas that Soviet policymakers were confronting in the Third World as well as the limits on future Soviet behavior in the developing world because of Soviet problems in the area of power-projection capability or the impact of regional instability on Soviet behavior.

Indeed, it is possible to argue that Soviet military and political involvement in such key Third World states as Afghanistan, Syria, Cuba, and Vietnam have led to problems in the regions of Southwest Asia, the Middle East, South America, and Southeast Asia. Soviet efforts to increase firepower in Afghanistan and to halt the flow of outside aid to the insurgents led to a serious refugee problem in the region and increased strains with both Pakistan and Iran. Indian opposition to compromising the traditional role of Afghanistan as a buffer between Indian and Soviet forces may have limited the Soviets' ability to increase their military effort in Afghanistan. Soviet exploitation of the Arab–Israeli confrontation and increased deployments of Soviet naval aviation and antisubmarine warfare and reconnaissance aircraft to Syria have led to a greater U.S. military presence in the region and hesitation on the part of Arab moderates to improve relations with the USSR. The deployment of Soviet naval task forces to Cuba as well as the operational roles of Soviet naval reconnaissance and antisubmarine warfare aircraft have limited Moscow's efforts to obtain additional ports of entry into South America and have compromised Moscow's efforts to expand its influence in Latin America and the Caribbean through political-diplomatic means. The use of Cam Rahn Bay as the largest Soviet naval forward-deployment base outside the USSR plus the use of Soviet naval and naval air assets in Vietnam to conduct military exercises in the South China Sea have spoiled Soviet efforts to improve relations with the states of the Association of Southeast Asian Nations (ASEAN). Soviet support for Vietnam's occupation of Cambodia has undercut Soviet initiative in Thailand particularly, but also in Indonesia and Malaysia. And Soviet military interventions in the Third World led to a sharp deterioration of U.S.–Soviet relations after 1975.

In addition to regional limitations caused by Soviet military support for key regional clients, the Soviets have confronted difficult policy choices because of Third World rivalries. In the Middle East, for example, the Soviets had to choose between Iran and Iraq in a war that continued until 1988 without deescalation. The Soviet tilt toward Iraq plus the Syrian tilt toward Iran have created additional problems in the Soviet–Syrian relationship. Soviet efforts to ingratiate itself with the two Yemens (the People's Democratic Republic of Yemen, or PDRY, and the Yemen Arab Republic, or YAR) have waxed and waned because of the military and political rivalry between Aden and San'a. The Soviets have encountered major difficulties in trying to balance the conservative and fragmented state of politics and society in the YAR with the tribal and radical politics of factionalism in the PDRY. Continued North Yemeni ties with Saudi Arabia and the coup d'état in South Yemen in 1986 indicate that the USSR cannot affect major events in the region and cannot persuade the Yemeni governments to take actions that benefit the Soviet Union. The Soviets have had similar problems in North Africa over the years in trying to balance their interests with Algeria and Morocco as well as with Algeria and Libya. On the Horn of Africa, the Soviets failed to prevent a war between Ethiopia and Somalia in the 1970s and have been unable to mediate differences between Ethiopia and the Sudan in the 1980s.

The Soviets have had the greatest difficulty in trying to influence the external and internal policies of the clients that have received the greatest amounts of Soviet support. In Egypt, for example, the Soviets became deeply involved in the operations of the Arab Socialist Union and the key institutional agencies in the army and the secret police, but this did not prevent President Sadat's decision to expel twenty thousand Soviet advisors and technicians present in the country and to allow the United States to broker a peace process with Israel under three U.S. presidencies. The Syrians have pursued their own interests in Lebanon and Jordan despite large amounts of Soviet military assistance, and Libya has confronted states large and small in ignoring Soviet advice to end Tripoli's political isolation in the Mediterranean and to moderate its political and military tactics. The Iraqi decision to invade Iran in 1980 was not appreciated in the Kremlin and led to an immediate suspension of Soviet military assistance to Baghdad. Thus, large amounts of military assistance to both Libya and Iraq have provided the Soviets with no assurance regarding the use of these weapons and no guarantee against domestic Arab opposition and resentment when increasingly sophisticated Soviet arms are used incorrectly by Arab military forces. Over the years, the Soviets have proven to be very sensitive to the charge of insufficient commitment from such clients as Egypt, Syria, and Libya.

On the other hand, the Soviets have encountered difficulties when they have tried to expand their presence and commitment to beleaguered clients, such as the Egyptians, that have not appreciated Soviet heavy-handedness. Egyptian journalist Mohammed Heikal has recorded Egyptian dissatisfaction with Soviet demands for special facilities at Mersa Matruh and Alexandria, Soviet exclusivity in the use of facilities at Cairo West airfield, and the general self-isolation of the Soviet presence in Cairo.[37] Heikal and others have argued that the "disadvantages of having so many Soviet experts in the country had become at least as apparent as the advantages," citing Soviet insensitivity in dealing with Arabs in particular and the virtual impossibility of establishing personal relationships with Soviet advisors and technicians. The exclusive Soviet position in Berbera led to similar problems with Somalia, as reflected by the expulsion of the Soviet presence there in 1977 and Siad Barre's unilateral abrogation of the Treaty of Friendship and Cooperation between the USSR and Somalia.

The Soviets also have been concerned with their inability to influence the economic-management plans of such client states as Cuba and Vietnam. There has never been much warmth or empathy between Soviet communism and their communist clients in the Third World who have found the Soviet model irrelevant and often counterproductive in the less developed areas. Soviet military and economic assistance for these states has been extremely generous over the years for good geopolitical reasons, but that in itself has not led to any commensurate influence or leverage over domestic political or economic decision making. The Cubans have always appreciated the anti-U.S. basis of Soviet policies toward Havana, and the Vietnamese have similarly perceived the anti-Chinese motives of the USSR in Hanoi. Both Cuba and Vietnam provide the Soviets with intelligence information on the United

States and China, respectively, valuable facilities for deploying reconnaissance aircraft and naval combatants in U.S. and Chinese coastal waters, and numerous facilities for Soviet military and civilian technicians.

The Soviets have provided the Cubans and Vietnamese direct and indirect economic subsidies, particularly the purchase of oil from the USSR at below–world-market prices both for internal use and for resale for hard currency. At the same time, the Cuban and Vietnamese economies have deteriorated sharply in recent years and there is no evidence that the Soviets have been able to achieve efficiencies in these Third World economies in order to ease the "burden of empire" for Moscow.[38] The escalating costs of aid to these Third World economies as well as their large foreign debts have caused the Soviets to become increasingly impatient with poor economic performance.

Both Cuba and Vietnam have become full members of CEMA and both have received growing amounts of Soviet aid and trade over the years. Yet, the declining growth of the Soviet economy and the increased burden of the continuing arms race with the West have led to increased constraints on Moscow's ability to provide economic assistance to these states. The rigidity of central planning and the difficulty in transferring Soviet agricultural and industrial expertise and technology—particularly to tropical countries with small-scale industry—has made Soviet economic relations with such countries as Cuba and Vietnam even more difficult. The Soviets have also been critical of unnamed Third World leaders for expecting the socialist states to finance dubious efforts to "force" socioeconomic change through rapid industrialization.[39]

The Soviets have conceded, then, that their preoccupation with developing basic industry—the traditional goal of Soviet economic aid—has been too costly for both patron and client, usually resulting in a decline in the standard of living and an alienation of the population. Indeed, Third World leaders have tended to blame the availability of Soviet credits for having induced large-scale economic projects that were beyond their financial and physical capacities. Whereas Soviet military aid has led to apparently unimpeded use of naval and air facilities in Cuba and Vietnam, there is no commensurate indication that Soviet economic aid has convinced the Cuban and Vietnamese leadership to maintain traditional roles as agricultural suppliers to the USSR or to cease efforts to diversity their economies.

It is noteworthy that the Soviets themselves have noted the completion of the "first stage" of the national liberation movement (which was a struggle for national freedom and therefore a military endeavor), acknowledged the impact of Soviet actions in the Third World on East–West relations, and repudiated the role of military power in settling regional conflicts. Soviet leaders clearly take a different view of developments in the Third World than they did in the 1970s. Soviet officials at the Institute of Economics of the World Socialist System (IEMSS) now argue that the USSR is at a disadvantage in economic competition with the West in the developing world. The Soviets appear to recognize the need to be more selective in choosing client states in the Third World.

At the 27th Congress of the Communist Party of the Soviet Union (CPSU), General Secretary Gorbachev indicated that Moscow's role in the Third World was far less important than addressing domestic economic concerns and improving relations with the United States. Gorbachev's formal remarks virtually ignored the Third World and, other than Afghanistan, made only passing reference to various regional conflicts that will continue to be potential problems for Soviet–U.S. relations. His deemphasis on Third World issues led such stalwart Soviet clients as Castro, Mengistu, and Angolan leader Dos Santos to remind the USSR that it could not back away from its international obligations. Castro reminded Gorbachev, for example, that "blood had been spilled" in the Third World and that the task of economic development in the underdeveloped world was just as important as avoiding nuclear war. Mengistu also urged the Soviets not to give the issue of regional conflict a lower priority than nuclear matters, and he put the Soviet leadership on notice that Moscow's Third World allies continued to expect Soviet support.

Gorbachev, however, has not repudiated the notion that political means must be sought for the resolution of regional disputes and that conditions must be created for greater Soviet involvement across-the-board in international politicking. At a dinner for Syrian president Hafez al-Assad in April 1987, Gorbachev emphasized that Soviet foreign policy had to be based on the "realistic analysis of the present-day world which has markedly changed recently" and the "diverse and conflicting forces of which world politics are comprised."[40] He acknowledged, for example, that the absence of diplomatic relations between the USSR and Israel could not be "considered normal" and that the use of military power in settling regional conflicts has become "completely discredited."

Gorbachev's announcement of a phased troop withdrawal from Afghanistan emphasized the importance of defusing those regional conflicts that have the greatest risk of compromising U.S.–Soviet relations. He stated that "implementing political settlement" in Afghanistan could be an "important rupture" in the chain of regional conflicts in Africa, the Middle East, Southeast Asia, and Central America. Moreover, in a series of articles (1988) by three members of the USA institute (the chief Soviet research establishment on the United States)—Deputy Director Vitaliy Zhurkin, section head Sergei Karaganov, and senior researcher Andrey Kortunov—the Soviets have argued that the "threat of premeditated nuclear aggression was decreasing, but that the threat of war may be increasing in part due to the struggle in regional sectors."[41]

This does not suggest that the Soviets will stop using their military assets to protect significant gains in Cuba, Syria, and Vietnam. Rather, Moscow may now recognize that military power alone will not resolve regional and bilateral conflicts and will not guarantee that Soviet interests can broaden from concentration in a few regional areas to a more active global role. In an interview in May 1987, Deputy Foreign Minister Vladimir Petrovsky disavowed the notion of a zero-sum game between the superpowers in the Third World and stated that Moscow could not "achieve a victory for itself by destroying someone."[42] Future Soviet actions in the Third World will test these attitudes.

Notes

1. See Melvin A. Goodman, "The Soviet Union and the Third World: The Military Dimension," in Andrzej Korbonski and Francis Fukuyama, eds., *The Soviet Union and the Third World: The Last Three Decades* (Ithaca, N.Y., and London: Cornell University Press, 1967), pp. 46–66.

2. Daniel S. Papp, *Soviet Policies toward the Developing World in the 1980s* (Washington, D.C.: U.S. Government Printing Office, 1986), pp. 352–54.

3. Ibid., pp. 169–73.

4. Henry S. Bradsher, *Afghanistan and the Soviet Union* (Durham, N.C.: Duke Press Policy Studies), pp. 210–13.

5. TASS, February 8, 1988.

6. Bradsher, *Afghanistan and the Soviet Union*, pp. 221–22.

7. Ibid., p. 255.

8. See Raymond Garthoff, *Detente and Confrontation* (Washington, D.C.: Brookings Institution, 1985), p. 902, re American–Iranian links prior to Soviet invasion.

9. *Izvestia*, July 29, 1983, p. 5.

10. *Izvestia*, October 17, 1985, p. 5.

11. *Pravda*, March 15, 1982, p. 5.

12. TASS, June 22, 1986.

13. Iranian ambassador Tabatabai finally arrived in Moscow in April 1983. During that month, Tehran also agreed to a visit by the chief of the Soviet Foreign Ministry's Middle East Department and permitted the resumption of Aeroflot service to Tehran. These overtures appeared to reflect Tehran's desire to prevent relations from deteriorating further and may have resulted from internal disagreement over the utility of provoking Moscow.

14. Treaty of Friendship between Persia and the Russian Socialist Federal Republic, signed in Moscow on February 26, 1921, Article Six.

15. Ibid., Article Five.

16. Melvin A. Goodman, *Regional Implications of the Soviet Invasion of Afghanistan.* Occasional Paper 176. (Washington, D.C.: Kennan Institute, 1984), pp. 7–9.

17. Ibid., pp. 9–11.

18. Georgi Mirsky, "The Middle East: New Factors," *New Times,* no. 48 (1973): 18–19. The other myths that Mirsky claimed were dispelled by the war were Israeli military superiority, Arab weapon inferiority, and that detente had no value. (Mirsky said that detente prevented an even worse "flare-up" in the Middle East.)

19. Robert Freedman, *Soviet Policy toward the Middle East since 1970* (New York: Praeger, 1978), pp. 141–65.

20. Ibid.

21. Dmitry Volsky, "Step toward Settlement," *New Times,* no. 23 (1974): 9.

22. *Pravda,* July 16, 1976, p. 3.

23. Quoted in Adeed Il Dawisha, *Syria and the Lebanese Crisis* (New York: St. Martin's, 1980), p. 137.

24. *New York Times,* April 30, 1987, p. 16.

25. Alvin Z. Rubinstein, *Red Star on the Nile* (Princeton: Princeton University Press, 1977), p. xv.

26. Jaime Suchlicki, *Cuba: From Columbus to Castro* (Washington, D.C.: Pergamon-Bassey, 1986), pp. 155–212.

27. Jorge Dominguez, *Cuba: Order and Revolution* (Cambridge, Mass.: Harvard University Press, 1978).

28. Edward Gonzalez, *Cuba under Castro: The Limits of Charisma* (Boston: Houghton Mifflin, 1972).

29. Papp, *Soviet Policies,* pp. 120–31.

30. Suchlicki, *Cuba,* pp. 155–212.

31. Gonzalez, *Cuba under Castro.*

32. Raymond Duncan, *The Soviet Union and Cuba: Interests and Influence* (New York: Praeger, 1985), pp. 51–52.

33. Carmelo Mesa-Lago, *The Economy of Socialist Cuba* (Albuquerque: University of New Mexico Press, 1981), pp. 77–108.

34. Robert Pastor, "Cuba and the Soviet Union: Does Cuba Act Alone?" in Barry W. Levine, ed., *The New Cuban Presence in the Caribbean* Westview, 1983), pp. 191–209.

35. W. Raymond Duncan, "Soviet Interests in Latin America," *Journal of Inter-American Studies and World Affairs* (May 1984): 168–75.

36. W. Raymond Duncan, "Castro and Gorbachev: Politics of Accommodation," *Problems of Communism,* 30 (March–April 1986): 45–57.

37. Mohamed Heikal, *The Sphinx and the Commissar* (New York: Harper & Row, 1978), pp. 275–89.

38. On the rising costs the Soviets face in Third World countries, see Jerry Hough, *The Struggle for the Third World: Soviet Debates and American Options* (Washington, D.C.: Brookings Institution, 1986).

39. Joseph Whelan, *The Soviet Union in the Third World, 1980–1982: An Imperial Burden or Political Asset* (Washington, D.C.: U.S. Government Printing Office, 1984), pp. 295–96.

40. *Pravda,* April 25, 1987, p. 2.

41. *Kommunist* (January 1988): 42–50.

42. *Washington Post,* May 29, 1987, p. 34.

Conclusion: Paradoxes of Soviet Power

Daniel N. Nelson

T hat the Soviet Union is today a global power, as it was not for the first thirty years after World War II, is a common observation. Strategic parity with the United States and a large numerical imbalance of conventional forces in Europe make the USSR's military might evident and imposing.

Simultaneously, however, it is widely understood that global Soviet involvement has produced incomplete control in core regions such as Eastern Europe, fragile influence in other locales such as the Middle East, and costly intervention as in Afghanistan. We know, indeed, that the growth of Soviet military and industrial capabilities in the last half of this century has not been transferable directly into political/diplomatic or economic realms.

Together, these assessments constitute a datum of contemporary analyses of Soviet foreign policy—that the USSR has greater power than ever before, while its capacity to affect the international environment remains substantially unidimensional. The appeal of the Soviet economic and political system, as Rajan Menon pointed out in his introduction, is a diminishing asset; as a consequence, a central motive of Gorbachev's reforms is to reinvigorate the Soviet system to strengthen its appeal to the Third World and to repair the underpinnings of Soviet military capabilities.

Power, as Menon concluded, is a multidimensional concept with many elements. Because there is unlikely to be one universal definition of power or one "systematic set of criteria" for evaluating it,[1] we have not sought to impose such evaluative criteria.

Yet, one *can* say without qualification that the property or capacity that we call power can be ascribed apart from its use and may explain international events without being a proximate cause of those events.[2] The extent or limits to Soviet power are thus demonstrable less through the USSR's actions in world politics than through enduring relationships in which the property of influence and control is inherent—exemplified by Jeffrey C. Isaac with reference to teacher–pupil, master–slave, and other dyadic relationships.[3]

In the foregoing chapters, contributors from several disciplinary perspectives have examined Soviet power from internal and external viewpoints, considering factors that affect the creation and projection of the USSR's capacity to shape the decisions or conduct of others. These contributors have not produced a clear consensus, which is as it should be. The portrait that emerges from these studies, and from other materials, is one of complexities and contradictions—for the USSR's might is, at once, its greatest weakness. The paradoxes of Soviet power are, in fact, profound.

Limits at Home

The boundaries of Soviet power are not, at least vis-à-vis its Eastern European cordon sanitaire, economic in nature. The "costs of empire" debate, to which Martin and Dina Spechler have added new dimensions, has been central to our larger concern about factors that restrain Soviet capacities to shape the behavior of others. The Spechlers' fresh look at this issue includes a critical assessment of previous analyses; they find that the USSR derives tangible benefits from WTO allies (e.g., Eastern Europeans' roles in the Third World). The cost-benefit calculation is, of course, subject to many judgmental criteria and complex issues, and it is certainly not a simple gain or loss proposition for the USSR.[4] But, according to the Spechlers, the degree of Soviet subsidization has been overstated previously because of a one-time scenario in which USSR oil prices were below world averages. By the late 1980s, the situation had changed considerably as Soviet oil prices for Eastern Europe, at $25 per barrel, have been much higher than world spot market prices. Short-term implicit subsidies may have existed in the 1970s, but they were *not* out-of-pocket monies literally sent to Eastern Europe.

Stephen White raises the question of leadership within the Soviet Union. White reviews the institutionalization of a system that limits the power of any single Politburo/Secretariat member, and he places the early Gorbachev years within the context of Soviet leadership development. It is clear from White's analysis that, notwithstanding the new general secretary's assertiveness and dynamism, substantial obstacles to his policies and views remain. The political legacy of Leonid Brezhnev is embedded thoroughly in Soviet bureaucracy, the values of which are even more anti-innovational than most. Against the recalcitrance of this institution, Gorbachev has spoken often. Further, the personnel changes Gorbachev effected in 1985–88 did not irrevocably secure his position. Students of Russian history know, of course, that leadership succession has been a problem that has weighted heavily in the somber past of Czarism. The Time of Troubles and innumerable regicides and fratricides all stemmed from the lack of clear-cut paths to monarchical succession.

The Soviet Union today has enormous resources underlying a patchwork of ethnolinguistic and political schisms and severe technological handicaps. Martha Olcott's analysis of Gorbachev's nationality policy and the political conflict that has emerged while he tries to reassert Moscow's control at all levels suggests the extent to which ethnicities and nationalisms drain sociopolitical resources. Cadre time, financial resources, and political capital are all used in the battle to reinforce the CPSU's democratic centralism. Often, the victories Gorbachev has won since 1985 have been pyrrhic, with the disruption of oblast or republic-level fiefdoms rekindling animus toward Great Russians and toward the Central Apparat that may take years to extinguish.

Related to the Olcott chapter are the well-known demographic trends that will soon mean that Great Russians no longer constitute an absolute majority in the Soviet population.[5] The ramifications of such a shift for the Soviet economy, the Red Army, and public policy are enormous. The younger labor force will increasingly be available in Asian republics, and the choice will be to move workers or move factories. At the same time, conscripts will have to be drawn increasingly from non–Russian-speaking minorities, including Central Asian Moslems. Not only do such demographic trends complicate long-term economic planning; doubts about Soviet military manpower and the reliability of some conscripts will inevitably rise.

Although the contributors in this book do not analyze this point, health and welfare deficiencies are of related importance. Inceasingly acknowledged in the USSR of Mikhail Gorbachev, such problems of public well-being affect productivity, exacerbate ethnic schisms (since republics in Central Asia have far higher infant mortality rates, lower male life expectancies, and other measures of poorer public health), and extract a high social cost.[6] Ethnic schisms and central–local friction, coupled with leadership uncertainties, have made the accumulation of power more difficult, as time and resources are squandered in political contests.

Resources, however, *are* plentiful in the USSR. From Moscow's perspective, the natural resources to be found in the USSR are a mixed blessing—encouraging waste and reliance on raw-material exports while at the same time being enormously supportive of the rest of the economy. Indeed, it was in October 1987 that *Izvestia* carried a report from the Institute of Economics of the World Socialist System of the USSR Academy of Sciences in which the USSR was characterized as a "raw-material appendage" of the world capitalist system. Western analysts had, of course, long ago seen the link between power and global capitalism.[7] As long as the USSR plays the role of a raw-material supplier to Western capitalism, it remains dependent in critical respects—dependent on world markets for gold, oil, gas, coal, or other minerals, *and* on an inexhaustible supply of these natural resources.

Judith Thornton approaches the USSR's technological base from the standpoint of its limited capacities to undertake research and development from indigenous institutions and enterprises, and its inability to apply technology to production techniques. Although Thornton acknowledges that Gorbachev's proposed reforms could affect positively the Soviet economy's ability to innovate, she notes that buyers are still "essentially assigned to suppliers" and that administrative intervention could short-circuit market-oriented reforms. These domestic obstacles remain and would complicate the absorption of Western technology even if direct ties to the world market were able to proceed in a less inhibited fashion than in past decades.

From all four of these contributions, then, one derives a portrait of Soviet power constrained most by Soviet policies and institutions, not by the arithmetic of objective economic costs. Uncertainties of leadership, as we know from Gorbachev's first several years, detract from the capabilities of a general secretary and the Communist Party as a whole to project influence and control. Two of the most gnawing problems that face the new generation of Soviet elites—the nationalities problem and economic malaise rooted in a lack of innovation and an outdated technological base—absorb political and socioeconomic resources. The Soviets, it would seem, can manage the economic burden of their empire; it is the political and economic burden of their own system that causes the hemorrhaging of Soviet power.

External Limits as Well

Outside the USSR, there are constraints on both the exercise of Soviet power *and* on the establishment or maintenance of "enduring relationships" in which power is inherent. The latter conditions, in fact, are often the self-imposed products of the USSR's own behavior in world politics and specific regions or states.

Christopher Jones argues, for example, that the Soviet Union does not want strong allies in Eastern Europe because strength would connote autonomy. Their military-political objectives, consequently, do not include aggressive designs, but rather emphasize control within Eastern Europe via an absorption of these states' high commands into Soviet theaters of military operations (TVDs), denying to national authorities command over national armies. The Soviets' own fear of autonomous developments within Eastern Europe, however, has engendered an alliance in which a lack of cohesion, unreliability, and a maldistribution of defense burdens are characteristic.[8]

The USSR's force-projection capabilities into the Third World as compared to those of the United States were considered by Michael Klare. Force structures and deployments by the Soviets do not, according to Klare, suggest an ability to engage in prolonged combat against determined resistance in the Third World. In fact, the imbalance in force-projection capacities documented by Klare implies that Soviet foreign-policy priorities in the Third

World are far different than those of the United States. Whereas the United States is prepared to intervene in environments hostile to U.S. presence, the USSR is confined to opportunistic intervention created by the need of a regime or movement for outside support.

Elsewhere, the USSR has accumulated a number of poor and crisis-prone client states. According to Melvin Goodman's discussion, the Soviet backing of unstable regimes requires the USSR to engage in counterinsurgency operations ill-suited to its ideological pronouncements. Goodman details the political problems created by the invasion of Afghanistan for Soviet relations with Islamic countries, the serious rifts between Castro and Soviet leaders at times during the 1960s–1980s, and the difficulties in Southeast Asia engendered by Moscow's support for the Vietnamese occupation of Kampuchea. These conditions, and more, add up to a significant "down-side" to Soviet successes.

A net assessment of Soviet influence in the Third World, then, may be less positive than it is often portrayed. While the USSR is unquestionably more able to act in corners of the world far from its borders and has received military and intelligence benefits from its presence in Africa, the Middle East, South Asia, and Southeast Asia, the regional and bilateral conflicts detailed by Goodman make stable and long-term power relationships difficult or impossible to secure. The USSR, under Gorbachev, appears to be beginning to recognize these limits. But, as Goodman concludes, the future will "test these attitudes."

Paradoxes of Soviet Power

What can we infer generally about Soviet power in the late twentieth century on the basis of analyses such as the contributions in this book? We can, I think, identify a number of self-contradictions within the spectrum of Soviet capacities to shape the decisions and conduct of others. I shall refer to these together as the paradoxes of Soviet power. Each paradox impedes the formation of an enduring capacity to control or mold actions of others. The paradoxes will be discussed under the headings of

nontransferability of Soviet power,

discontinuity of Soviet power,

permeability of Soviet power,

temporality of Soviet power,

economic subjectivity of Soviet power, and

political subjectivity of Soviet power.

Nontransferability

Although Leonid Brezhnev's eighteen-year rule saw the USSR achieve nuclear parity while maintaining numerical superiority in European-theater conventional forces, the growth of military-related industry was without parallel in the rest of the Soviet economy. It is now clear that the USSR's unswerving commitment to military equality with the United States mortgaged the Soviet future and condemned it to underdevelopment. Soviet underdevelopment, which spans the entire gamut of the USSR's society and economy untouched by direct military applicability, creates a unidimensionality of power that was bequeathed by Brezhnev to the next generation of leadership. The Soviet Union's military strength cannot infuse strength elsewhere in the USSR's society and economy; it has, instead, drained from all other sectors both human and material resources. While this may be an axiom for all superpowers, it is visible in especially poignant ways in the USSR—a superpower that did not know how to drill for its own oil, could not build its own gas pipelines, cannot create its own microelectronics industry, is unable reliably to feed its own population, has one of Europe's most poorly developed road systems, and has exhibited (at least during the 1970s to mid-1980s) a period of declining life expectancy.

A superpower so deficient in the basic infrastructure of economic and social well-being certainly is not strong across the board. With the USSR's future development contingent not only on domestic economic and political reform, but on the lifeline of Western technology, credits, and investments, the Soviet Union's dependence on developed capitalist states reveals starkly the nontransferability of its military power.

Discontinuity

The USSR, at least for the two decades after Khrushchev was deposed, was unremitting in its drive for military growth. Because of this emphasis on expanding USSR's armed forces, gaps in Soviet development that had been inherited from the Stalinist era pervade the USSR's economy. Soviet capacities to shape the behavior of others, even as they became larger, became noteworthy as well for their substantive gaps in areas outside military forces.

Considering how large the Soviet economy is, it has relatively little influence on the world economy.[9] Even after a sharp rise in Soviet trade during the 1970s and 1980s, the Soviet Union still imports goods with a value only 5 percent of its GNP, while exports consist largely (80 percent or more) of raw materials. Imports are held down by the Soviets' own conservative economists who counsel limiting indebtedness plus Western reluctance to transfer technology with military applications. Both the narrow range of its exports and the relatively small value of its imports reduce the potential Soviet role in the world economy. Of course, the USSR also has a severely depressed domestic consumer economy endemic to a system so tied to extensive development.[10] The noncovertibility of the ruble and other CMEA currencies detracts further from the Soviet role in the world, placing the USSR and its closest associates outside the circles of international financial and monetary policy.

The lacunae of Soviet power include, as well, gaps in the USSR's role in the Third World because its aid is skewed greatly toward the provision of military hardware and training. In 1984, for example, the USSR delivered over $7 billion worth of military assistance while it disbursed only $1.595 billion in economic aid to noncommunist less developed countries (LDCs). Even if one adds trade credits and concessional credits/grants (a total of $2.350 billion in 1984), military programs outweigh nonmilitary ones by almost 2:1.[11]

Other characteristics of Soviet economic relations with LDCs also undercut the USSR's role. The economic assistance proffered by the USSR tends to focus on industrial development, with little earmarked for small-scale enterprises or agriculture. In addition, Moscow may allow short-term credit, but at high interest and often with mandatory repurchase agreements with the Soviet Union or other CMEA states.[12] By the early 1980s, these stiff credit requirements had created the awkward situation that more money was being repaid to the USSR than the USSR disbursed as economic aid.[13] In short, aid from the USSR, if not in the form of armaments or military training, does not come cheaply.

It is not surprising, then, that Soviet (and Warsaw Pact) economic assistance to LDCs is highly concentrated in certain client states. In 1984, "five countries (Afghanistan, Ethiopia, Guinea, Iraq, Syria) . . . absorbed about 75 percent of the new commitments" made by the USSR.[14] Four of these states were engaged in ongoing military conflicts, with regimes that either existed at the behest of Moscow or depended heavily on Soviet armaments. Military dependency on the Soviets explains, in large part, the concentration of other forms of aid as well. Such concentration, however, has meant that Soviet influence has been focused on strategically less important states while "prizes—South Korea, Taiwan, Argentina, Brazil, Indonesia, or Mexico—that have large populations and greater economic and military potential, have been outside Soviet efforts.

The Soviets have the capacity, it is clear, to support the military needs of client states and to target a few for economic assistance. This capacity expanded during the 1970s and 1980s into regions of the world that were earlier beyond the Soviet reach. But if the USSR can now "reach" beyond its periphery, to use Zbigniew Brzezinski's evocative metaphor, can it "grasp"?[15] The dichotomy between the reach and grasp of Soviet power is an outgrowth of its discontinuity; were it not for the deficiencies in Soviet economic and technological capacities, the USSR could seek to shape the behavior of other nation states with many more tools. The ties Moscow could establish with ruling strata in other states might well extend beyond the narrow echelon of party, military, and security elites. As it stands, however, "Soviet economic assistance is not as generous as it would first appear" and, as developing states realize this, then constraints on the "USSR's ability to provide aid . . . [will] limit the influence, security and geopolitical/strategic advantage the USSR can gain through economic levels of policy."[16]

Distinctions between reach and grasp are evident as well in the area of force-projection capabilities.[17] Were the USSR to see its interests threatened in Central or South America, Africa, or much of East, South, and Southeast Asia, it would have few of the kinds of military units and equipment needed to intervene if opposed. It is revealing that as recently as 1982, the USSR, had it been in Britain's position, might not have been able to mount an operation to retake the Falklands; the Soviets had very limited naval infantry, no aircraft carriers comparable to the two used by the British, and no island bases in the South Atlantic. Being able to create a presence in a locale and to support indigenous or proxy troops in combat are capabilities quite distinct from a force-projection capability integral to one's own armed forces. In this regard, there are discontinuities in Soviet military power as well. Overall, of course, the USSR surely maintains a substantial numerical advantage in most categories of conventional arms, and it would be foolhardy to extrapolate from some disadvantages in Soviet power projection to other kinds of inventories or deployments.[18] Nevertheless, no regime in Moscow can yet presume to have the upper hand in any far-flung environment where combat is likely.

Today the reach has been extended, and Soviet arms, technicians, teachers, and engineers are present in Nicaragua, Kampuchea, Angola, and elsewhere. Because of missing links in Soviet power, however, Moscow's "grasp" is decidedly weak—and the very effort of the 1970s and 1980s to globalize Soviet power may have contributed to a loosening of the Soviet grip within a region of vital concern—Eastern Europe. It has been more than coincidence that, among its six Warsaw pact allies in Eastern Europe, the USSR has sought increasingly during the 1970s and 1980s to counter its wavering hold by denying national control of national armies and ensuring that the command of all Eastern European forces would, in crises, pass to the Red Army's TVDs.[19]

The gaps in Soviet capacities to shape others' behavior—discontinuities that are the natural consequence of military power's nontransferability—are thus evident as the USSR expands the number of its client states, while preventing the emergence of autonomous allies. In that sense, the USSR's weakness, not strength, is revealed by its effort to ensure subservience rather than cooperation.

Permeability

Discontinuities of Soviet power mean, simultaneously, the permeability of those capacities. No array of capacities across all dimensions—military, economic, and political/diplomatic—will provide an impervious shield against economic setbacks, social malaise and unrest, or the efforts of other powerful states to affect politics within the USSR or within its client states.

Particularly because of gaps in Soviet power, however, the relationships in which power can be effected will be buffeted, if not disrupted, by countervailing interests. Stalin, for example, was unable to intimidate Tito notwithstanding hundreds of thousands of Red Army troops nearby in 1948, while later Soviet regimes have seen leaders backed by Moscow in Africa (such as Patrice Lumumba or Kwame Nkrumah) defeated or deposed, and have been themselves ignominiously ousted from erstwhile client states (from Egypt by Anwar Sadat). Domestically, the USSR has been unable to destroy, even during the Brezhnev era, movements of intellectual, religious, and national dissent supported by world public opinion.

The interstices of Soviet power are those discussed throughout this book: leadership uncertainty, ethnic mistrust and rivalries, technological backwardness, weak clients posing as allies, inadequate power-projection capabilities, and political dilemmas engendered because of involvements abroad. Through these openings, as it were, transude challenges to the leading role of the party, to economic growth, to Warsaw Pact cohesion, and to the USSR's ability to hold on to its position in Third World environments.

Temporality

If not embedded in enduring relationships, the capacity to shape decisions and behavior of others will be tested constantly. As there are degrees of such relationships, there are also degrees of challenges; yet, the power of the USSR in Eastern Europe—while limited by discontinuities of Soviet power outside the military/security arena—is less uncertain than the power of the Soviet Union in other parts of the world. Aside from mere proximity, the Soviets have inherited the role of a regional power that the Russian Empire held since the partition of Poland in the late 1700s. "Long before there was a Soviet Union," writes Robin Remington, "national security concerns combined with religious-cultural pan-Slavism" had made the region of Eastern Europe "high on the list of Czarist Russian foreign policy priorities."[20]

Power outside a lasting relationship will be ephemeral since, for one to be powerful, another must conform or submit; bases for power are not created or maintained through momentary shows of force or transient interventions. There is a tacit recognition of such a principle in Soviet military and economic assistance patterns—i.e., long-term consistency in servicing particular clients. The USSR is assiduous in its efforts to cultivate deeply rooted dependencies that come to be almost immutable patron–client relationships.

Yet, Moscow often fails in that endeavor, because its military power is nontransferable, yielding incomplete capacities to affect others' behavior. Further, the USSR tactically has erred by supporting clients already in tenuous positions that lose in a struggle with domestic opponents (in Indonesia in 1965, for example) or by attempting to accelerate or deepen Soviet influence in a manner so unsubtle that indigenous elites unite to expel the Soviet/Warsaw Pact personnel.

Power, then, does not last in any environment unless an underlying relationship exists that can be nurtured. Americans were not sufficiently "powerful" in Vietnam, notwithstanding ten years of warfare and up to half a million troops. Without any military intervention, however, the United States probably has been more able to shape decisions and behavior in the Philippines (indeed, more able than is Japan, which has more trade with the Philippines, and than is China, which is far closer) because of a long-term relationship between the United States and Filipinos.

The creation of Soviet client states in Angola and Ethiopia in the middle to late 1970s through Moscow's intervention and the use of Cuban combat troops in both countries was based on opportunities rather than an outgrowth of lengthy Soviet association with political organizations in either state.[21] The presence of thousands of Cuban troops may have been Castro's idea as much as, if not more, than Leonid Brezhnev's.[22] At the very least, the underpinnings of Soviet power in such environments do not auger well for a permanent capacity to shape decisions and behaviors.

One of the Soviets' key relationships has been the linkage to India, including a Treaty of Friendship and Cooperation dating from the Indira Gandhi years. Yet, the Soviet role connotes little or no power in the subcontinent; U.S. backing of Pakistan, in 1971 and later with massive arms shipments to General Zia, has pushed India toward the Soviets as a supplier of arms and as an aid for large-scale industrial projects. It is a relationship of convenience, not of power. The Indians use their ties to Moscow as a balance vis-à-vis both Pakistan and China, while the Soviets use New Delhi both to counter efforts in the subcontinent and to thwart Chinese interests.[23]

Unable to transfer its military might to other dimensions, and thus plagued with gaps—discontinuities—in its capacity to control or influence, the Soviet Union's power remains permeable, subjected to ongoing challenges at home and abroad. The temporality of Soviet power in distant settings, where Moscow's commitment is recent and costly, thus becomes likely.

To this point, the paradoxes of Soviet power are those we see from the outside looking in, as observers of Soviet political and social processes. Far more paradoxical, are assessments that Soviet decisionmakers may themselves make regarding their own capacities and the power of the USSR. Principles incompatible with the capacities to shape the behavior of others may be economic or political in nature. Calculations of economic cost and political will may lead those who have power to abandon it or to so lessen commitments implicit to relationships of power that capacities dissipate.

Economic Subjectivity

The power of a patron presupposes clients. There is, however, a cost associated with holding such power—not only, of course, "out-of-pocket" expense, but rather the expenditure of various forms of resources. Even for hegemonic states, commitments of resources to those over whom power is held is implicit in the relationship. Loans or grants to ensure economic viability, aid programs to educate students or train workers and technicians, and developmental projects to build factories, roads, or irrigation canals may be only a fraction of the costs associated with power relationships maintained by the USSR or any modern nation-state.

Ultimately, however, the principal costs arise when the political regime with which the patron/hegemon is linked becomes endangered. For Moscow, this has been the case in Angola, Ethiopia, and Afghanistan—and, for the USSR's own client, Vietnam, a similar problem followed the 1978–79 invasion and occupation of Kampuchea. The costs of empire in Eastern Europe, once thought to be weigh heavily on the USSR[24], were transitory and appear now to pose minimal difficulty for Moscow. Further, the Spechlers' analysis in this book makes it clear that the direct, cash costs for support of Third World clients and the war in Afghanistan do not reach a high level relative to past Soviet military budgets.

Yet, what in Brezhnev's years was an acceptable cost may not continue to be acceptable. No longer acceptable in the Gorbachev era may be expenditures that, while affordable in a strictly budgetary sense, produce little of value and durability. It may be, as well, that Russians view unbearable burdens differently than Americans and that their tolerance of sacrifice is higher.[25] Yet, there is certain to be variation in the meaning of sacrifice or loss incurred as a consequence of a state's power, i.e., the economic subjectivity of Soviet power.

At some point, the amount a society and economy must pay—or perceives it must pay—to continue a relationship of power may appear to be greater than that relationship is "worth." Alternatively, further adding to capacities for influence and control to ensure the stability of a relationship may abut other priorities or needs. In the Soviet Union, this cost-benefit calculation will be made within a more narrow stratum of the population than in competitive democracies, but the calculation will be made nonetheless.

Political Subjectivity

Perhaps most important among the self-contradictory traits of Soviet power—or of any state's power—is its "political subjectivity." That is, the power of the USSR exists only to the extent, and in a form, allowed by domestic Soviet politics. Soviet power is affected as well by the political conditions of client or subservient states, parties, or movements insofar they are disposed to recognize Moscow's capacities. But political subjectivity is even more complicated.

Gross measures of power are not good predictors of outcomes because raw capacities of political actors are mediated by many subjective factors, the most basic of which is political will. A hegemonic or patron nation-state—a superior in a power relationship—must have the political will to perform that role. Such political will may be generated by two sources. First, the powerful require political myths that justify their capacities. Second, those myths must be reinforced with increments to national prestige, pride, or legitimacy gained from *maintaining* the capacity to affect the decisions and behavior of others. Lacking either justifying myths or their reinforcement through heightened prestige, pride, or legitimacy, the domestic politics of a system cannot support power, even if the raw capacities are present. Were this to happen, repercussions will be felt elsewhere; insofar as Soviet reforms under Khrushchev or Gorbachev are a de facto confession of Moscow's fallibility, the legitimacy of Soviet power in Eastern Europe and among communists generally will be reduced as ideological myths are tarnished.

Superpowers must justify their power to their own populations and to the world. Modern political myths provide that justification. During the past several centuries, myths appropriate to the mass politics of literate, industrialized societies have emerged—myths as recurring themes and ideas, real or fictional, that appeal to a people by expressing commonly felt emotions or cultural norms. Modern political myths have wide audiences and are repeated with great frequency to underpin complex societies and polities. The myths themselves have become thoroughly interwoven with the power of those who project them, necessitating their protection by the power that these myths justify. The sociopolitical place of myth remains the same, however, as in preliterate societies. "Truth, clothed in myth" is seen as fundamental or divine, "justifying the order of society and consoling for its hardships."[26]

Americans have developed their national political myths for more than two centuries. Indeed, it may be argued, as did Arthur Ekirch, that one can trace the "idea of mission" from Puritan leaders through early American statesmen,[27] an idea later transformed by the "self-centered doctrine of manifest destiny."[28]

From the epic poems (*beliny*) of Kiev, Novgorod, and other centers of pre-Muscovite Russia, the notion that recurs over and over again is that of omnipresent danger from the outside, an external threat made all too real by the almost three centuries of Mongol occupation. At the same time, Russia's danger demanded internal order, discipline, and maintenance of its distinctiveness from the outside. Russian uniqueness, closely identified with Orthodox Christianity, had to be guarded strictly.[29] Much later, in the nineteenth century, Slavophiles created an ideology that opposed efforts to westernize Russia—an ideology that at once postulated the superiority of Russian Orthodoxy and the mission of Russia to defend all Slavic peoples.

Lenin's Bolsheviks were also, in their own way, believers in exceptionalism, in their own moral superiority, and in their historic mission. To the extent that the Bolsheviks retained Marxism when they achieved power in 1917, it was to further enhance the myth of their own superior righteousness; the Soviet Union was to be the harbinger of equality, social justice, and progress, and it was the model for workers around the world.

The political myths of uniqueness, righteousness, and mission recur in the histories of the United States and the Soviet Union. Lacking conviction derived from these sources, the commitment or knowledge of an adversary may more than compensate for the ostensibly greater power of the the other.[30] Thus, the United States's decade-long war in Vietnam and the USSR's equally prolonged combat in Afghanistan have been tragic episodes in which the exercise of power has led to vastly destructive interventions. In fact, the raw capabilities of the superpowers were inappropriate for these wars, and instruments of modern warfare were applied against peoples who absorbed immense suffering because of their own myths and intense commitments.

Ironically, then, the same intangible factors that are requisites for the political will of powerful nation-states are the bane of those states' capacities to control others' behavior.

For the USSR, its emergence from the Eurasian land mass to become a global actor during the past several decades has meant political costs with each step. These costs cannot be tallied; yet, analyses such as those by Melvin Goodman in this book, buttressed by other discussions of noneconomic costs and benefits of the USSR's "empire," place the issue of political subjectivity at the forefront of limits to Soviet power. Often, the Soviet Union's capacity to affect outcomes of conflicts and the direction of political processes has been exercised with positive consequences (as viewed from Moscow). In Bruce D. Porter's study of Soviet involvement in Third World conflicts from 1945 through 1980, it was found that, at the level of tactical and military operations, Soviet activity "in local conflicts has been highly successful," with Moscow's clients almost always being victorious in the time period studied.[31] The same study, however, found that the USSR's record in "political and diplomatic outcomes . . . has been much more ambiguous."[32] The Soviets did not always achieve lasting political influence and, concludes Porter, "military and diplomatic outcomes [of interventions by superpowers in Third World conflicts] may be diametrically opposite."[33]

After almost a decade of combat in Afghanistan against the *mujahedeen,* however, the USSR's string of military successes has ended and the diplomatic costs of exercising power have escalated. And, rather than achieving a secure foothold in sub-Saharan Africa or the Horn of Africa, Soviet/Cuban intervention has succeeded only in immersing the USSR and Cuba in seemingly unending conflict. Mikhail Gorbachev appears to have recognized that forceful demonstrations of Soviet power elicit only heightened political will from opponents and, unless clear national interest is evident, sap that same intangible quality from the USSR. At the 27th CPSU Congress in 1986, and in the subsequent years, Gorbachev has given little attention to "wars of national liberation" and other struggles that used to garner a great deal of rhetorical support—and often military aid—from Soviet leaders. When Gorbachev spoke of Afghanistan as a "bleeding wound" for the Soviet Union, his thoughts were unlikely to have been focused on Red Army casualties. Rather, domestic disenchantment with the Soviet military role in Afghanistan plus diplomatic damage in the Moslem and nonaligned world may have been the "blood" to which Gorbachev referred.

It has not been Afghanistan alone that has tested the USSR's political will as a superpower, nor the *mujahedeen* alone who exhibited the heightened will of those who resist Soviet intervention. Neither, for that matter, have the prolonged conflicts in Africa or Southeast Asia taught Soviet leaders something about the political/diplomatic costs of their power. Indeed, these conflictual environments have served to sharpen a much broader, generically *political* trend that serves to counterpoise Soviet power.

The morass of ongoing military conflicts in the Third World environs has reinforced and made more urgent the waning efficacy of Soviet ideological influence throughout the world. Once again, this is not a variable amenable to empirical measurement. Yet, analysts generally agree that states that previously flaunted their Marxism have abandoned much of their ideology and turned to the United States, Western Europe, and Japan for "aid and economic developmental models."[34] Even in countries such as Iran where reliance on the West is shunned, the appeal of the Soviet model peaked long ago. The same incompleteness of Soviet power discussed earlier has meant that the USSR's own economic system and its path to development have appeared less attractive since the mid-1970s than in the first seveal postwar decades. It is revealing that the USSR's clients and new members of the socialist "commonwealth" are in the lowest socioeconomic stratum among all nation-states and have made little or no economic progress since the advent of a Soviet-regime. This datum of contemporary politics (which is certainly recognized by Soviet scholars) plus the poor performance of Soviet and Eastern European economies have accelerated the abandonment of state-directed economic policies.

The ideological slippage of the Soviet position has been more than economic in origin. Because of the USSR's confrontation with Islam in

Afghanistan, its efforts to crush a national liberation movement in Eritrea, its support of a Vietnamese occupation army in Kampuchea, and other cases similar in the unleashing of Soviet arms against Third World adversaries, the Soviet Union has lost much of its revolutionary legitimacy and political appeal in the underdeveloped world that it had possessed for decades. No longer can the USSR claim that, unlike Western capitalist states, it is a power free of the urge to dominate. Mikhail Gorbachev surely recognizes these issues and the choices available to him and the Communist Party of the Soviet Union.

Those choices do not present inviting paths—for, it would seem, the USSR can either continue to expend economic and political capital on its current stable of clients or it can seek to become a more mainstream part of the international community. The latter strategy, which necessitates the resolution or mitigation of conflictual issues with major powers coupled with an active immersion into world diplomacy and trade, appears to be Gorbachev's intention. But this strategy, too, will invoke substantial short-term political costs at home and abroad. The USSR must withdraw from Afghanistan, resolve various disputes with China, open its military establishment for verification of arms control accords, and so on—all of which will be opposed strongly by antireform elements within the USSR as well as by Soviet clients around the world for whom such policies may connote defeat.

The political subjectivity of Soviet power, then, suggests no easy course for the maintenance of the USSR's capacity to shape decisions and behavior around the world. Although Gorbachev is cognizant that the Soviet Union must effect a substantial change in its world role to maintain its current capacities, those changes will disrupt some relationships of power in order to save others.

Summary

To attribute power to a particular state does not preclude some weakness in such a state. However, power that is narrowly based—not grounded, at once, in military prowess, economic capacities, sociocultural authority, and so on—will not be as enduring. Also, it is not tautologous to note that power cannot endure outside a relationship in which other people, groups, or states exist in an ongoing submissive and inferior position. Intervention that enables a superpower to control a small stratum of elite political actors, while engendering a civil war that cannot be extinguished, creates no lasting environment for power. This is the lesson of Afghanistan. By the same token, diplomatic treaties and military ties offer no guarantee of permanent influence or control in another sociocultural milieu.

The Soviet Union's capacity to shape the decisions and behavior of some nation-states, political parties, and movements is substantial and is unquestionably greater from a military standpoint than at any time in the CPSU's seventy-year rule. As argued here, however, that capacity is seen to be self-contradictory. Unable and probably unwilling to transfer resources from the military to other realms of socioeconomic needs, the USSR became, to use Paul Dibb's term, an incomplete superpower.[35] The discontinuities among its capacities have meant that, notwithstanding enormous resources for nuclear and conventional forces, Soviet power is highly permeable and frequently not very durable in venues beyond the Soviet periphery.

Further, it would seem that the economic and political costs implicit to their globalism may be part of a reassessment of Soviet priorities. The "empire" largely achieved by the Red Army in Eastern Europe no longer drains the Soviets and, as Martin and Dina Spechler argued, the cost was never principally out-of-pocket. But subjective economic and political costs, especially the latter, may now be understood more clearly in Moscow. Thus far in his tenure, Mikhail Gorbachev has effected no evident change in long-term Soviet priority for military expenditures; his rhetoric, however, has suggested reduced emphasis on an purely military perception of security—aiming for "sufficient defense" rather than a balance favorable to the USSR.

All contributors to this book would no doubt underscore the common-sense observation that the 1990s are certain to be years in which the Soviet Union remains a superpower sharing few interests with the United States. The capacities developed by the USSR since World War II, especially since the 1960s, to become engaged globally have not malfunctioned and have not become dangerously overloaded.

This has not been, in other words, a pathology of Soviet power. The capacities of the USSR, albeit narrowly based, are not disintegrating; instead, they are "seriously flawed."[36] Rather than disintegrating, Soviet power will change and evolve as the USSR's leaders adjust to, and compensate for, the limits discussed in this book. The direction of such change will depend, in part, on the political fortunes of Mikhail Gorbachev. But the appeal of the Soviet model of development and the relevance of Soviet ideology (e.g., Moscow's support for "wars of national liberation") have waned. In this sense as well, the future of Soviet power will depend on exogenous effects—the cumulative effect of changes in all relationships in which the USSR has had, or sought to have, the capacity to shape decisions and behavior of others.

There are clear signs that, as long as Mikhail Gorbachev remains general secretary, the USSR will pursue an active diplomacy, exhibiting new flexibility and dynamism in interactions with the United States and Western Europe. Throughout Africa, Asia, and even Latin America as well, we should expect to see efforts to broaden the scope of Soviet political influence while reducing the political and economic costs of the USSR's global involvement. Hence, Foreign Minister Shevardnadze and others have visited many locales around the world establishing new bases for contacts, while strenuous efforts have been made to resolve issues with China, extract Soviet troops from Afghanistan, and accomplish other goals. Of course, Soviet flexibility in arms control surprised many in 1986–87, while accelerating movement toward an INF accord.[37] Meanwhile, on the Soviet home front, no one should interpret *perestroika* as anything else than an effort to reinvigorate the Soviet Union from within, while reinforcing the leading role of the Communist Party.[38]

These are not the actions of leaders who are recoiling from power. Rather, the activism at home and abroad are steps being taken because the limits to Soviet power were, for perhaps the first time, recognized as being endemic to the Soviet system itself rather than a function of "capitalist encirclement" or some other threatening phenomenon that only military might could stave off. For the first time, the paradoxes of Soviet power have been acknowledged in the Kremlin—an acknowledgment that is benign neither for the Soviet population nor for the West.

Notes

1. Robert Legvold, "The Nature of Soviet Power," *Foreign Affairs,* 56, no. 1 (October 1977), as reprinted in Robbin F. Laird and Erik P. Hoffman, eds., *Soviet Foreign Policy in a Changing World* (New York: Aldine, 1986), p. 35.

2. Terence Ball, "Power, Causation and Explanation," *Polity,* 8, no. 2 (winter 1975): 189–214.

3. See Jeffrey C. Isaac, *Power and Marxist Theory* (Ithaca, N.Y.: Cornell University Press, 1987).

4. Paul Marer, "The Political Economy of Soviet Relations with Eastern Europe," in Sarah Terry, ed., *Soviet Policy in Eastern Europe* (New Haven: Yale University Press, 1984), pp. 155–88.

5. In 1970, Russians were 53.4 percent of the Soviet population; by 1979 they were 52.4 percent. See Ann Sheehy, "The National Composition of the Population of the USSR According to the Census of 1979," *Radio Liberty Research,* no. 123/80 (March 27, 1980). One estimate of demographic trends and the future possibility of a non-Slav majority was by Mikhail S. Bernstam, "Demographic Depression in the USSR and the Welfare State," in Robert Conquest, ed., *The Last Empire: Nationality and The Soviet Future* (Stanford, Calif.: Hoover Institution Press, 1986). Bernstam estimates that by around 2080, all Slavs will account for only 41 percent of the Soviet population as opposed to almost 70 percent in the early 1980s, while Great Russians would decrease from slightly more than 50 percent to only 27 percent.

6. See Mark Field, "Soviet and American Health Care: An Uneasy Comparison," in Daniel N. Nelson and Roger B. Anderson, eds., *Soviet–American Relations: Understanding Differences, Avoiding Conflicts* (Wilmington, Del.: Scholarly Resources, 1988).

7. For example, see James Caparoso, "Dependence, Dependency, and Power in the Global System," *International Organization,* 32, no. 1 (1978).

8. Daniel N. Nelson, *Alliance Behavior in the Warsaw Pact* (Boulder, Colo.: Westview, 1986), pp. 71–107.

9. Legvold in Laird and Hoffman, p. 37.

10. In his book *USSR in Crisis: The Failure of an Economic System* (New York: Norton, 1983), Marshall I. Goldman discusses the concentration of raw materials and semifinished products in Soviet exports (p. 134) and considers at many points the poor consumer sector of the USSR's economy (e.g., see p. 29). Some of the difficulties of Soviet economic ties with the world, especially Soviet fear of indebtedness, are mentioned by Timothy Colton, *The Dilemma of Reform in the Soviet Union,* rev. ed. (New York: Council on Foreign Relations, 1986), pp. 207–8.

11. U.S. Department of State, *Warsaw Pact Economic Aid to Non-Communist LDCs, 1984* (Washington, D.C.: U.S. Department of State, Bureau of Intelligence and Research, 1986), pp. 2–3, 19.

12. U.S. Department of State, p. v.

13. Daniel S. Papp, *Soviet Policies toward the Developing World during the 1980s* (Maxwell AFB, Ala.: Air University Press, 1986), p. 114.

14. U.S. Department of State, p. v.

15. This metaphor was, I think, first used by Zbigniew Brzezinski in his article "The Soviet Union: World Power of a New Type" in Erik P. Hoffman, ed. *The Soviet Union in the 1980s: Proceedings of the Academy of Political Science* (Montpelier, Vt.: Capital City Press, 1984), p. 155.

16. Papp, p. 114.

17. This topic is covered in depth in Rajan Menon, *Soviet Power in the Third World* (New Haven: Yale University Press, 1986), ch. 3.

18. See, for example, the account of Soviet conventional capabilities in John M. Collins, *U.S.–Soviet Military Balance, 1980–1985* (Washington, D.C.: Pergamon-Brassey's, 1985), pp. 108–17.

19. These trends during the 1970s and 1980s are discussed by Jeffrey Simon in his introductory chapter in Jeffrey Simon, ed., *Force Mobilization in NATO and the Warsaw Pact* (Washington, D.C.: National Defense University Press, forthcoming 1988).

20. Robin Alison Remington, "Politics of Accommodation: Redefining Soviet–East European Relations," in Roger E. Kanet, ed., *Soviet Foreign Policy in the 1980s* (New York: Praeger, 1982), p. 105.

21. The shift of Soviet support from Somalia to Ethiopia in 1976–77 was based upon "strategic covetousness and political myopia" according to Alvin Z. Rubinstein. The Soviets were "tempted" by the "self-proclaimed 'Marxism-Leninism' " of Col. Mengistu's regime. Likewise, the USSR had minimal contacts with southern African left-wing parties or movements before the mid-1970s. See Alvin Z. Rubinstein, *Soviet Foreign Policy since World War II,* pp. 180–81.

22. In the early to middle 1960s, Cuban troops had been in Ghana to operate a guerrilla-training facility and in Algeria to assist with internal security according to Papp, p. 12. "Cuba's African presence during the 1960s may . . . be most accurately viewed more as an indication of Cuba's own revolutionary fervor than as an arm of Soviet foreign policy" (p. 13). The continuing deployment of 40,000 or more Cuban military personnel in Angola, and as many as 12,000 in Ethiopia in the 1980s has certainly lent support to Soviet interests and has been made possible only through the

logistics and the financial contributions of Moscow and WTO states. Although authors such as Jiri Valenta and Robert S. Leiken have argued that Cuban options in Africa are determined by the Soviets and are part of a Soviet global strategy, others think that the Cubans are guided by their own interests that differ substantially from the Soviet Union. See selections of Valenta's and Leiken's views in Joseph G. Whelan and Michael J. Dixon, *The Soviet Union in the Third World: Threat to World Peace?* (Washington, D.C.: Pergamon-Brassey's, 1986), p. 315. For a different view, see Wayne S. Smith, "Time for a Thaw," in *The New York Times Magazine* (July 29, 1984). A more scholarly presentation of the argument that Cuba behaves autonomously is found in Peter Shearman, *The Soviet Union and Cuba,* Chatham House paper 38 (London: Routledge and Kegan Paul, 1987).

23. Edward A. Kolodziej and Roger E. Kanet, "The Soviet Union and the Developing World," *Swords and Plowshares,* Bulletin of the Program in Arms Control, Disarmament and International Security (University of Illinois, Urbana), 2, no. 1 (October 1987). See also the authors' chapters in *The Limits on Soviet Power in the Developing World: Thermidor in the Revolutionary Struggle* (London: Macmillan, 1988).

24. The study most often cited to support the notion that costs of empire loom very large for the USSR was the Charles Wolf, Jr., et al. study referred to by Dina and Martin Spechler in their chapter in this book. A brief summary of the original Wolf study from 1983 appeared in an opinion-page article by Wolf in *The Wall Street Journal* (January 30, 1984), p. 32.

25. John P. Hardt (senior specialist in Soviet economics, Congressional Research Service), as cited in Whelan and Dixon, p. 404.

26. Guy Hunter, *Modernizing Peasant Societies* (London: Oxford University Press, 1974), p. 250.

27. Arthur A. Ekirch, Jr., *Ideas, Ideals, and American Diplomacy* (New York: Appleton Century Crofts, 1966), pp. 22–39.

28. Ibid., p. 29.

29. Riasanovsky, for example, cites seventeenth-century Muscovite Archpriest Avvakum's statement that: "By the gift of God among us there is autocracy; . . . [and] in Russia under our pious princes and tsars the orthodox faith was pure and undefiled, and in the Church was no sedition." Nicholas Riasanovsky, *A History of Russia,* 4th ed. (New York: Oxford University Press, 1984), p. 196.

30. One might consult David Baldwin's article, "Power Analysis and World Politics," *World Politics,* 31 (January): pp. 161–94, for a discussion of how the commitment and knowledge of an opponent may compensate for the power of another.

31. Bruce D. Porter, *The USSR in Third World Conflicts* (New York: Cambridge University Press, 1986), p. 236.

32. Porter, p. 237.

33. Porter, p. 238; this argument is developed in much greater depth in Menon, *Soviet Power in the Third World,* op. cit.

34. See Kolodziej and Kanet, "The Soviet Union and the Developing World."

35. Paul Dibb, *The Soviet Union: The Incomplete Superpower.* Studies in International Security 23 (Basingstoke, England: Macmillan, 1986).

36. Legvold, in Laird and Hoffman, p. 30.

37. Soviet dynamism regarding arms control proposals, especially since 1985, is

discussed in Jack Mendelsohn, "The Soviet and American Record on Arms Control in the 1980s," in Nelson and Anderson.

38. Implications of "restructuring" for the USSR and the United States are considered in Daniel N. Nelson, "The Perils of Perestroika," *Foreign Service Journal* (November 1987).

Index

About the Contributors

Melvin A. Goodman is professor of international security studies at the National War College in Washington, D.C. He has been an analyst for the Central Intelligence Agency and the Department of State and has published articles on Soviet foreign policy in various journals and books. He is currently working on a book on the military dimension of Soviet policy in the Third World.

Christopher Jones received both an M.A. in Soviet studies and a Ph.D. in political science from Harvard Univesity. He is the author of *Soviet Influence in Eastern Europe: Political Autonomy and the Warsaw Pact* (1981) and coauthor with Teresa Rakowska-Harmstone of a forthcoming study on the dynamics of ethnic and political issues within the Warsaw Pact. He is associate professor at the Henry M. Jackson School of International Studies at the University of Washington. He has contributed articles on strategic issues to *Orbis, World Politics, Survey, Arms Control Today* and several edited collections.

Michael T. Klare, who holds a Ph.D. from the Union Graduate School, is the Five-College Associate Professor of Peace and World Security Studies (a joint appointment at Amherst College, Hampshire College, Mr. Holyoke College, Smith College and the University of Massachusetts at Amherst) and the director of the Five-College program in peace and world security studies. He is author of *War Without End* (1972), *American Arms Supermarket* (1985), *Low Intensity Warfare* (1988) and is a regular contributor to *Foreign Policy, The Nation,* and other journals.

Martha Brill Olcott, associate professor and chairman of the department has been a member of the faculty of Colgate University since 1975. Since receiving her doctorate from the University of Chicago, Olcott has written over a dozen articles on Soviet politics and Central Asian affairs. Olcott is the author of *The Kazakhs* (1987), which was selected as one of the best scholarly books of 1987 by the American Library Association; she is also the editor of the forthcoming *Soviet Nationality Practices in the 1980s* (1988).

Dina Rome Spechler, Ph.D. Harvard University, is an associate professor of political science at Indiana University. Among her recent publications are *Permitted Dissent in the USSR, Domestic Influences on Soviet Foreign Policy* and articles in *World Politics, Studies in Comparative Communism,* and many edited volumes. Current research pertains to superpower involvement in Third World conflicts and economic constraints on Soviet foreign policy.

Martin C. Spechler, Ph.D. Harvard University, has taught at Harvard and the Hebrew University of Jerusalem and is now associate professor of economics at Indiana University–Purdue University at Indianapolis. His current research concerns the economic burden of Soviet foreign policy, Tsarist economic history, Soviet planning of technical change, and regional economic development.

Judith A. Thornton, who received her Ph.D. from Radcliffe (Harvard University) is professor of economics and director, Institute for Economic Research, University of Washington, Seattle. Her books and articles concern the economic analysis of the Soviet-type system, the theory and practice of economic planning, and the diffusion of technology. Currently, she is a member of the Committee to Study International Developments in Computer Science and Technology, National Academy of Science. Recent articles and monographs include "Chernobyl and Soviet Energy," *Problems of Communism,* November–December 1986 and *Technological Choice in Soviet Electric Power* (1987).

Stephen White is a reader in politics and associate of the Institute of Soviet and East European Studies at the University of Glasgow, Scotland. He was educated at Dublin and holds doctorates from both Glasgow and Oxford universities. He is joint editor of *Coexistence* and a member of the editorial boards of *Soviet Studies* and the *Journal of Communist Studies.* His recent publications include *Communist Politics: A Reader* (coedited with Daniel N. Nelson, 1986) and *Ideology and Soviet Politics* coedited with Alex Pravda, 1987).

About the Editors

Rajan Menon received his doctorate from the University of Illinois (Urbana) and is associate professor of international relations at Lehigh University. He is the author of *Soviet Power And The Third World* (1986) and contributor to numerous journals and edited volumes. During 1988–1990 he is working on a book focusing on Soviet security policy in Northeast Asia—first as a research scholar at the Wilson Center's Kennan Institute for Advanced Russian Studies and then as an international affairs fellow of the Council on Foreign Relations.

Daniel N. Nelson, Ph.D., The Johns Hopkins University, is professor of political science at the University of Kentucky, Lexington, Kentucky. He is the author or editor of more than a dozen scholarly books concerning communist party states. His recent single-authored books include *Romanian Politics in the Ceausescu Era* (1989), *Elite-Mass Relations in Communist States* (1988), and *Alliance Behavior in the Warsaw Pact* (1986); recent edited works by Nelson include *Soviet–American Relations* (1988) and *Communist Politics: A Reader* (with Stephen White) (1986). His articles have appeared in journals such as *World Politics, Journal of Politics, Problems of Communism, Soviet Studies,* and others.